CONTEMPORARY SOCIAL THEORY

General Editor: ANTHONY GIDDENS

Published titles

Tony Bilton, Kevin Bonnett, Philip Jones, Ken Sheard, Michelle Stanworth and Andrew Webster, *Introductory Sociology*

Simon Clarke, *Marx, Marginalism and Modern Sociology*

Emile Durkheim, *The Rules of Sociological Method* (ed. Steven Lukes, trans. W. D. Halls)

Boris Frankel, *Beyond the State?*

Anthony Giddens, *A Contemporary Critique of Historical Materialism*

Anthony Giddens, *Central Problems in Social Theory*

Anthony Giddens, *Profiles and Critiques in Social Theory*

Anthony Giddens and David Held (eds), *Classes, Power and Conflict*

Jorge Larrain, *Marxism and Ideology*

Ali Rattansi, *Marx and the Division of Labour*

Gerry Rose, *Deciphering Sociological Research*

John Scott, *The Upper Classes: Property and Privilege in Britain*

Steve Taylor, *Durkheim and the Study of Suicide*

John B. Thompson and David Held (eds), *Habermas: Critical Debates*

John Urry, *The Anatomy of Capitalist Societies*

Forthcoming titles

Martin Albrow, *Max Weber and the Construction of Social Theory*

David Brown and Michael Harrison, *Industrial Sociology*

Chris Dandeker, *Capitalism, Bureaucracy and Surveillance*

Emile Durkheim, *The Division of Labour in Society* (trans. W. D. Halls)

Anthony Giddens, *Between Capitalism and Socialism*

David Held, *Bureaucracy, Democracy and Socialism*

Geoffrey Ingham, *Capitalism Divided?*

Terry Johnson, Clive Ashworth and Chris Dandeker, *The Structure of Social Theory*

Douglas Kellner, *Herbert Marcuse and the Crisis of Marxism*

Claus Offe, *Social Class and Public Policy*

Ali Rattansi and Dominic Strinati, *Marx and the Sociology of Class*

John Scott, *Documentary Research*

Michelle Stanworth, *Gender and Class*

John B. Thompson, *Language and Ideology*

CONTEMPORARY SOCIAL THEORY

General Editor: ANTHONY GIDDENS

This series aims to create a forum for debate between different theoretical and philosophical traditions in the social sciences. As well as covering broad schools of thought, the series will also concentrate upon the work of particular thinkers whose ideas have had a major impact on social science (these books appear under the sub-series title of 'Theoretical Traditions in the Social Sciences'). The series is not limited to abstract theoretical discussion – it will also include more substantive works on contemporary capitalism, the state, politics and other subject areas.

Theoretical Traditions in the Social Sciences

This new series introduces the work of major figures in social science to students beyond their immediate specialisms.

The Rise and Fall of Structural Marxism

Althusser and his influence

Ted Benton

University of Essex

MACMILLAN

First published 1984 by
Higher and Further Education Division
MACMILLAN PUBLISHERS LTD
London and Basingstoke
Companies and representatives
throughout the world

Printed in Hong Kong

British Library Cataloguing in Publication Data
Benton, Ted
The rise and fall of structural Marxism
1. Althusser, Louis
i. Title
335.4′092′4   B2430.A474
ISBN 0–333–31280–5
ISBN 0–333–31281–3   Pbk

Contents

Preface

Louis Althusser was born in 1918, near Algiers. He went to school there and at Marseilles. Most of the war was spent in a prisoner-of-war camp, and after it Althusser went on to complete his studies at the Ecole Normale Supérieure, under the supervision of Gaston Bachelard. He subsequently became a distinguished philosophy teacher at the same institution. Though briefly a member of the Catholic student movement before the war, he has been a member of the French Communist Party since 1948.

Althusser's political activity has been described as naive and sporadic,[1] and it was no surprise, apparently, to find him quite absent from the scene during the 'events' of May 1968, perhaps the most significant political moment of post-war France. In so far, then, as Althusser has had political influence, it is principally through his writings and those of his associates. There has always been, indeed, a political intent in these writings, despite their frequently abstract and technical character. This is especially true of the series of essays and seminar papers, dating from the early and mid-1960s, and collected together in *For Marx* (trans. Ben Brewster, London, 1969) and *Reading Capital* (trans. Ben Brewster, London, 1970, and including in this edition, essays by both Althusser and Etienne Balibar). Althusser describes these contributions as 'interventions',[2] but, as we shall see, they can be seen as political interventions only in a way far removed from the more overt and explicit attacks on the Communist Party leadership which Althusser published in the 1970s.

In 1980 Althusser was admitted to St Anne's Psychiatric Hospital in Paris, after confessing to the killing of his wife. This confession, and confusion surrounding his wife's death, stunned both friends and colleagues, and the event was, of course, widely reported in the international press. Althusser had suffered from deep, recurrent depressions for more than thirty years.

This book started out as a projected introductory text on Louis Althusser and that tradition in Marxist thought associated with his name. My qualifications for undertaking such a project were no greater than those of many other English-speaking intellectuals and activists on the Left. Like them, I too had struggled to make sense of Althusser's ideas, to establish a critical position in relation to them, but at the same time to consider what use they might have in my own trades-union and political activity in Britain. Beyond this, I make no claim to any special expertise in French intellectual or political life. I have never met Althusser, and had only a brief acquaintanceship with the late Nicos Poulantzas.

These facts about the situation and perspective of the author, rather than any large questions of principle, serve to explain many of the decisions as to inclusion, exclusion, emphasis and parenthesis in the treatment of topics in this book. I have decided, for example, to say very little of a biographical nature about the leading contributors to the tradition of structural Marxism. This is not because I apply to them some of their own more unqualified dismissals of the role of conscious 'subjects' in the production of theoretical innovations. It is, rather, that by training and by disposition I am better fitted to write a book of theoretical analysis and criticism than one of biography. I do, indeed, think that the personal life-histories of 'subjects' are of great pertinence to their intellectual formation, though I am a long way from those colleagues for whom the terrible personal tragedies both of Louis Althusser and his wife and of Nicos Poulantzas[3] have been taken as a final justification for an ill-informed and unthinking dismissal of their intellectual contribution.

I have also decided to say relatively little about a body of work, stemming, like Althusser's work itself from both structuralist and Marxist origins, which has had an important and influential contribution to make in the fields of literary and dramatic criticism, and, more broadly, in aesthetic and cultural analysis. Among this body of work, the contributions of the Birmingham University Centre for Contemporary Cultural Studies deserve special mention. This, again, reflects no judgement on my part about the relative importance of these fields of inquiry, compared with such fields as contemporary political analysis, philosophy of science, anthropology and historical materialism, which I do try to deal with. Rather, it is simply that with my 'given' personal and scholarly limitations, a book which dealt at all adequately with these matters would have been even longer in gestation, and may, indeed, never have been delivered.

Finally, I want to say something about the way my idea of what this book should be about has changed in the course of writing it. As I have already said, it *began* as a projected introductory text. I thought such an introductory text was probably of value, given the extreme difficulty of some of the work of Althusser, Poulantzas and their associates for readers unfamiliar with the intellectual and political context in which those texts were produced. A second reason for such an introductory text was that I felt that the internal disarray of the Althusserian 'camp', and the emergence of influential 'post-Althusserian' and 'post-structuralist' writers had provided an opportunity for some unjustifiably harsh and often malevolent retrospective judgements on Althusser's work to gain quite undeserved credibility.

The pervasive judgement that Althusser's work simply re-enacts Stalinism in modern dress, for example, seems to me to be outrageous.[4] Althusser himself once characterised his aim in these terms: 'to make a start on the first *left-wing* critique of Stalinism, a critique that would make it possible to reflect not only on Khrushchev and Stalin but also on Prague and Lin Piao: that would above all help to put some substance back into the revolutionary project here in the West'.[5] True enough, the claim to have embarked on the *first* left-wing critique of Stalinism is stunning in the narrowness of its historical scope, but the seriousness of the opposition to 'Stalinism' and the commitment to a development of Marxist analysis to the point where this convenient term of political abuse can be replaced by adequate means of thought and action are surely beyond question. In a parallel philosophical assessment Alasdair MacIntyre has written of 'the profound gratitude that we all owe to Althusser for having brought French Marxism back into dialogue with the rest of French philosophy'. He goes on to say that: 'So far as French philosophy was concerned, he de-Stalinised Marxism more thoroughly than any other Marxist did'.[6] I share MacIntyre's view, and, with some reservations, Althusser's self-assessment, and I have devoted a good deal of this book to arguing the point.

The work of writing this book, which I had at first thought of as little more than the labour of setting down on paper a more or less well-defined view of the value and limitations of Althusserian Marxism, opposing, at the same time, some of the current misrepresentations of it, turned out to be a more complex and engaging effort of personal 'settling of accounts'. In the course of this 'settling of accounts' I have both shifted my own intellectual and political perspective, and come to see much more clearly the implications of moves I had already partly made. Undoubtedly the wider context of a crisis of Marxism itself as well as the fundamental alteration in the terms of British political debate and action induced by the success of 'Thatcherism' are relevant to these shifts in perspective.

Attempting a systematic re-evaluation of structural Marxism in this new context has made me aware in a way that I was not before of the importance of issues and areas of debate effectively foreclosed by that tradition. I have in mind here some important questions which *do* have a place in other traditions of Marxism. One such area has to do with the recognition that human beings, however distinctive their historical and cultural activity, are nevertheless products of nature and continue to be dependent on nature for their physical and spiritual well-being. Though not without its own problems, the philosophical materialism of Marx and Engels at least provided a perspective within which these broad prospects of human survival and historical advancement could be thought about. This is almost (though not *entirely*) lost in Althusser's Marxism through the unstable importation of ideas from French 'conventionalist' philosophy of science, and the effective abandonment of ontological speculation in favour of epistemology and a rather narrowly circumscribed 'science' of historical materialism. This loss has been doubly disastrous, in that it deprived an influential current of Marxism of the intellectual means for coming to terms with two fundamental aspects of our contemporary world. These are, on the one hand, the practical threat posed by the growing and systematic destruction of the human environment, and, on the other, a growing movement of radical (though generally non-Marxist) opposition within the 'advanced' societies which sees our relation to our environment as the central issue confronting us. I remain convinced that there is much in the 'classics' of Marxism that is enormously illuminating on these questions, and find myself returning again and again to the 'pre-scientific' early works of Marx and Engels for help in thinking about them.

But there are other issues with which the classics of Marxism offer little help. Questions including, for example, the nature of 'non-class' forms of social oppression such as those based on gender and race, or the nature of those 'mechanisms' by which the loyalty of the oppressed and exploited to their oppressors and exploiters is secured. The old explanations in terms of 'fetishism' of commodities and control over the means of production and distribution of ideas now look hopelessly limited and threadbare (though not, I think, wholly mistaken). It is precisely here (and especially where Gramsci's work was used) that structural Marxism made real advances over the Marxist classics. Ideas such as 'interpellation', and the 'relative autonomy' of ideology, as well as the attempt to link psychoanalysis with Marxism (not, of course, the first time this had been tried!) did provide means with which 'class-reductionism' and 'economism' could be opposed within Marxism.

Here, though, it seems to me that the 'opening up' of Marxism has subsequently been combined with the more general crisis of Marxism in such a way that some of the more valuable ideas and priorities of classical Marxism are in danger of being lost. It is, for example, very important indeed, theoretically and politically, to recognise and understand the specificity, the distinctiveness, of the forms of oppression faced by women. Comparable considerations apply to the position of ethnic minorities, and to individuals whose sexuality is socially stigmatised. What also has to be recognised is that the resistance of such individuals and groups will employ symbolic forms, will establish priorities, and will develop organisational forms which cut across and sometimes conflict with those of the 'traditional' class-based Left. This much the post-Althusserian (and post-Marxist) Left insists upon, and, I think, rightly so. But it is one thing to recognise these realities, to take them seriously, and to begin the work of dialogue which may take us closer to a practically realisable vision of a future to which all these diverse currents of opposition make their distinctive contribution. It is quite another to revel in the discovery of the impossibility of the project of the class-based 'traditional' organisations and discourses of the Left as if this negative task of demolition were the whole of our task, and as if the achievements of the traditional Left amounted to nothing.

This is not the place to repeat those historical achievements – they should be apparent to anyone with the least grasp of historical reality. But for the present, it is important to temper a justified opposition to 'class-reductionism' with the realisation that however *specific* the forms of racial and sexual oppression, they are none the less clearly marked and shaped by their co-presence in a society characterised by class domination. Though these forms of oppression cannot be *reduced* to class, they cannot be wholly understood in abstraction from it, either. And in political practice, too, it has been a disastrous failure, still not really recognised, on the part of the 'traditional' Left that it has never found adequate means of dialogue with those whose experience of exclusion, oppression or lack of fulfilment in society somehow did not articulate with the symbols of class oppression and economic exploitation. But to see this is not the same thing as to deny the immense and pervasive presence of class oppression both as a reality and as a part of the lived experience out of which practical political opposition is constituted. The belated 'discovery' of the significance of other forms of oppression is a spring-board from which the culture and politics of the Left may be enriched, and its popular appeal widened. But this will not happen if these 'discoveries' are made at the cost of 'forgetting' (either in theory or practice) the traditional role of the Left in interpreting, articulating and turning into effective practical struggle the experiences of class exploitation and oppression.

Well, these few paragraphs sketch out a position – of course, only a provisional one – that my thinking and writing have brought me to over the last four years. I say a little bit more – but not nearly enough – in the final chapter of this book. In the rest of the book these ideas are implicit, but not often explicitly. This is in part a reflection of the fact that serious writing is a process in which you are hardly ever sure where you are going until you get there, and, assuming you *do* arrive, it is only then that it is possible to see that you should have chosen a better place from which to begin. That we do not, after all, choose our own starting-point is one thing, at least, that Althusser was right about.

It is conventional and, of course, proper, to preface such works as this with 'acknowledgements'. This is a task which I find particularly difficult. It is not that I am loath to admit to having been influenced by others. The problem is almost the reverse. I have always pursued the ideal of 'thinking for myself' but in doing so I have always been aware that even the most independent thinker cannot avoid using means of thought provided by others. More than this, I have often come to see that a thought which I had experienced as 'my own' was already present in the writing or conversation of another. It is in the nature of the situation that the listing of such influences is bound to be incomplete and uncertain. That much said, I do want to acknowledge the help of Linda George and Mary Girling for devoting many hours to making sense of large parts of my handwritten draft and converting it into a readable typescript. My mother, Hilda Benton, also worked on the rest of the typescript and for this as for so much else I am immensely indebted to her. Shelley, Rowan and Jay deserve my apologies for all the times when I failed to reconcile my commitment to them with my commitment to finishing this book. All three of them both contributed to and obstructed the writing of this book in ways that are much too complicated for me to be able to understand at the moment. Several members of staff, especially, but not exclusively, in the Sociology Department at Essex University have given time to discussing the topics of this book with me. I would particularly like to mention Tony Woodiwiss, Harold Wolpe, David Rose, Mike Weston, Mike Freeman, Alison Scott, Michael Harloe, Maxine Molyneux, Penny Rickman, Bob Jessop, Bob Little, Joan Busfield, Joe Foweraker, Ernesto Laclau, Cutz Venn and Ian Craib for their intellectual help and/or personal support. David Lee and David Rose, especially, spent hours with me in coffee bars and elsewhere talking through my problems in writing this book. Their help is especially appreciated because of the very difference of their perspectives from my own. Anthony Giddens, a very patient editor, has also been exemplary in his combination of incisive and pertinent criticism with personal encouragement. In this respect, thanks are also due to John Winckler and Steven Kennedy. In the longer term, too, I know I owe an enormous debt to successive 'cohorts' of students, both graduate and undergraduate, whose sustained criticism has been indispensable to me. Especially important have been a series of seminars, in the early 1970s, in the Essex Sociology MA. Those seminars were very important for me in initially getting to grips with Marxist ideas, and with Althusser's work in particular. Through their published work and unbeknown to them, Norman Geras and Alex Callinicos were also of great help in this. The help of my colleagues Roy Enfield and Andrew McCulloch at that time was also a very important formative influence on me. More recently, my colleague Ian Craib and students taking part in the 'Sociology of Knowledge' course in this Department have provided me with the kind of creative intellectual stimulus that I find it hard to imagine would have been given elsewhere.

Department of Sociology
University of Essex   TED BENTON

1

Introduction

This book is about the work of a Marxist philosopher, and has something to say about the vicissitudes of an intellectual tradition arising from it. Writing a book of this nature requires certain important decisions to be made at the outset. Althusser is a *Marxist* philosopher, a member of the French Communist Party, and has been an increasingly outspoken critic of its leadership. No serious work of interpretation and evaluation can possibly avoid confronting the question of the pertinence of Althusser's work to the political issues and conflicts of his time and place. At the same time, however, Althusser is a *philosopher*, an intellectual, working within the Marxist tradition. This means that his work has also to be situated in the intellectual space defined both by competing versions of the Marxist intellectual heritage and by prevailing non-Marxist intellectual challenges and resources.

This work of interpretation and evaluation, then, will have to engage with Althusser and his followers both politically and intellectually. And it is here that the most crucial decision has to be made: do we evaluate Althusserian intellectual work from the standpoint of its pertinence to a given political project, or do we give priority to intellectual evaluation, to the questions of the consistency and validity of Althusser's arguments, to the cogency of his critiques of others and the adequacy of his re-definition of historical categories? Here I can only state my view – I shall argue for it elsewhere in this book – that there is an irreducible specificity to theoretical work. Like Althusser himself, I take the view that theoretical work is a social practice, with its own distinct relations, means, and objects. Though theoretical work is influenced by social and political events and processes, and, in turn, has effects on them, it is in no sense *reducible* to such external influences or effects. Intellectuals work with ideas, with methodological rules, with arguments, with various means of collecting and evaluating evidence, and it is by means of these resources and critical tools that their work should be assessed. This work, then, will be principally concerned with intellectual evaluation.

But it is also true that theoretical work is produced within a social and political context, and has political effects and uses. French intellectual life, especially, is politicised in a way that is rarely true of, say, British or American intellectual life, and, conversely (Althusser's complaints on this score notwithstanding), French political culture has an unusually high intellectual quality. There are connections, of course, between the struggles fought out in the seminar room and in the exchanges between academic texts, and those fought out on the streets or in the party organisations. But there are no one-to-one correspondences, only complex, intersecting, cross-cutting and overlapping linkages between positions and tendencies in the two domains. It will be necessary to say something of these connections, and also to say something of the political meanings and effects of Althusser's work, as well as that of his followers. No serious analysis could fail to do so. My decision to adopt a primarily intellectual, rather than political, mode of evaluation is designed to oppose, in the clearest possible way, an increasingly influential body of critical work which operates through slur and innuendo, through the attribution of political guilt by association, and through political character assassination, rather than through the intellectual values of respect for the integrity of a text, and rigorous evaluation of the evidence. In the end, my opposition to such methods of 'intellectual' confrontation itself comes down to a matter of political values. If Althusserianism is to be condemned as a new Stalinism, or as the old one in disguise, then this has to be argued through an analysis of what Stalinism itself is, and of what in Althusserian thought and political values betrays its complicity with the evils of Stalinism. To apply the methods of Stalin to kill off his ghost is to corrode the personal and intellectual conditions for a living, open and diverse intellectual culture on the Left. In his own, often idiosyncratic, often contradictory way, such an open and diverse intellectual culture is what Althusser has fought for, no less than critics such as E. P. Thompson who chose to fight on different grounds.

Well, all rules are made to be broken. Having asserted the autonomy of theoretical work and the primacy of intellectual means of criticism, the purposes of my first chapter require a temporary withdrawal. Althusser's most important and influential writings (the essays collected together in English translation as *For Marx*, the collection of seminar papers by Althusser and some of his collaborators published in a truncated version in English as *Reading Capital*, and the collection of essays, *Lenin and Philosophy and Other Essays*)[1] span the decade of the 1960s. The earlier of these writings have as their context two events of decisive political importance: first, the revelations and denunciations of the crimes of the Stalin period issued by Khrushchev at the Twentieth Congress of the Communist Party of the Soviet Union. This congress was a watershed in the history of the Communist movement, East and West. The 'de-Stalinisation' it promised turned out to be rather less than the hopes it inspired. But for intellectuals, especially those who had, for whatever reasons, remained within the Communist Parties of the West, a new freedom of criticism and of intellectual movement became possible. Not, as we shall see, a complete intellectual liberation, but enough of a change to make possible a whole series of encounters between Marxist and non-Marxist intellectual traditions, and, perhaps still more significantly, critical encounters with Marxist orthodoxy itself.

The second event of political importance, the international division within the Communist movement, the split between the Chinese and Russian leaderships, added its effects to the effects of the first. To the newly acquired, if still limited, freedom of intellectual manoeuvre, were added new objects and means of intellectual controversy. Increasingly China could be looked to as a model of socialist construction which challenged the paradigm status of the Soviet pattern. The political importance of China's alternative had all the more significance against the backdrop of the now inescapable knowledge of the human price which had been paid for the 'socialist achievement' of the Soviet Union. With this new interest in the Chinese movement came also an interest in the theoretical work of Mao Tse Tung. An attempt to interpret this body of work, and introduce it into the debates of the French CP is already evident in Althusser's early essay 'Contradiction and Overdetermination',[2] but it has an even more central presence in the critical revisions of his earlier positions which Althusser commenced in the late 1960s. These revisions were stimulated both by the French student movement and social crisis of the late 1960s and by the Chinese Cultural Revolution of that period.

'Orthodox' Marxism and philosophy

To understand the direction taken by Althusser's work in response to these political realities, we also need some idea of the intellectual oppositions and resources available at the time. If it was still true in 1978[3] that official theoretical work in the French Communist Party (PCF) was largely subordinated to the requirement of legitimating policy options already settled in advance by the political leadership, then how much more restricting must have been the intellectual environment of the Party prior even to the limited 'de-Stalinisation' of the late 1950s? We get some hint of this in Althusser's own commentary[4] on the special predicament of Party philosophers in those days. The range of intellectual sources legitimated by 'orthodox' Marxism – essentially, selected texts of Marx, Engels, Lenin and Stalin – whilst it might allow at least a subsistence diet for economists, economic historians and even political theorists, spells near-starvation for the philosopher.

The 'orthodox' tradition allowed three basic options for philosophy. First, to take Marx and Engels in the *German Ideology* at their word,[5] and abandon philosophy in favour of the science of history. A second alternative, given that historical materialism presents itself as a science, is to abstract from the great scientific works of the tradition, most especially *Capital*, their distinctive logic and methodology: to write, in other words, the famous volume on 'dialectics' which Marx promised but never delivered. Or, third, to continue the tradition established in Engels's later work on philosophy and the natural sciences. For the 'orthodox' tradition this work had become systematised and codified as a distinctive Marxist world-view, 'dialectical materialism'. This form of materialist philosophy is supposed by its advocates to spell the end of philosophy as *a priori* speculation in favour of a generalisation of the up-to-date results of the sciences – natural and human. Nature, human history, and human thought are all united in their common exemplification of universal dialectical laws, and in their ultimately material nature. Though each science has its own domain, and its own specificity, there is a fundamental logical, methodological and doctrinal unity binding together all of the sciences, and constituting the basis for a philosophical world-view of a radically new type.

In this form, 'diamat', was one means whereby the 'revisionist' Marxism of the Second International became linked with a biologically-inspired evolutionism and with empiricist philosophy of science. But it also proved its usefulness as the official world-view of the Soviet state, as a dogmatic 'scientism' which legitimated technocratic authority, and, among other things, was implicated in the Lysenko scandal. This last involved the purging of an entire generation of Soviet geneticists on the grounds of the undialectical character of their work, with disastrous results, not just for the science of genetics, but also for Soviet agriculture.[6]

Apart, then, from some significant East European (especially Polish) work in logic and philosophy of science, the 'orthodox' tradition of Marxism has left little room for serious philosophical work. This essentially political circumstance has meant that almost all that is worthwhile in Marxist philosophy has required some form of synthesis between Marxism and non-Marxist traditions of thought. This has further meant that such philosophical work has been carried out by philosophers working independently of (and often in opposition to) the state, in the East, and the Communist Parties, in the West. This has been so, at least, until the relative easing of restrictions on Party intellectuals since the Stalin period.

The non-Marxist sources which have been used by independent Marxist philosophers have been immensely diverse – from the empiricism and evolutionism of Eduard Bernstein,[7] through the Neo-Kantian influences on Lukács[8] to the existentialist and phenomenological bearings of Merleau-Ponty and Sartre. It is to these last two writers that I shall turn, since their work was of decisive importance in establishing independent Marxist theoretical activity in France in the post-war period. Althusser's critical vocabulary and in many respects his positive attempts at the construction of alternative concepts constitute an effort to detach the legacy of Marxism from the tradition defined by these two thinkers. Paradoxically, though, as we shall see, Althusser's philosophical opposition to them masks a partial solidarity with their political project.

Independent Marxism: Sartre and Merleau-Ponty

For both Sartre and Merleau-Ponty, the war-time occupation of France and work in the resistance brought a new political dimension into their philosophical work. The immediate post-war period saw a collaboration between them in the editorship of a very influential periodical of the independent political Left – *Les Temps Modernes*. Merleau-Ponty's commitment to Marxism was relatively shortlived and had been thoroughly abandoned by 1955. Sartre, on the other hand, engaged in a much more prolonged attempt to constitute a Marxist philosophy in keeping with what he saw as the political requirements of the situation. Though both philosophers were relatively uncritical in their tactical and political support for the Soviet Union in the immediate post-war period, there can be no doubt that their philosophical projects are defined overwhelmingly in opposition to the Stalinist version of Marxism.

These independent Marxist intellectuals saw an inherent connection between the development of an authoritarian state structure in the Soviet Union and, on the one hand, the failure of the Western Communist Parties to lead a successful revolution, and on the other, the sclerosis of Marxist theory imposed by the orthodox tradition. The appropriation of Marxism by this orthodox tradition had to be challenged, and ways found of comprehending the fate of socialist revolution, East and West, in terms of a refurbished Marxism.

The key features of Stalinism considered as a theoretical tradition were, for these independent Marxists, its inheritance of the 'naturalism' and 'scientism' of dialectical materialism, its associated economic and technological determinist account of historical process, and its conception of historical materialism as a science. The dialectical materialist thesis of a unity between human history and the natural world denies what is specific to the former: the part played in it by the creative activity of human beings and social groups. The indifferent application of the concepts of the dialectic to nature and to human history, too, divests these concepts of their distinctive value – the rendering intelligible of human practice. The associated Stalinist conception of history as the outcome of 'iron laws' rooted in the economic contradiction between forces and relations of production and of the ineluctable advance of the former likewise denies a creative, directing, meaning-bestowing role for human subjectivity in the historical process. Instead of Marxism as a theory of revolutionary self-emancipation, we have a self-proclaimed science which imposes a direction upon history from above, in the name of 'iron laws' which will tolerate no opposition.

Stalinism cannot conceive revolution as *self*-emancipation of the working class, and its conception of historical materialism as an esoteric science detaches it from any genuine mutuality with the lived experience of the oppressed and exploited. This separation of Marxist science from the daily concerns and experiences of the masses is what renders the Western Communist Parties at best unresponsive, at worst overtly repressive in the face of spontaneous movements of political opposition, and consequently makes them incapable of revolutionary leadership.

The break with 'orthodox' Marxism required for such a root-and-branch rejection of Stalinism has to be fundamental. The lineage of Marx, Engels, Lenin and Stalin had to be thoroughly disrupted, even to the point of a reconstruction of the work of Marx himself. Determinist and scientistic elements are undoubtedly present in Marx's own conception of history, and were not gratuitous and alien impositions of Lenin's and Stalin's. The reading of Marx had to be selective, and the means of selection employed were deep-rooted ethical and political values articulated through phenomenological and existentialist philosophical categories.

In Merleau-Ponty's case, Husserl's phenomenological conception of consciousness as 'intentional' – as necessarily consciousness *of* something – is given shape in the form of a concept of historical practice as bestowing meaning on and transforming its object. Through this concept a link is made between the phenomenological tradition and a version of Marxism in which the emphasis is on the *making* of history by 'man'. There are no 'iron laws' and created history is always fragile and contingent.

Sartre's existentialist philosophy[9] also placed human subjectivity at the centre of the intellectual stage. Inert, passive, material nature is opposed to the free creative power of the human subject: mere 'being' is contrasted with 'nothingness' – the power to 'negate' that which merely exists. Those oppositions of Sartre's earlier philosophy are both carried through and transformed in the later encounters with Marxism. Here human subjectivity and freedom are no longer abstract universals but are historically located and contextualised. But material nature remains an undifferentiated category, designated inert and passive. Dialectical reason applies to human individual and social practice, or 'praxis', alone. The dialectical materialist tradition is denounced for detaching dialectics from the field of intelligible practice. Like Merleau-Ponty, Sartre rejects the scientistic and determinist self-understanding of Marxism, seeking to develop that side of Marxism which recognises the possibility of the free and creative making of history by social actors, in a way which always holds surprises in store for the theoretician.

In their practical relations to nature, human beings necessarily interpret objective conditions of their action, and are constrained by them, but in intentionally modifying nature they in turn impress something of their own humanity upon it. Worked-nature, however, has a reciprocal effect on human actors and, at least under conditions of material scarcity, they become themselves thing-like, passive, inert, in relation to nature. This ordering of human relations by worked-nature, the 'practico-inert', imposes self-alienation, isolation and passivity on human subjects. Such nature-ordered and external relations between human beings are designated 'series' by Sartre, and contrasted with 'fused' groups which arise when actors spontaneously recognise common goals and arrive at mutual recognition and reciprocity as they do so. Such communal action defines itself against all fixed and alientated relationships, and is capable of bearing a human praxis which imposes its own meanings and creates its own future. Sartre gives the storming of the Bastille by the revolutionary crowd in the Paris of 1789 as his example of such a group-in-fusion. But, historicised though it is, we can see in Sartre's conception of the fused group the embodiment of the earlier philosophical conception of freedom as negativity; freedom is equated with the most radical renunciation of all fixed and settled existence.

However, though the 'fused group' may be a concept capable of grasping a moment of revolutionary mass action, it cannot carry the whole weight of comprehending the new form of social existence it may bring into being. Here, Sartre introduces a new concept – that of 'organised group practice' – wherein a division of labour between actors is sustained through recognition of a common purpose. Though elements of exteriority arise in these relationships, collapse into serial relations is not inevitable. But where this tendency is present the division of labour will be established through the authority of pure sovereignty which comes to replace the spontaneous community of objectives of the fused group. Here is the beginning, at least, of a set of categories for understanding Soviet bureaucracy and the 'cult of personality', not as something inevitable, as the 'routinisation of charisma', but as a possible faltering and reversal of a revolutionary process. The possibility always remains of the spontaneous re-emergence of free communal action.

Against the economic determinism of orthodox Marxism, Sartre argues that human subjectivity, consciousness, is formed not just in the process of production, but in participation in a whole range of institutional practices. The conscious life, the personal identity, of each individual has to be seen as a result not of a single class determination, but of a series of 'mediations' the most important of which is the family. But set against this promising basis for a non-economistic marxism, Sartre fails to escape economism in his conception of revolution itself. Human practice imposes meanings through what Sartre calls 'totalisations': interpretations of the conditions of action in the light of the aims and intentions of action. The possibility of human creation of history requires that history be given a single meaning, that the totalisations inherent in each individual project do not cancel each other out in some meaningless chaotic resultant, but somehow coalesce into a synthetic unity. Sartre roots his conviction of this possibility in the idea of the working class as a 'universal' class: a class whose emancipation carries with it the emancipation of all other classes and sectors of society. This, in turn, rests upon a conception of the mode of economic production as the central determinant of social cleavages and struggles.

Politically, these philosophical Marxisms counter the 'scientism' of orthodox Marxism by situating theory *directly* within the historical process itself, as the self-consciousness of actors who live their freedom as 'negation' of existing states of affairs. Their basic theoretical categories embody the central political and moral values of human freedom and creativity, of mutuality and of the intelligibility of social life to its creators. What is perhaps the most important difficulty of 'orthodox' Marxism – how can the science of Marxism make contact with the lived experience of the working masses? – has its solution written into the very basis of humanist philosophical Marxism. But this is done at a cost. The radically non-determinist concept of human freedom which is employed means that theory loses the capacity to illuminate and guide practice at the level of concrete strategies and tactics. All that is possible is an interpretation of history from the standpoint of a free-floating ethical identification with the exploited and oppressed: the hoped-for source of the negation of what exists. In rendering these fundamental ethical commitments as themselves beyond rational evaluation in terms of their practical realisability, these positions are capable of dogmatic degeneration no less than 'orthodox' Marxism.

Against the 'iron laws' and 'scientific' knowledge which, for them, constituted Stalinism, phenomenological and existential Marxisms posited a 'subject-centred' history, and the lived-experience of the historical actor as the source of cognition. Despite the historicisation of subjectivity, and its attribution to the communal action of collectivities, the philosophical ancestry of this conception of self and of cognition is clear. Descartes' *'cogito ergo sum'*[10] is an assertion of the ultimate cognitive primacy and self-transparency of the contents of consciousness. In this unmediated presence of the self to itself is to be found the certainty by which all other knowledge-claims are to be measured. Descartes' epistemological[11] reconstruction of the world of external objects and other selves on the basis of this certainty, and under the guarantee provided by God the non-deceiver, can also be taken as the source of a philosophical tradition in which the self is the starting point not just for knowledge, but for the constitution of the world itself. The philosophical 'subject' is here the self-subsistent source of *knowledge* of the 'object' which it simultaneously *constitutes*. This philosophical legacy passes through the work of Hegel and into the earlier work of Marx, and, by a different route, passes into the phenomenological and existential Marxism of post-war France.

French structuralism

Stalinism is not the only tradition of thought which stands opposed to subject-centred history and subject-constituted knowledge. In France, Comte and, above all, Durkheim represent a nineteenth century tradition for which human subjects are constituted by their social milieu. The consciousness of the individual subject is made up of representations in which the imperatives of an external social order are internally inscribed. Subjectivity does not carry with it the means of its own intelligibility, and objectivity, so far as it is obtainable has to be established in opposition to the 'pre-notions' through which the actor lives his or her social existence. Social science must relate to its object much as the natural sciences relate to theirs: as an external facticity. The inheritors of this alternative paradigm of knowledge and of subjectivity as socially constitut*ed*, rather than constitut*ive* have been, in the twentieth century, the diverse 'functionalist' and 'structuralist' currents of social thought. The structuralist contemporaries of Sartre and Merleau-Ponty, though less influential in the immediate post-war period, had none the less already produced an impressive body of work in linguistics, anthropology, psychology and adjacent disciplines by the time (the late 1950s and early 1960s) the intellectual tide turned in their favour.

Indeed, the consummation of the prolonged courtship of existentialism and Marxism, Sartre's monumental *Critique of Dialectical Reason*,[12] came too late to bear the fruit it had promised. By this time, intellectual attention had turned, in a disciplinary sense, away from history and towards psychology, anthropology, linguistics and philosophy. In terms of perspective, this was also a shift from the subject as bestower of meaning to the subject as *prisoner* of meaning. The principal source of the 'structuralisms' which came to dominate the French intellectual scene from about 1960 onwards was the structual linguistics of Saussure[13] and Jakobson. Central to this way of thinking about language are two theses, both of which have the effect of radically challenging phenomenological and existentialist ways of thinking about the relationship between meaning and subjectivity. First, a linguistic 'sign' is held to be separable into two components, a 'signifier' and a 'signified'. The mark or sound which signifies is held to be arbitrary in relation to the idea, or concept, which it signifies: the word 'trees' signifies the idea of a tree by virtue of convention only, it doesn't have to resemble it in shape, sound, colour, and so on. It follows that the *identity* of a sign is given neither by the object to which it refers, nor by the intention of its user, but only by the system of differences and oppositions which constitutes the language to which it belongs. The displacement of 'subject' as bestower of meanings implied by this is clear. What is also significant from the standpoint of our theme in this book, is the simultaneous exclusion of the extra-linguistic referents of signs from the concerns of structural linguistics.

The second important thesis of structural linguistics is based on the distinction between language and speech. Any specific utterance may communicate a message only on condition that it satisfies the complex of rules for the combination of signs which constitutes the language in which the utterance occurs. Only set against the context of the set of other possible combinations allowed in this sign-system can this *particular* utterance communicate a message. The meaning of an utterance, then, cannot be the direct expression of the inner states of the subject. On the contrary, the subject may use language to convey a meaning only to the extent that he or she 'submits', or becomes 'subject' in a second sense of the term, to an externally established and, in this (rather misleading) sense, 'coercive' sign-system.

The work of Levi-Strauss in anthropology extends Saussure's analysis of the sign and signification (a possibility sanctioned by Saussure himself) beyond language to other social practices such as kinship, economic relations, food, and myth, all of which can, Levi-Strauss argued, be treated as activities in which 'messages' are constructed through the constituting rules of a 'code'. The object of structural anthropology is to arrive by analysis at these codes, and, further, to show the homology of the codes within a culture. To show, in fact, that rules of transformation enable the derivation of one rule system from another. The unrealised supposition of Levi-Strauss's anthropology is the ultimate reducibility of the diversity of human cultural practices to a unitary and universal 'depth-grammar' of the mind. The decentring of the 'constitutive' role of the conscious subject is extended, then, in Levi-Strauss, beyond linguistics, into every field of social practice, and with it is effaced the internal cognitive link between subject and the world it creates. The human sciences stand to their objects in a relation comparable with that of the natural sciences to theirs.

In an explicit critique of Sartre's conception of history, Levi-Strauss[14] calls attention to the Cartesian[15] legacy in it. To start historical interpretation with the conscious project of the historical actor (individual or collective) is to remain its prisoner. Just as Descartes can escape from the 'prison' of his own conscious life, and therefore of solipsism,[16] only by the rationally illegitimate device of an external guarantee, so a consistently humanist approach to history must remain trapped within the cultural premises of its place and time. The greater the historical distance, or the greater the differences between cultures, the less becomes their mutual intelligibility. Cultures and historical forms are either incommensurable, or they are interpreted selectively from the standpoint of the project of the present. This latter option, the one in fact adopted by Sartre, entails imposing a spurious continuity upon discrete historical forms and periods, and swallows up the specificity of those periods and other cultural forms in a kind of 'intellectual cannibalism'.

This closed, internal relation between Sartre's conception of history and the project of a contemporary historical agency enables Levi-Strauss, the anthropologist, to analyse it as directly comparable to the mythical thought of primitive peoples.[17] In myth, structural anthropology sees a means whereby individual subjects are bound together in their submission to the symbolic representation of the founding and integrity of their social order. But the integration of their lived experience with the intelligible categories of the myth, the means whereby the order sustains itself, is no guarantee of the *truth* of the myth. On the contrary, the characteristic structuralist detachment of signification from reference implies that whatever 'truth' the myth attains will be disclosed not to the consciousness of the believer, but only to the anthropologist who applies to it structuralist methods of analysis. Sartre's man-made history is a myth of modern times. Like the myth of the primitives, Sartre's myth answers to a social imperative. The myth of the French Revolution may be necessary to stimulate revolutionary action in our own day, to enable individuals to play the part of historical actors, but this is no mark of its truth. For the myth to be true would require that contemporary schemes of interpretation were congruent with the imperatives of action, and this congruence, if ever present at all, must be quite contingent, and may already have passed away.

History is to be understood, now, not as the project, or as the resultant of the projects, of conscious subjects, since the cultural systems within which historical action is performed are prior to and independent of the projects of the individual actors whose very subjectivity they constitute. Only in virtue of their subordination to the constituting rules of those cultural practices are subjects capable of devising 'projects' at all. Whatever meaning and movement history displays is imparted or endowed not by historical actors, but by the totality of rule systems within which they are located and enmeshed.

But the structuralist challenge doesn't end here. The sovereignty of the 'constitutive' subject is traced right to its source: in the theory of the human psyche itself. Jacques Lacan, a colleague of both Levi-Strauss and Althusser at the prestigious Ecole Normale Supérieure, was the leading advocate of a re-working of Freudian psychoanalysis, in which the nature and significance of the unconscious was taken to be Freud's fundamental discovery. Against 'ego-centred' versions of psychoanalysis, Lacan employed the basic concepts and distinctions of structural linguistics to show that the conscious life of the individual is not self-sufficient, and does not carry the means of its own intelligibility. Not only does analytic practice necessarily work through the use of language, but the unconscious itself is 'structured like a language'. The phases through which, for Freud, the individual achieves its identity as a gendered human subject are interpreted through the categories of structural linguistics as phases in the subjection of this subject to the authority of the culture – the symbolic order. In the pre-oedipal phases desire is related to objects whose images are themselves already cultural, whilst the resolution of the oedipal phase itself requires submission to the rules of the symbolic order as a condition of the communicability and hence satisfaction of desire. But this very submission requires that the original desire is repressed, is excluded from the conscious life and speech of the subject. To the psychoanalyst, however, such phenomena as dreams, slips of the tongue and neurotic symptoms can be made to reveal the 'silent' discourse of the unconscious which 'doubles' that which is spoken. Here the Freudian concepts of 'condensation' and 'displacement' are given a linguistic rendering as 'metaphor' and 'metonymy'.

Althusser, humanism and Stalinism

The power of these arguments, deployed by close and respected colleagues could hardly have failed to play a part in Althusser's intellectual formation. The essays written by Althusser between 1960 and 1965, and collected together in *For Marx* centre on the critical themes introduced by structuralism: is Marxism necessarily 'humanist' or 'historicist' in its philosophical basis? What is the relationship between Hegel and Marx? What is the relationship between the earlier and the later works of Marx? What Althusser embarks upon, in these early essays, is a thorough re-working of the most basic categories of Marxist thought in the face of the structuralist criticism. Althusser does not explicitly align himself with structuralism. When he later employs structuralist terminology he simultaneously distances himself from what he calls 'structuralist ideology'. Nevertheless, the essays concede virtually the whole territory previously occupied by Marxism in its phenomenological and existentialist forms. No attempt is made to defend these Marxisms from the structuralist critique. On the contrary, arguments, sometimes with a clear structuralist ancestry, sometimes derived from the classics of Marxist–Leninism, but always complementary in their effects, are given a specific focus in the refutation of humanist and historicist Marxisms.

How can Althusser, a self-professed Marxist philosopher, ally with structuralism to the extent of complementing its already effective assault on Marxist positions? By the single tactic of denying that those positions were, all along, Marxist positions. Marxism had been conquered from within by alien ideologies, and so, by implication, the weaponry now on offer from the structuralists justifies a tactical alliance with them to enable a recapture of Marxism for itself. Marxism is not a 'historicism': history is not, for Marxists, a project of conscious self-emancipation, but an autonomous 'terrain' opened up for scientific analysis by the classics of Marxist theory, and whose laws of motion do not readily disclose themselves to the consciousness of historical actors. Marxism is not a humanism: Marxism was *established* in Marx's rejection of the philosophical humanism of his early years, and is now *threatened* by the current 'retreat' into philosophical humanism by intellectuals faced with the ethical, political and intellectual realities of Stalinism. Socialist humanism, it is suggested, expresses a proper denunciation of the inhumanity of Stalinism, but the construction of a non-Stalinist socialism will require a political strategy, and this, in turn, will require a scientific analysis of what Stalinism was and what were its conditions of possibility. This scientific analysis is precisely what the humanist philosophy does not have to offer.

In this complex intellectual manoeuvre, Althusser, as he later recalls,[18] has political as well as intellectual objectives. The wake of the Twentieth Congress revelations and subsequent de-Stalinisation had both motivated and provided room for subject-centred, 'humanist' and 'historicist' philosophical forms of Marxism to surface inside the PCF and for Party intellectuals to follow the example of Sartre and Merleau-Ponty into a re-examination of Marx's earlier works as a source for the humanitarian values and ethical principals which Stalinist Marxism so clearly lacked. Althusser's opposition to this as a response to the challenge of Stalinism is rooted in his commitment to the conception of Marxism as a science: an indispensible means of guidance and direction for communist politics. Without this guidance, Marxist politics must descend into mere opportunism. Though Sartre's anti-Stalinism is leftist in direction, its voluntarism prevents any development of a consistent tactics or strategy. But the examples of opportunism in the PCF which clearly worried Althusser most were of a rightist nature – the dialogue between Christians and Marxists, and the alliance policies of the Party leadership. The poor level of development, and humanist misappropriation of Marxist theory were, for Althusser, at the root of this opportunism, and so had to be opposed as a matter of political as well as intellectual priority.

Althusser's adoption of intellectual means to fight a political battle is hard to square with his insistence on the specificity and 'relative autonomy' of these practices. A full explanation of it would no doubt make reference to Althusser's professional and personal formation as a prestigious figure in French academic life. Academics are prone to the illusion that the authority their words command in the classroom is an autonomous property inhering to the words themselves: a kind of fetishism arising from the social relations of academic institutions. Althusser, in a partial later insight into this, criticised his earlier work as 'theoreticist' in its failure to theorise the relationship between theory and politics. Nevertheless, this was, indeed, Althusser's 'project'. The series of texts, 'Theorie', in which Althusser's main writings of this period (*For Marx* and *Reading Capital*) were published was designed to oppose 'opportunism' in both theory and politics, to rectify the supposed lack of intellectual culture in the French Party and to combat intellectual tendencies supposedly inimical to Marxism.

Notwithstanding the later shifts and reversals of theoretical positions there is a discernable and consistent direction in Althusser's interventions – both intellectual and political – which is already present in these writings of the early 1960s. The complexity of the intellectual and political 'fields' within which these interventions were made, however, and their frequently disguised and oblique character has led to an understandable confusion among critics and commentators. 'Humanist' Marxists, both within and outside the PCF had identified Stalinism with the view of Marxism as a science, and with the associated denial of an autonomous, creative role for human subjectivity in the making of history. Althusser makes the centre-piece of his philosophical interventions the defence of Marxism's scientific status and the associated claim that history must be conceived as a 'process without a subject'. For the humanist Marxists of the time, and for their successors in the subsequent debates about the meaning of 'Althusserianism', this meaning is unmistakable: it is Stalinism in a new, structuralist vocabulary.[19] A number of Althusser's erstwhile collaborators to the left of the PCF, initially influenced by Althusser's cautious espousal of Mao's theoretical contribution and of the Chinese model, subsequently broke organisationally from the PCF to associate themselves with the various Maoist factions and parties which briefly flourished in France. For them, too, Althusser's continuing membership of the PCF and failure to push his theoretical self-criticism sufficiently far were enough to justify a repudiation of his work as 'Stalinist' and 'revisionist'.[20] Finally, and again not surprisingly, Althusser's work has been represented as Stalinist by writers in the Trotskyist tradition or strongly influenced by it. Part of what is at work in these analyses, some of them quite sophisticated, is a tendency to treat Althusser's theoretical contribution as no more than an articulation of the strategic dilemma of the PCF.[21] Indeed, the absence of any serious engagement with Trotsky's own work in Althusser's writings must be read as 'symptomatic' in Althusser's sense of the word. Trotsky is by far the most important of Althusser's predecessors in the attempt to provide a leftist critique of Stalinism, and a historical materialist, scientific analysis of the genesis and demise of Soviet socialism, yet Althusser's caution in the face of his Party leadership allows him only the occasional, presumably rather daring, mention of Trotsky's name.

Set against all this, there is no mistaking Althusser's enthusiasm for the widening of the terms of intellectual debate made possible by 'de-Stalinisation.[22] Indeed, given what we have seen of the paucity of options available to a philosopher in the orthodox tradition, it is hard to see how Althusser, a philosopher, could be anything but anti-Stalinist. Moreover, the attack on 'socialist humanism' defines its objectives clearly: the ethical content of humanism is endorsed. What is rejected is the abandonment of the theoretical tools necessary to explain and effectively oppose Stalinism as a historical reality. A number of Althusser's conceptual innovations can be related to this task. For Althusser the key defect of Stalinism as a theoretical formation is its economism and technical determinism. There are two main lines of argument against this in Althusser. First, the Marxist thesis of the 'determination in the last instance' by economic relations is reinterpreted by Althusser not as an *historical* law, but rather as a thesis about the causal relations between the elements in a society, considered *in abstraction from* their historical movement – that is to say, in structuralist language, synchronically. Understood in this way, the correlate of 'determination in the last instance' by the economic, is the 'relative autonomy' of the super-structures. This idea of 'relative autonomy', whatever its limita-tions, is of great importance in allowing for due weight to be given to a whole range of cultural and political struggles, practices and objectives. With particular relevance to Stalinism and the Soviet state it carries the implication that transformation of capitalist economic relations is insufficient for thoroughgoing social revolu-tion. Social and political struggles for the revolutionising of cultural life and against state bureaucracy remain necessary, as the Chinese case shows, even where there is a socialist infrastructure. In this respect, at least, there is a close parallel between Sartre's concept of 'mediations' and Althusser's thesis of 'relative autonomy' both in their theoretical and in their political objectives.

The second line of argument against Stalinism is to argue that it misappropriates Marxism in a way which exactly mirrors the humanist misappropriation. Whereas the latter represents the his-torical process as a journey of the human subject through self-alienation to final self-consciousness and self-emancipation, the former repeats this teleological structure, only with the ever ad-vancing forces of production in the place of the human subject. History is still an evolutionary succession of phases, in which original inner potentials are successively realised through historical time. Against this is set a properly Marxist conception of 'history without a subject'. No social form has its necessary transcendence inscribed in its origins. The direction of historical change is open and contingent. Revolution is a precarious achievement, and even when achieved, its advance may be impeded, halted or reversed. Undoubtedly, as we shall see, Althusser has great difficulty in coherently theorising this conception of an open and contingent history, but its radical departure from the certainties of the Stalinist form of 'orthodox' Marxism is clear. What is more doubtful is whether the critique of historicism is effective against all forms of humanist Marxism – Sartre himself, for example, sees the possibility of the imposition of meaning on history as a fragile, contingent and partial achievement.

Finally, Althusser's later work confirms and elaborates this op-position to Stalinism. The criticisms of the Soviet Union become more outspoken,[23] and there is an increasingly bitter engagement with the problems of authoritarianism in the structure and practice of the PCF itself. The nècessity for open debate in the Party, for the breaking down of barriers to communication laterally between different branches and sections of the rank and file membership, for a genuinely *democratic* 'democratic centralism', and for a positive and open approach to spontaneous mass actions (1968 is the obvious example) where the party leadership too often is suspicious and hostile to whatever it does not control, are asserted with great vigour. These and other demands are linked with the elaboration of a socialist strategy which is both revolutionary (that is, avoids the 'right-opportunism' of Eurocommunism and social democracy) and genuinely popular and democratic (that is, avoids the authoritarian-ism and bureaucracy of Stalinism).

When these considerations are given their due weight it seems to me that Althusser's basic project – intellectually as well as political-ly – has been consistently opposed to Stalinism.[24] But it is an opposition to Stalinism which takes seriously the question of what *kind* of opposition, in theory, and in practice, is most adequate to its historical tasks. Althusser offers a 'third way' – *neither* Stalinism *nor* humanist Marxism and 'opportunism'. The question of the nature and viability of this 'third way' is clearly an important one in a world haunted by economic depression, the threat of nuclear extinction and environmental crisis. It is the question which will dominate the rest of this book. Clearly, Althusser, the 'subject' who engages in political polemics and writes texts is opposed to Stalinism. But the theoretical content of those texts and polemics may still escape the intentions of their author. For some, the concept of 'relative au-tonomy' allows the convenience of a limited criticism of the Soviet Union whilst continuing to recognise it as a socialist society, as if Stalinism were a disease of the superstructures which had not infected the socialist infrastructure. For others, Althusser's failure, through all his self-criticism, to develop a conception of ideology adequate to sustain the idea of an independent 'spontaneous' class struggle on the part of the masses is the mark of his ultimate failure to escape from the Stalinist deformation of Marxism. In the end, the key question faced by all those Marxists sufficiently orthodox to think of Marxism as a science is 'How can Marxist science become a living force in history without a betrayal of the very values it sets out to establish?' Deny the premises of humanist Marxism, and the link between Marxist theory and the consciousness of those it aims to serve becomes contingent and tenuous. The decisive question, it seems to me, for the viability of any proclaimed 'third way' between humanism and Stalinism is how the question of that link is to be resolved. Fail to resolve it at all and theory has no relevance to socialist practice ('theoreticism', Althusser calls this). Resolve it through imposition via a coercive party or state apparatus and you have Stalinism.

Just as humanist and historicist Marxisms had to disrupt the 'orthodox' lineage of Marx, Engels, Lenin and Stalin, so Althusser's 'third way' has to disrupt the same lineage, but in a different place. For humanist Marxism little in Engels, Lenin or Stalin is above suspicion, and even Marx has to be interrogated pretty thoroughly. For Althusser, on the other hand, this concedes, paradoxically, too much to Stalin: it concedes the legitimacy, especially, of Stalin's use of Lenin. For Althusser, Lenin as analyst of the 'current situation', as synthesiser and developer of Marxist political analysis, as strategist and even as philosopher, is indispensible. It is above all Lenin who needs to be rescued from the grip of Stalinism. A significant discontinuity has to be established, then, between Lenin and Stalin, and an 'authentically' Leninist theoretical and political tradition re-established within the French CP. On the other hand, it has to be conceded that there is ample textual support for both humanist 'readings' and economic and technical determinist ones, for that matter, in Marx and Engels themselves. Discontinuities, theoretical distances have to be established within, as well as between the classic texts of the 'orthodox' tradition. Althusser's 'disruption' of the 'orthodox' lineage goes further, as we have seen, with the introduction of Mao as a seminal figure in the tradition, and also in a selective use of the work of the Italian Marxist Gramsci,[25] especially in the conceptions of the state and ideology.

What Althusser is engaged in here is a retrospective restructuring of a whole tradition of intellectual and political practice. It is an immense task, and it poses a number of important problems. In the remainder of this chapter I shall focus on two of these, which turn out, in the end, to be only one. First, in the three-cornered battle for an 'authentic' Marxism, we have an established 'orthodox' lineage, and two competing restructurings of it. The orthodox tradition has the authority which comes from control of an administrative apparatus. Of its two rivals, one has the self-proclaimed authority of the ethico–philosophical principles which constitute it, whilst the other is in search of a source of authority. The task before Althusser is to establish a series of discontinuities, differences, dislocations within and between texts; on the basis of these discriminations to establish a principle of selection (*this* is acceptable, authentic, validated – *that* is not) and, finally, to establish the credentials of the principle of selection. Intellectual means are required, both to identify and interpret the discriminations and to validate the principles by which the selections are made.

The second problem has to do with Althusser's specific intellectual formation as a philosopher. The abandonment of humanist Marxism means the breaking of the bond through which that tradition linked Marxist theory, the subjective experience of historical actors, and their transformative action. This theoretical strategy had attempted, in one and the same movement, to found the possibility of Marxism as a *historically effective* theoretical formation, and to establish its *truth*. The abandonment of a phenomenological foundation for Marxism, then, creates two problems where previously there had been only one. One problem, the relation between theory and politics, is indeed, a centrally important problem, but it belongs to political theory and practice, and is no longer a philosophical question. The other question, that of the cognitive value of historical materialism remains a philosophical question, but has to be posed again, not in the context of a theory of the conscious life of acting 'subjects' and their interpretive schemes, but as a question of *epistemology* or, what for Althusser is the same thing, the philosophy of science.

It is here that the two problems of Althusser's theoretical programme converge: how is the authenticity of Althusser's restructuring of the Marxist tradition to be established? Answer: by recourse to epistemology and philosophy of science. A criterion of 'scientificity' is required to distinguish the acceptable from the unacceptable, and to re-constitute the tradition as a scientific one. And the second problem – what role is left for philosophy with the abandonment of phenomenological philosophies of history? – has the same answer. Marxist philosophy is to be an epistemological theory through which concepts and propositions are authenticated as 'scientific' or assigned the status 'ideology', non-knowledge.

Though, in one sense, this is a very powerful role for philosophy to assume, in other respects, it represents a drastic narrowing of the field open to philosophical work by comparison with both alternative ways of viewing the Marxist tradition. Both 'orthodox' Marxism and the existentialist Marxism of Sartre assigned philosophy the role of theorising basic questions of existence not fully resolvable within the confines of historical materialism – questions about the world of nature, its historicity, and the place of human kind and its history in nature. The 'dialectical materialism' of the orthodox tradition and Sartre's opposition of the regions of 'being' proper to nature and to free, 'negative' beings, were both philosophical ontologies which, [26] whatever their shortcomings, did at least confront these fundamental questions about the relationship of human beings to their inner and outer nature. By contrast, Althusser's restriction of Marxist philosophy to epistemology obstructs even the posing of such questions *as* philosophical questions. This may not seem too serious if the prospect remains open of posing these and related questions not as philosophical ones, but as scientific questions which nevertheless are of an interdisciplinary nature. The questions I have in mind are questions about human ecology and natural history. How far, for example, do the social processes through which societies reproduce and maintain themselves depend on the satisfaction of certain conditions in external nature, and how far, under some circumstances, may social processes undermine those conditions? How far are the social processes through which agents are constituted, socially distributed, allocated to positions of dominance and subordination and so on, rooted in biological differences between individuals (age, sex, race, and others)? As I shall later argue, the theoretical means Althusser employs in the attempt to settle his epistemological problems serve to obstruct the posing of such important questions not just as philosophical, but also as scientific ones.

But what are these intellectual means? They are, in fact, drawn from two sources outside Marxism, but synthesised and re-worked by Althusser in a distinctive contribution to Marxist philosophy. One external source we are already familiar with: the range of intellectual positions commonly put together under the name 'structuralism'. The other source, complementary to the first in several respects, is a distinctive French tradition in the philosophy of science which is best described as 'historical epistemology'. This tradition is itself part of a broader tradition in the philosophy of science commonly referred to in the literature as 'conventionalism'.

Conventionalism and historical epistemology

The crisis in the physical sciences of the late nineteenth century, resulting in the emergence of relativity theory and quantum mechanics early in this century had traumatic effects not just in physics, but also in the wider culture. In philosophy, the shock of the displacement of Newtonian physics (together with its metaphysics and its epistemology) was registered in a revival in the fortunes of 'conventionalist' philosophies of science. It was in French philosophy of science (most notably in the work of Duhem and Poincaré) that this 'conventionalist' approach was furthest developed.[27] The classical philosophies of science, 'rationalism' and 'empiricism' had attempted to establish a clear distinction between (justified) scientific belief, and the non-scientific (faith, opinion, prejudice . . .) in the procedures by which science accepts into the corpus of established knowledge only demonstrably provable propositions: propositions provable, that is, either by formal derivation from indubitable premises, or by formal operations on empirical evidence. On the empiricist view, especially in its inductive form (scientific laws are generalisations from observed instances), the history of science should be intelligible as a progressively and continuously accumulating body of knowledge.

Against these classical philosophies, conventionalism argues that the body of established scientific theory at a particular moment is 'underdetermined' by empirical evidence and formal reasoning. In other words, it is always possible, in full logical consistency, to account for the available empirical evidence in terms of more than one set of theoretical assumptions. Theories of perception, too, may be employed to establish the incoherence of the idea of 'theory-neutral' observation, which would be required if empirical evidence were to play the kind of role of final arbiter between competing theories to which empiricism generally assigns it. This 'underdetermination' of theory by formal reason and experience places a new emphasis on the *constructed* character of scientific theory and on the creative role of scientific practices, and/or its practitioners. This leaves room for ethical or aesthetic values, instrumental or other 'extrinsic' conditions and considerations to enter essentially into the process of scientific theory-construction and change, and in this way the outcome of such a process can be seen, in broad terms, as the adoption of a *convention* to employ a set of concepts and laws in future scientific research. These concepts and laws are not *imposed* on science by logic and systematic experience.

Conventionalist philosophies of science, then, differ from most 'classical' philosophies of science in that they allow room for the sciences to be taken seriously as historical phenomena, subject to transformation and locked into relationships with other social practices. It is in this historical dimension that French philosophy of science has (until relatively recently, with the work of N. R. Hanson, T. S. Kuhn, P. Feyerabend and other English-speaking philosophers) been distinctive. It has established the requirement of any philosophical account of science that it be adequate to the interpretation of concrete (and especially revolutionary) episodes in the histories of specific sciences: hence the term 'historical epistemology'.

The writings of the French historian and philosopher of science, Gaston Bachelard, which are the immediate source of Althusser's most important 'borrowings' are no exception to this. The task of creating a philosophy adequate to science at each moment of its history is taken most seriously. Philosophies of science, according to Bachelard, are in one aspect *effects* of innovations in science, but, in another, they may become obstacles to the further advance of science. Only a new philosophy can distinguish within the discourse of a post-revolutionary science what is truly scientific, and defend this achievement from contamination by the philosophical residues of a previous phase in the history of that science.

For Bachelard, science is an achievement wrested only out of a struggle against what may be thought of as the natural inclinations of the human mind. The common-sense conceptions we form in our everyday life, our tendency to take our experience at face value, our tendency to assume that the world is spontaneously intelligible, our susceptibility to be captivated by a peculiarly vivid impression, and so on, belong to the sphere of 'reverie' and are the content and materials of art and poetry. Objectivity in the sciences, however, requires a continual struggle against the *positive power* of these inclinations of our through.[28] Two characteristics of science follow from this. First, scientific knowledge is not, as empiricism sometimes depicts it, the opposite of ignorance, but, rather, of a tenacious web of *error*. Second, and following from this, the history of science cannot be a continuous process of accumulation of knowledge, but must be a discontinuous revolutionary process, through which earlier conceptions are rejected, displaced, and replaced by new theoretical constructs. The transformation, too, must be one which involves the whole theoretical system of the science – it is not a change which can affect concepts one by one, piecemeal. This is because the concepts and problems which make up a theoretical structure are not identifiable independently of their location within the whole. This interdependence of the concepts which make up a theoretical structure, and the way in which they enable the posing of certain problems, whilst excluding others from consideration has been noted not just by Bachelard but also by others both within and outside the French epistemological tradition. Using the term 'problematic' to characterise it, Althusser attributes the concept to Jacques Martin. This is an important concept in Althusser's work, and we shall have occasion to return to it.

But the 'web of errors' which a new set of scientific concepts and their associated problems has displaced does not simply cease to exist. At every point, according to Bachelard, science is threatened by 'epistemological obstacles' which impede its progress. We are given no general theory of these obstacles, however, but rather a list and some historical examples. They include 'natural' and common-sense tendencies of thought – 'animism', 'realism' (which, for Bachelard, seems to mean 'empirical realism', the thesis that reality reveals itself in its appearance, rather than the thesis that there exists an external reality to which concepts may or may not correspond), as well as philosophies, such as positivism and rationalism, through which scientific innovations are accommodated to such natural tendencies of the mind. Such philosophies, though they present themselves as *universal* philosophies of *the* scientific method, are pertinent only to a certain phase in the history of each science, thereafter constituting epistemological obstacles, vehicles through which common-sense non-scientific images and notions invade scientific discourse.

A philosophy adequate to the requirements of the present phase of a science, then, must be a philosophy which 'negates' all previous philosophies. In particular, it must resist the temptation to convert the transitory constructs of scientific activity into a fixed ontological system which will then obstruct further scientific transformations. This characteristic of scientific theoretical formations, that they are susceptible of development in the form of further transformations, distinguishes them from pre-scientific theoretical formations, where the structure of problems and solutions is 'closed' and therefore lacking in the capacity for such an inner dynamic. Finally, the dynamic in scientific systems of thought is to be found in a 'dialectic', or dialogue, between the formation of scientific concepts and hypotheses and their 'concretisation' in instrumentation which produces, in the scientific experiment, the phenomena of scientific observation. In Bachelard's conception of scientific experiment as 'phenomeno–technics', scientific theory is not seen as an attempt to account for 'data' given to experience, but, rather, through the technical realisation of scientific concepts nature is made to exhibit phenomena which would not otherwise be available for observation.

Bachelard's commitment to some doctrines of conventionalism, especially his rejection of empiricism and realism, and his conception of scientific theory as an open-ended, developing construct of scientific practice, enable him to abandon any concept of scientific objectivity as a correspondence between the concepts of a theory and a real world existing externally to, and independently of, theory. It is here that a central problem arises for all conventionalist philosophies of science, and for historical epistemology in particular. If neither rational proof nor empirical evidence can be called in to 'guarantee' a correspondence between scientific knowledge and external reality, if theoretical schemes are simply historically constituted conventions, then how can any special cognitive value be justifiably assigned to scientific findings? All we have are numerous co-existing conventional conceptions of reality, none of which can claim any more right to be believed than any other. In short, conventionalism has difficulty in stopping short of radical relativism or agnosticism. The details of Bachelard's own attempt to resolve this problem by way of a measure, not of the correspondence of scientific ideas to reality, but of their distance from the 'web of errors' from which they started, need not detain us.

Althusser, historical epistemology and Marx's 'science'

These concepts for thinking about scientific activity have an evident utility for Althusser's programme. In particular, Althusser needs conceptual means first to analyse the historical process of formation of a scientific discipline, second to establish the difference in cognitive (epistemological) status of the concepts of a newly founded science by comparison with the ideas and 'notions' of its prehistory, and, last, to distinguish, within a single text, the effects of two, or even more mutually incompatible theoretical schemes, or 'problematics'. Bachelard provides a conception of the history of each science as marked by discontinuities, ruptures and transformations, especially significant among which being that rupture through which a scientific discipline is initially formed from the 'web of errors' which preceded it. But Bachelard's conception of this discontinuity is not just an historical concept; its application also serves to locate a shift in the cognitive, or 'epistemological' status of the complex of concepts and problems constituting the discipline: hence the term which Althusser adopts, the 'epistemological break'. Applied to the history of Marxist thought, this concept should serve to locate both the historical moment of the emergence of 'historical materialism' in the texts of Marx, and also to indicate the shift in cognitive status to a scientific theory which occurs with this break. Correlatively the texts composed prior to this historical moment can be assigned to the *pre-history* of Marxism, as not truly 'Marxist', though composed by Marx. Furthermore, the persistence after the 'break' of concepts and problems of this pre-history is to be expected on the Bachelardian view: the philosophical effects of displaced stages in the theoretical lineage continue to threaten the achievements of later theoretical transformations in the form of 'epistemological obstacles'. The work of a philosophy which is partisan in support of the new science is to identify and wage war on these obstacles.

Althusser himself characterised his 'double intervention' in these terms:

The object of the first intervention is to 'draw a line of demarcation' between Marxist theory and the forms of philosophical (and political) subjectivism which have compromised or threaten it:

above all, *empiricism* and its variants, classical and modern –
pragmatism, voluntarism, historicism, etc. . . .

The object of the *second intervention* is to 'draw a line of
demarcation' between the true theoretical bases of the Marxist
science of history and Marxist philosophy on the one hand, and,
on the other, the pre-Marxist Idealist notions on which depend
contemporary interpretations of Marxism as a 'philosophy of
man' or a 'Humanism' . . . Behind the details of the arguments,
textual analyses and theoretical discussions, these two interventions reveal a major opposition; the opposition that separates
science from ideology . . .[29]

At first reading, this appears to be a direct application of
Bachelard's concepts of the epistemological break, the problematic,
epistemological obstacles, the relation of philosophy to science, and
so on, to the example of Marxism considered as a science. However,
the application has not left the concepts unaltered. For one thing, a
concept which plays an important part in Bachelard's analysis of
science, that of the 'scientific city', the institutionalised collective
character of scientific research, which is essential to the overcoming
of the epistemological obstacles affecting the individual psyche, is
absent from Althusser's conception of science. For Althusser, the
'autonomy' of science *vis-à-vis* ideology and the other social practices is a purely conceptual and epistemological autonomy, apparently unrelated to any specific system of social relations or mechanisms.

A second respect in which Bachelard's epistemology is transformed by Althusser is that science is not opposed, in Althusser to
'reverie', or, ultimately, as in Bachelard, to the natural inclinations
of the human mind, but, rather, to ideology. This is not a concept
which appears in Bachelard, but is a concept with a specific place in
the 'problematic' of historical materialism (the *word*, of course,
predates this). The obstacles which impede the advance of historical
materialism are not, in Althusser's use of these ideas, rooted in the
(universal) individual psyche, but in the theoretical articulation of
the ideologies (religious, ethical, political, and so on) through which
individuals 'live their relationships to their conditions of existence'.
But even this is not quite right. Althusser does not speak here of the
specific ideologies against which a specific science has to struggle in
the process of its formation, but of a general opposition between

science and ideology, a single, and presumably universal opposition which 'lies behind the detail'. In this respect Althusser seems closer to the 'philosophical conscience' which returns to Bachelard in his attempt to avoid relativism, than he does to the Bachelard who is concerned to analyse the historical processes of sciences in their concrete specificity, and to reject the claims of the 'philosophies of guarantees'.

But, as we shall see, this is not something incidental, a merely 'local' problem in Althusser. It is quite essential to his whole philosophical programme. On the one hand the ideas of historical epistemology are required if the necessary re-structuring of the Marxist theoretical tradition is to be achieved, if the necessary 'mutations' in theoretical problematics are to be identified. Moreover, the concept of a scientific problematic as 'open', and therefore subject to further transformations even after the founding of the science, shows a way to oppose the dogmatising of historical materialism. Science cannot be used as a set of eternal truths without ceasing to be science. The very criterion of scientific status is openness to revision. But if, in this respect, historical epistemology is a useful ally against Stalinism, as well as against 'humanism', it is, in the same breath, quite *useless* against Stalinism. What this whole exercise is about is providing an authority for a *particular reading* of Marx in *opposition* to others. What is needed is a criterion which will validate *these* concepts, problems and propositions as scientific against the claims of the rest. In short, while Althusser remains true to historical epistemology, he has difficulty in avoiding relativism (there are *differences* between the problematics of the earlier and later Marx – that is all), but relativism is no use if the requirement is for a seal of scientific *authority*.

There is another problem for whose solution Bachelard is no help. In replacing Bachelard's 'common sense' and the 'natural' tendencies of the human mind with 'ideology' as the source of epistemological obstacles, Althusser actually renders the problem of establishing a relationship between scientific theory and popular consciousness even more intractable. If the 'common sense' in which individual subjects 'live' their lives is a 'web of errors' against which science has to continually struggle to maintain itself, then how is an open and 'living' relationship between science and popular struggles ever to be established? Only if 'common-sense' is allowed (as, in fact, Gramsci recognises) to contain positive cognitive content, albeit bound up with mystification and illusion, can this problem be resolved, either in theory or in practice.

Finally, Bachelard appears to provide the theoretical means whereby the co-existence of incompatible theoretical schemes in a single text is to be identified. The concept of problematic is of obvious value here, especially if it is used in a structuralist way as what 'underlies' and determines the questions posed and answers given in an 'empirical' text, in such a way that the problematic is not immediately apparent but has to be inferred by a distinct *technique* of reading. Borrowing from structuralist psychoanalysis this technique of reading may be called 'symptomatic', recalling the analyst's treatment of the 'empirical' text of a dream or slip of the tongue as symptomatic of its subterranean unconscious determinants. Structural linguistics, too, can help here, in the shape of Saussure's thesis of the arbitrary connection of the signifier and the concept signified. The utility of this whole array of techniques and distinctions is to establish one thing: the 'reading' of Marx (or any other work, for that matter) established through their use may not be 'refuted' by the mere device of using 'quotations' against it. Old words may signify new concepts, incompatible problematics may simultaneously determine a single, *apparently* continuous discourse.

A final point needs to be made, before we go on to look at the results of Althusser's importation of structuralism and historical epistemology to serve in Marxism's internecine warfare. What makes the whole strategy of importation necessary is the vicious circularity in which Althusser is caught if he stays within the terms of Marxist theory itself. Althusser seeks to validate his reading of Marx as scientific. For this he needs to found a Marxist philosophy (epistemology) adequate to the task. But the founding of a Marxist philosophy itself requires that the authentically 'scientific' and authentically 'Marxist' texts can already be identified. In practice, as we have seen, Althusser breaks the circle by introducing independent elements of historical epistemology and structuralism. But how, it might then be asked, can Althusser possibly claim to be engaged in an exercise of eradicating the alien, unscientific accretions from Marxism, when he himself has to draw upon equally un-Marxist (even bourgeois!) sources to carry it through consistently? Althusser's response to this is to once again close the circle. These philosophical means are required only to give explicit philosophical expression to concepts already present 'in the practical state' in the works of Marx and Engels themselves. But this is, of course, no help. By what credentials does this structuralist 'reading' of those concepts in their practical state defend itself against the rival humanist and Stalinist readings? Of course, there is a way out of this circle. It is to detach the question 'What is authentically Marxist?' from the question 'What is authentically scientific?' Perhaps we are here up against one of the limits to Althusser's anti-Stalinism.

Part I
Althusser

2

Althusser and Marxist Philosophy: Science and Ideology

For Althusser, as we have seen, Marxist philosophy, or Theory (with a capital 'T') was supposed to be an indispensable means for any adequate interpretation of the works of Marx (or, indeed, any other text). In order, then, to *establish* the principles and methods of Marxist philosophy it is first necessary to *employ* them. Althusser recognises the circularity of this intellectual process, but denies that it is a vicious circularity: the interpretation achieved by the employment of the results of that interpretation is tested in the process. I have argued that whatever the significance of this claim of Althusser's, in practice he escapes from his circle by a series of conceptual borrowings mainly from French conventionalist philosophy of science, historical epistemology and from structuralism.

So far I have dealt in a preliminary way with several of these conceptual borrowings: the concepts of 'problematic' and 'epistemological break' from historical epistemology, and a structuralist way of making the distinction between scientific and ideological theoretical formations in terms of the place in them of conceptions of the 'subject'. Althusser justifies these borrowings from alien philosophical territory partly by claiming to uncover the concepts in their practical state (that is, not theoretically recognised and articulated, but nevertheless present) in a number of classic Marxist texts, and partly by the open admission that Marxist philosophy has yet to be established and can benefit from its confrontation with other philosophical traditions. In every case, the borrowings are of *particular concepts* (which, as we have seen, are transformed in the process) and not of the whole philosophical problematic. Only this latter would 'bind' or 'imprison' the borrower.

To investigate this claim, and to see what the consequences of Althusser's philosophical investigations are for his overall conception of Marxist theory and political practice, it will be necessary to see what Althusser does with the concepts he borrows. How does he combine them together with one another and with concepts he himself contributes?

Knowledge as production

Althusser's most important contribution to the analysis of theoretical work is his conception of knowledge as a form of 'production'.

Theoretical work is, according to Althusser, a social practice, along with other social practices (ideological, political, economic, 'technical', and so on) which together make up a complex whole, 'society'. Each of these practices is held to have the structure of a production: that is to say, in each, some raw material is transformed by human labour utilising certain instruments, or means (of production), into a specific kind of product. Within a practice so defined, Althusser says, it is the 'moment' or 'element' of the labour of transformation itself which is 'determinant'. Theoretical work is to be thought of, at least in its structure, as analogous to other forms of social practice with which it is combined or articulated in society. But it is distinct from them in having its own specific raw materials, means of production, product, and, presumably, form or type of human labour.

The raw materials of theoretical practice are concepts, notions, facts which are either the products (by-products) of other social practices (especially ideological practices) or the products of previous phases in the work of theoretical production. The means of production employed to work upon and transform these raw materials into 'knowledges' are the currently established set of concepts, principles, laws, and so on, of the theoretical discipline concerned. Finally, the product takes the form of new concepts, laws and analyses which may henceforward play the part of the means of production in succeeding phases of theoretical work.

This conception of knowledge as 'production' has considerable advantages as a means of analysing theoretical work. It enables the analysis of conceptual change within a discipline not as some mysterious act of genius, nor as the direct effect of the application of logic to experience, but as a result of real intellectual labour, using identifiable conceptual instruments. The possibility, at least, is opened up of a much broader conception of scientific rationality than is available in the main alternative (empiricist) traditions for thinking about the nature of scientific activity. Also Althusser's conception has the dual advantage of providing means for thinking about the *specificity* of theoretical work within a discipline, with its own inner dynamic, whilst at the same time (through the reference to extrinsically produced raw materials) referring to its necessary articulation and interchange with other social practices.

Althusser's distance from empiricism is emphasised in his insistence that the raw materials of theoretical practice are never 'pure data', but are always products of previous social practice of one kind or another. Here is a reference not only to the Marxist conception of the nature of the 'raw' materials of economic practices (that is, they are always products of previous labour processes), but also to the conventionalist doctrine that the 'facts' with which a science deals are always 'theory-laden': all observation and experience has an unavoidable conceptual element (at least, it must have some conceptual content if it is to figure significantly in scientific thought). In this Althusser is in line with most contemporary thinking in the philosophy of science. Althusser in one text marks this point by referring to raw materials, means of production, and product of theoretical practice all as 'Generalities' (Generalities I, II, and III).[1]

It is, however, in his employment of this conventionalist critique of empiricism that Althusser gets himself into some of his most serious philosophical difficulties. Using an important but highly ambiguous methodological text[2] written (but not published) by Marx as his guide, Althusser argues the case that theoretical practice takes place 'entirely in thought'. By this he means to say that the whole process, raw materials→transformation with means of production→product, whilst it may, *in some sense* involve a *reference* to an external, independent reality (of which the product is a 'knowledge'), nevertheless takes place without, so to speak, directly touching, or 'taking up' that independent reality. In transforming the *concept* of matter, the scientist does not transform matter; to invent the oxygen theory of combustion is not to invent combustion by oxygen. A clear distinction must be drawn, in Althusser's view, between the objects of scientific investigation as they are conceptualised through the means available to a science – conceptual means which are eminently subject to revision, even abandonment (for example, phlogiston) – and the real-world things, processes and mechanisms which continue independently of our thinking about them, and remain unchanged by our changed conceptions of them.

Althusser variously refers to this distinction between the internal and the external objects of knowledge with the contrasting terms 'concrete-in-thought' and 'real-concrete', or 'object of knowledge' and 'real object'. The existence of real-world objects, independent of our thought about them is a premise of the classic materialist works in the theory of knowledge, especially those of Engels and Lenin. Althusser could hardly abandon it. On the other hand, his adoption and extension of the conventionalist critique of empiricism commits him to denying that independently existing real-world objects are *directly* appropriated in thought. This would be to concede that there could be such a thing as theory-neutral perception or observation.

For Althusser, empiricism appears to be a very broad tradition indeed, seemingly including virtually every tradition in epistemology except his own. In Althusser's characterisation, empiricism is a conception of knowledge in which a 'subject' conducts an operation – 'abstraction' – upon an external object, as a result of which part, the *essential* part, of that object is appropriated. Empiricism, then, presupposes a distinction within the real object between what is inessential (its superficial appearance) and what is essential. Knowledge abstracts the inner, essential core of its object, so that, in Althusser's rather bewildering expression, for empiricism knowledge is 'already *really* present in the real object it has to know ...'[3] Strictly speaking, it seems that Althusser is defining as empiricist those theories of knowledge which assert an actual *identity* between knowledge and its object, in which case his critique, such as it is, would apply only to certain rationalist philosophers (such as Spinoza) some idealists (such as Hegel) and to some Hegelian Marxists (such as Lukács), and then only on some readings of their works. To cover conventionally recognised empiricists, Althusser would have to include doctrines for which knowledge takes the form of representations, copies, reflections, and so on, of external reality. Here the relationship is one of correspondence rather than strict identity. In any event, the main point of Althusser's characterisation and critique of empiricism appears to be to show that it entails a denial of the productive, transformative character of the 'knowledge process': knowledge is an intellectual construct not a receptacle of the imprints of what lies outside it.

In its negative aspect it seems to me that this critique, despite its obscurity of expression, has much to commend it, but in his efforts to avoid the errors of 'empiricism' Althusser over-reacts. All that is necessary to sustain the conception of knowledge as productive, transformative activity, and at the same time to retain the idea of knowledge as knowledge of something external to and independent of itself, is to recognise that one and the same thing (object, substance, process, mechanism, and so on) may be referred to through a variety of *different*, even *mutually incompatible* means of conceptualisation: the *same thing* may go under *different descriptions*.

A good deal, but not all, of the productive work in science consists in the generation of new forms of conceptualisation to better characterise what was previously known through alternative forms: for example, the shifts from Aristotelian to Copernican and then Newtonian conceptions of the sun and its planetary system. True, it is necessary to allign oneself with one of these conceptions in order to refer to the identical object which is 'known' to each of them. But that it *is* an identical object, 'known' to each of them is shown in the means available *within astronomy* to establish (complete or partial) identity of reference between such phrases as 'the planetary system' and 'the heavens', 'orbits' and 'spheres', and so on. Althusser, however, seems to overlook this possibility, avoiding 'empiricism' at the cost of a wholescale duplication of the universe into those real objects which exist external to thought and those inner 'objects of knowledge' which are the 'appropriation in thought' of the external objects.

Paradoxically enough, this radical distinction which Althusser insists upon immediately poses for *him* the central question of the classical subject/object epistemologies, the 'philosophies of guarantees' which he has sought to abandon. This question is, given that there is a radical separation between knowledge and its external object, how do we 'know' that the internal object *really is* the knowledge of (really does correspond to) the external object? 'Experience' as the infallible mediator between the external world and the 'knowing subject' is ruled out for Althusser, as also is the rationalist (and ultimately theological) guarantee of the 'clear light of reason'. These answers to the central question of classical epistemology (the quest for a criterion by which to recognise genuine knowledge) share with all other answers the second-order problem:

how, in turn, is the epistemological guarantee *itself* guaranteed? Althusser, following the traditions of French conventionalism and historical epistemology, is quite right to reject the very terms of the original question, but, as we have seen, his own distinction between internal and external objects of knowledge makes it unavoidable.

Althusser's conception of knowledge as production could be rendered consistent in only two ways: the distinction between internal and external objects of knowledge may be abandoned in a realist, or materialist direction (I have suggested, in the notion of 'same thing – different description', one device which makes this possible), or it may be abandoned in an idealist, or conventionalist direction. In this latter strategy the internal (conceptual) object of knowledge is privileged, and what counts as 'real' is a function of what is *conceptualised* as real in current knowledge. The historian and philosopher of science, Thomas Kuhn, comes close to this position when he says that, in a certain sense, the world of scientists after a scientific revolution is a *different world* from that of their predecessors.[4] Althusser himself alternates uneasily between both strategies. Sometimes he denies there is anything at all problematic in the object of knowledge–real object relationship, and sometimes asserts that specific sciences stand in no need of external guarantees or tests of their validity.[5] These are both conventionalist responses, and take Althusser down the slippery slope to relativism: any discipline (classical political economy, rational theology, phrenology, astrology ...) which sets itself up as 'scientific' and provides its own internal criteria of validity, its own independent means of establishing its status as knowledge must have that status accepted at face value. Such a relativist, or conventionalist conception of science is, of course, absolutely useless for Althusser's *political* project of establishing the scientific credentials of one tradition, or 'reading' of Marxism *as against* the claims of rivals.

Elsewhere Althusser attempts to resolve his epistemological problem by terminological fiat: it is somehow an intrinsic property of a scientific, as distinct from an ideological mode of theoretical production that its products *are* the cognitive appropriation of their external object. The impressive phrase 'mechanism of the knowledge effect'[6] attempts to conceal the otherwise rather blatant emptiness of this 'solution'. I have attempted to show elsewhere that, short of the abandonment of this real object – object of knowledge distinction in a materialist, or realist direction, Althusser's epistemological problem remains insoluble.[7] I shall need to return, in a moment, to the epistemological problems of Althusser's theory of knowledge, since they emerge sharply in his treatment of the Marxist conception of ideology. Meanwhile, however, two more difficulties in Althusser's notion of knowledge as production must be mentioned.

First, Althusser's characterisations of what it is about knowledge that justifies its inclusion as a form of production are not always consistent with one another. Most importantly, the characterisation I have so far given (raw materials–transformation by human labour–means of production–product) vies with another character-isation in Althusser in which prominence is given to the *structure of social relations* within which this production process takes place:

> This thought is the historically constituted system of an *apparatus of thought*, founded on and articulated to natural and social reality. It is defined by the system of real conditions which make it, if I dare use the phrase, a determinate *mode of production* of knowledges. As such it is constituted by a structure which combines ('Verbindung') the type of object (raw material) on which it labours, the theoretical means of production available (its theory, its method and its technique, experimental or otherwise) and the historical relations (both theoretical, ideological and social) in which it produces.[8]

The first account of the structure of knowledge as production, which omitted all mention of its social relations of production has rightly been criticised as 'technicist' (that is, as representing the production of knowledge as a mere technical process in which means are employed to achieve a certain useful object). If, on the other hand, the analogy with Marx's notion of economic produc-tion is to be taken seriously then clearly the question of the social relations within which production takes place must be given priori-ty. All modes of economic production mentioned by Marx involve economic agents in social relations which are 'independent of their will,[9] and in all antagonistic modes of production (that is to say, modes of production in which the surplus product of the producers is appropriated by a class which owns, or controls the means of economic production) a distinction has to be drawn between the technical aspects of the social relations of production, which would be required irrespective of the exploitative or antagonistic character of the mode of production, and those other aspects of the social relations of production, which are necessary to the preservation of the existing social form of class domination and economic exploitation. In the capitalist mode of economic production this distinction is marked in the distinction between the 'labour process', considered as a process whereby specific 'concrete labours' result in the production of specific useful products, and the 'mode of production' in the broader sense, in which labour power as a quantifiable commodity is set to work to add value to commodities which are then sold by the owner of the means of production who thereby realises an economic surplus. Although an analysis of the social relations of exploitation (essentially, property relations) presupposes that the commodities produced do have some utility (that is to say, meet some specific requirement on the part of a potential purchaser) it isn't necessary to the analysis of this aspect of the social relations of production to specify what 'use value' the items have. The supposed contradiction between production for use and production for profit is regarded, in some interpretations of Marxism, as the source of the central dynamic in capitalist societies.

To return, though, to Althusser's analysis of knowledge as production. In the first version it certainly seems to treat knowledge as if it were a 'labour process' only, and in abstraction from anything analogous to property relations, social relations of exploitation, or, more broadly, *class* relations. Of course, for a Marxist writer this is a rather damning omission, and Althusser's critics have been quick to point out how well it conceals the social significance of Althusser's own position as a professional employee in one of France's foremost academic institutions: a bourgeois social position *par excellence*! In qualified defence of Althusser, though, texts such as the one I quoted above which *do* include reference to the social relations of knowledge production are also present in Althusser's work. What is missing however, in his works up to 1965 at any rate, is any systematic account of what these relations are, how they affect the cognitive value of the knowledge produced, how they relate to the social relations of economic exploitation, and, more broadly, to class relations in society. Only in Althusser's later, revised position do we begin to get answers to such questions as these. Whether they are adequate answers remains to be seen.

A second problem in Althusser's conception of knowledge as production is related to this first one. It concerns the relationship between the structure of relations within which production takes place, and the agency of the labourer whose labour power ('thought power') is set to work in the production process. At one point, as we have already seen, Althusser speaks of the 'moment' or 'element' of the labour of transformation itself as 'determinant'.[10] But this is a most imprecise formulation: determinant of what? and what is to be included in this 'moment' or 'element'? On the face of it the quotation could be seen as giving priority, at least in the case of the production of knowledge, to the creative activity of the scientist. But this is decidedly not the position Althusser advances elsewhere. In *Reading Capital*, for example – the source of the quotation in which Althusser includes social relations of production in his conception of knowledge as production– it is the *structural conditions* (conceptual and social) of thought which determine what a scientist can or cannot think (just as, in Althusser's conception of 'symptomatic reading', it is the structure of the relationship between the problematic(s) underlying the text and that employed by the reader which determines what is visible or invisible to the reader).

The thought of the individual scientist (which is presumably the analogue of the labour of the individual labourer) achieves what it achieves merely as the functionary, so to speak, of the structural conditions in which it takes place. Using Marx's critique of the category 'value of labour' as an example, Althusser argues that Marx's critique required not just 'an acute or attentive gaze', but presupposed a transformation of problematics. He goes on:

The fact that this *'change of terrain'* which produces as its effect this metamorphosis in the gaze, was itself only produced in very specific, complex and often dramatic conditions; that it is absolutely irreducible to the idealist myth of a mental decision to change 'view-points'; that it brings into play a whole process that the subject's sighting, far from producing, merely reflects in its own place; that in this process of real transformation of the means of production of knowledge, the claims of a 'constitutive subject' are as vain as the claims of the subject of vision in the production of the visible; that the whole process takes place in the dialectical crisis of the mutation of a theoretical structure *in which the 'subject' plays, not the part it believes it is playing, but the part which is assigned to it by the mechanism of the process* – all these are questions that cannot be studied here.[11]

Important questions to be put aside, one might think! But even as they stand, these indications as to the status of the agency of 'subjects' in the production process of knowledge are demonstrably faulty. First, the implication of opposition between the subject's *belief* as to the part it plays and the 'part assigned, to it' is that this opposition exhausts the possibilities. To follow Marx's dictum that 'one does not judge an individual by his consciousness of himself' *appears* to entail assigning to individuals no independent agency, *vis-à-vis* the structural conditions of their activity. But clearly this move is not required in logic. Individual 'subjects' may believe many different things about the part they play in the activities in which they participate. But why must they *necessarily* misrecognise it (even, presumably, when they are informed by a historical materialist understanding of their own social practice)? Further, sustaining a distinction between 'the part individual subjects *believe* they are playing' and 'the part individual subjects *actually* play' doesn't at all commit one to the thesis that individual subjects *actually* play no significant (that is, independent) role at all. The extreme forms of structural determinism which are to be found in places in these early texts by Althusser are not, as they are some-times presented, the logical outcome of Marx's methodological precepts but are, rather, signs of Althusser's submission to certain contemporary structuralist doctrines which have no necessary con-nection with the Marxist tradition.

Having said this, these structural determinist formulations are nevertheless worth investigation in their own right, especially as their occurrence in Althusser's writing about knowledge is only a specific (though particularly problematic) instance of Althusser's general position on the relationship between social structure and agency. It will be necessary to turn later to this question, but for the moment some of the problems implicit in Althusser's position may be noted. First, since the activity of the individual (or, for that matter, collective) 'subject' is held to be a function of its structural conditions, it follows that the real work (in the sense of causal efficacy) of theoretical transformation is achieved by the play of problematics and their social conditions of existence. If this is so, then it should be a matter of complete indifference who the agent (scientist) is in whose works this result is achieved: the qualifica-tions, mental powers, value-position, training and so on of that individual (or collectivity) should be strictly irrelevant to the onward march of the conceptual movement. Paradoxically, there is more than a hint of Hegelianism in this supposedly anti-Hegelian position, and in the specific case with which Althusser is most concerned, the repetitious references to Marx's 'extraordinary rigour' and perspicacity would be rendered entirely superfluous if Althusser's discourse were self-consistent.

More seriously than this, though, Althusser's undifferentiated subsumption of individual agency under the agency of external structures obliterates a number of important distinctions. To return to the analogy with economic production. Marx certainly asserts that in their productive activity, 'men' enter into relations which are 'independent of their will'. This is supposedly a general statement covering all (except, possibly, the socialist mode) modes of production. Nevertheless, Marx also regarded as one of the distinguishing features of the capitalist mode of production its subordination of labour to the conditions of production: in manufacture this subordination is 'formal', an effect of the division of labour, and becomes 'real' with the subordination of labour to the rhythms and operations dictated by machinery with modern factory production. These differentiations and many others, between forms and types of subordination of labour need to be made even to characterise labour processes adequately, let alone modes pf production, in the full sense, in which class and relations of exploitation impose other types of domination and subordination. The truth implicit in Marx's dictum is that action is inconceivable independently of its structural conditions, but it is a characteristic elision of conservative thought to draw from this the conclusion that action is *no more than* its structural conditions. What is also hidden in this elision is the distinction between the necessity for *some* structural conditions and the non-necessity of any *particular set* of such conditions.

Science and ideology: the epistemological break

So much, then, for the moment, for the advantages and difficulties of Althusser's conception of knowledge as production. I have already given a brief account of two other concepts of Althusser's theory of knowledge, which he derives from external sources: the concepts of 'problematic' and of the 'epistemological break'. The three concepts are, of course, closely logically integrated with one another: the idea that theoretical discourse is governed by an underlying problematic, which determines what can and cannot be said/seen within it carries with it a conception of knowledge as a social construct, as produced, rather than 'impressed' upon the mind, whilst the notion that knowledge must advance discontinuously, by qualitative leaps or revolutions is implicit in the idea of a problematic as a *structure* of concepts and problems which binds together and gives unity to its constituent elements. Change must be a more or less immediate overthrow and replacement, rather than a cumulative process of piecemeal addition or correction.

As we have already seen,[12] though, the concept of an epistemological break has itself undergone some changes in its incorporation into Althusser's 'problematic'. There are two specific changes which most centrally concern us here: the first is that the relationship between a science and its pre-history is, in Althusser, mapped onto the Marxist contrast between science and ideology, whilst the second is that the obstacles which continue to threaten the advance of a science after the moment of its foundation, conceived of by Bachelard as psychological in origin are, for Althusser, also rooted in ideology. To begin with the first modification, the implication is that an important distinction has been made between the 'qualitative change', the epistemological break proper, that marks the transition from ideology to science, and the subsequent 'recastings' of the problematic of a science once it has been established (Althusser's favourite exemplars of the two are the shift from Aristotelian to classical physics in the seventeenth century, and the development of quantum mechanics and relativity theory around the turn of the present century, respectively).

If we concern ourselves, following Althusser, with the characteristic features of the epistemological break proper, the shift from ideology to science, then two further implications can be derived from his account. First, ideology (in the sense of whatever-it-is that is the precursor of a scientific discipline) must itself be a form of theoretical practice, which is worked on and transformed to produce the problematic of a science. This implication is, indeed, embraced by Althusser, who speaks of the distinct ideological and scientific 'modes of production' of knowledge. Secondly, though, despite their having in common their status as theoretical practices, science and theoretical ideology are radically distinct in their epistemological status: the problematic of a theoretical ideology involves a tissue or 'web' of errors, which the founding of the scientific problematic displaces. The location of an epistemological break in the history of a branch of knowledge, then, serves both the periodise that history, and to indicate a qualitative change in the *cognitive status* of the discourse in that field. It is at this point that there recurs the same epistemological problem which infected Althusser's critique of empiricism. To *apply* the concept of epistemological break, in Althusser's use of it, is to commit oneself not just to an historical, but also to an epistemological judgment: a judgment as to the cognitive status of the problematic which emerges from the break. What is the criterion by which this judgment is made, and what is the justification of that criterion?

Althusser alternates between two main strategies. In the first he makes the contrast between science and ideology a matter of the different relationships the two types of discourse (or problematic) have to social practices external to knowledge, and the related structural differences in their problematics. Althusser's alternative strategy involves reverting to a classical epistemological distinction in terms of the 'falsehood' or 'deformation' of ideology *vis-à-vis* its scientific counterpart. The former strategy involves Althusser in the claim that ideological discourses do not possess an internal principle of intelligibility. In order to understand an ideological discourse it is necessary, certainly, to relate it to its broader 'ideological field', but beyond this it is necessary to understand the peculiar pattern of presences and absences – questions posed, questions excluded – in terms of a relationship between the ideology and the real social problems and structures which sustain it.

This account of ideology, which concerns principally ideology in its theoretical state – theoretical ideology – may be related to what Althusser says in exposition of the Marxist category of ideology itself, most explicitly in the text 'Marxism and Humanism'.[13] In this text Althusser says that ideology differs from science in that in the former the 'practico–social function is more important than the theoretical function ...'[14] This practico–social function is that through and in ideology 'men' are formed, transformed and equipped to respond to the demands of their conditions of existence.[15] This is supposed by Althusser to be a historical necessity in all forms of society – including communist (albeit that new *forms* of ideology may be expected to emerge here). Though Althusser puts this necessity rather obliquely, the argument seems to be that in any society in which there is a division of social labour (that is, any society) there must be some means by which agents are allocated to positions in that division of labour, equipped with forms of consciousness (beliefs, values, commitments, dispositions, skills and so on) which fit them to carry out the function assigned to that position. Ideology, as an objectively existing 'structure of representations' is the necessary element in which agents 'live' their relationship to their real position in society. The representations, images, concepts, and so on, through which they 'live' this relationship do, indeed, refer to the real relationship but they do so in an 'imaginary' form. Ideology in this sense could never be replaced by science since what is involved is not simply a matter of cognition, but the binding together of elements of cognition and misrecognition with motivations, commitments and dispositions.

When, in theoretical ideology problems are articulated and given answers, an adequate analysis of the structure constituted by those problems and answers must necessarily make reference, beyond the theoretical ideology to the ideological field in which it is rooted, and, beyond that, to real problems in the relationship between the lived experience of 'subjects' and their real conditions of existence. In another text, Althusser expresses this succinctly in terms of the provision by theoretical ideologies of questions to match the answers *already* required by interests extrinsic to the domain of theory.[16] This domination of theoretical ideologies by the need to 'service' the demands of extra-theoretical interests and practices has implications for the structure of their problematics: the problematics of theoretical ideologies are 'closed' by contrast with the openness of scientific problematics.[17]

This contrast between openness and closure of problematics isn't given any extended development, but one thing that seems to be implicit in it, since the 'answers' given in an ideology are already presupposed in their questions, is that theoretical ideologies can have no inner dynamic: in so far as there is theoretical transformation, then this must be an effect of a dynamic existing in the world of real conditions of existence and 'lived' relationships to them. This, in turn, seems to challenge Althusser's very conception of theoretical ideologies as a form of 'practice': it seems that they are a form of practice in which nothing gets produced, except shadows of what occurs elsewhere. Equally difficult, in the light of this, would be any serious account of how a (non-existent) ideological practice could transform itself into a scientific theoretical practice. Self-reproduction, perhaps in variant forms, appears to be the limit of the transformative possibilities open to an ideological theoretical practice.

On the other hand, the 'openness' of the scientific practice is something that must, on Althusser's own account, be a feature of all genuine theoretical *practices*: if real (conceptual) transformation takes place, then it follows that there must be conceptual and epistemological unevennesses and dislocations between raw materials, conceptual means of production and product of theoretical practice. This feature of scientific discourses as complex, uneven and internally contradictory systems of concepts and problems is implicit in Althusser, and is, in my view, a promising and fruitful way of understanding the nature of scientific discourse. But it follows from the above arguments that if theoretical ideologies are also to be taken seriously as theoretical practices, and as constituting the pre-history of sciences, then these, too, must be recognised as characterised by an 'openness' in their problematics, and so this way of making the science–ideology distinction fails in its present form.

But there is a more fundamental problem, from Althusser's point of view, in this attempt to distinguish science and ideology in terms of the 'practico–social function' of the latter. This is that, whilst avoiding the awkward implications of admitting that these categories are epistemological ones, it commits Althusser to abandoning his claim to be engaged in the recovery of Marxist philosophy. This is because, deprived of their epistemological 'purchase', and treated, instead, as categories of social and historical analysis, such concepts as science, ideology, knowledge as production, problematic and epistemological break cease to be *philosophical* categories, and become, instead, categories belonging to a region (theory of theoretical practices and their history) of historical materialism – the proclaimed science of history.

Is there a Marxist philosophy?

This brings us, at last, to the basic question underlying these early texts of Althusser's: is there such a thing as Marxist philosophy, and if so, what is it? Althusser's dilemma seems to be that, on the one hand, to make the science–ideology distinction a sociological–historical one is to admit that there is no Marxist philosophy (the thesis of the death of philosophy against which Althusser polemicises), whilst, on the other, to make the distinction an epistemological one (to make it turn on the question of the relative statuses as *knowledge* of the two types of discourse) is to reinstate the problem of classical epistemology: what guarantees the epistemological status of the philosophical theory which judges the epistemological status of the sciences? Althusser's way of 'resolving' this dilemma is to advance a conception of Marxist philosophy by contrast with all other, ideological philosophies, as a scientific philosophy: Theory (with a capital 'T') is the general theory of Marxism 'in which is theoretically expressed the essence of theoretical practice in general, through it the essence of practice in general, and through it the essence of the transformations, of the "development" of things in general'.[18] This conception of Marxist philosophy turns out, somewhat surprisingly in view of the detour via various modern non-Marxist philosophical traditions, to be none other than a rather orthodox (if somewhat pallid and shame-faced) rendition of the 'dialectical materialism' of the later works of Engels, mediated through the philosophical works of Lenin, Stalin and, more directly, Mao. On this conception of Marxist philosophy the laws of the dialectic (which Engels claimed to have detected in their idealist form in the work of Hegel) are truly universal laws in the sense that they govern the processes of human thought, the movement of human history, and also of the history of nature itself. This conception of philosophy is inseparable from an ontology, a scientific 'metaphysics', in which human history is viewed as an aspect of the history of nature, and human thought as the reflection in the human brain of these two histories.[19] Given such a 'materialistic' metaphysic the proposition that all three domains should be governed by identical 'laws of motion' need not come as a surprise.

What is surprising, however, is that Althusser should espouse it. The historical epistemology upon which Althusser relies so heavily represents philosophies as effects of revolutions in scientific problematics which serve to consolidate the hold of a given phase in the development of a science, and so reappear as epistemological obstacles which retard further advances. In the form echoed by Althusser, dialectical materialism has all the hallmarks of such an epistemological obstacle – it generalises and turns into a philosophical ontology the results of a given phase in the history of the sciences. Paradoxically enough, the necessity of Marxist philosophy is urged by Althusser precisely as a weapon with which to *defend* scientific advances in Marxism against ideological incursions such as humanist and historicist philosophies of history. Perhaps the only merit of this conception of Marxist philosophy as 'Theory', the theory of theoretical practice, is that it provides the verbal 'solution' to Althusser's dilemma over the status of his theory of knowledge: the theory is *both* 'scientific' and philosophical, it is a 'scientific philosophy'. As we shall see, this conception of philosophy came in for some very strong criticism – not least from Althusser himself in his later writings. Althusser's dilemma over the status, in particular, of his science ideology distinction also subsequently received critical attention. But this is to anticipate: our next task is to investigate the periodisation of Marx's works which the application of Althusser's theory of knowledges and their history produces, and to outline the interpretation of the Marxist conception of history which they claim to validate.

3

Marx's 'Epistemological Break'

Althusser's central project in his philosophical writings of the early and mid 1960s, as we have seen, was the recovery and development of a Marxist philosophy. This is seen not simply as an end in itself, but as a means of drawing a boundary between the Marxist science of history, historical materialism, on the one hand, and the various epistemological obstacles, principally ideological philosophies, which invade and impede its progress, on the other. Since the problematic of historical materialism was constituted in the works of Marx, and yet a major source for the most powerful of the philosophical ideologies ('historicism' and 'humanism') against which Althusser's work is pitted is also the works of Marx, it follows that Althusser's project turns on devising the means for a selective and critical reading of these same writings of Marx. The instruments Althusser uses for this purpose are the ones we have so far discussed: the concepts of science and ideology, theoretical practice, problematic, epistemological break, and their cognates.

To anticipate, and to oversimplify: Althusser seeks to locate an 'epistemological break' in Marx's intellectual career (more properly, in the historical series of Marx's works), such that those texts produced before the break can be designated works of theoretical ideology, whilst those after it are governed by the newly founded scientific problematic. Of course, all of Marx's writings from his Doctoral dissertation to the 1844 *Manuscripts* cannot be lumped together as effects of a single ideological problematic. Althusser distinguishes within this early period works dominated by a Kantian–Fichtean (liberal–rationalist) problematic, and works resting upon Feuerbach's anthropological problematic, as well as a single text (the 1844 *Manuscripts*) which is dominated by the Hegalian problematic. Secondly, the transition from ideology to science, though a qualitative break, is not consummated in a single moment, so that in addition to what Althusser calls the 'Works of the Break' (two texts composed in 1845: the *German Ideology* and the *Theses on Feuerbach*) is a series of *transitional* works from 1845 to 1857, the period of the 'Mature Works' dating from the first drafts of *Capital*.[1] Since the establishment of the new problematic is a more or less extended process, and since, also, the emergence of a new problematic does not abolish the existence or 'effectivity' of its predecessors, we should not be surprised to find passages and formulations even in the mature works which take us back to the earlier problematics: the mere 'empiricist' citing of quotations from the later works is insufficient to refute Althusser's thesis of the epistemological break.

Another way in which Althusser's thesis might be put to the test would be by setting it against Marx and Engels' own comments on their intellectual development. Althusser himself does, indeed, take these comments seriously, but they have no specially privileged status in his view, and must be themselves subject to critical scrutiny. That this really is necessary is evident from the paradoxical and sometimes contradictory character of Marx and Engels' formulations on these questions. In their 'mature' works, Marx and Engels do often refer to their relationship to Hegel as if it were very close:

> The mystification which dialectic suffers in Hegel's hands, by no means prevents him from being the first to present its general form of working in a comprehensive and conscious manner. With him it is standing on its head. It must be turned right side up again, if you would discover the rational kernel within the mystical shell.
>
> In its mystified form, dialectic became the fashion in Germany, because it seemed to transfigure and to glorify the existing state of things. In its rational form it is a scandal and abomination to bourgeoisdom and its doctrinaire professors, because it includes in its comprehension and affirmative recognition of the existing state of things, at the same time also, the recognition of the negation of that state, of its inevitable breaking up; because it regards every historically developed social form as in fluid movement, and therefore takes into account its transient nature not less than its momentary existence, because it lets nothing impose upon it, and is in its essence critical and revolutionary.[2]

But the metaphors through which Marx here thinks his relationship to Hegal cannot be taken as precise or adequate characterisations. The metaphor of a 'kernel within a shell' and that of an 'inversion' suggest that the dialectic 'in its rational form' can be arrived at as the outcome of a simple operation or transposition of the dialectic, in its Hegelian, 'mystified' form. Not only are the images Marx uses seemingly incompatible (the operations of 'inversion' and 'extraction' are not the same) but each, as Althusser points out, spirits away the *work of theoretical labour* involved in the achievement of Marx's 'immense theoretical revolution'. Furthermore, the thinker who most unambiguously 'inverted' Hegel's philosophy was Feuerbach, whose materialism was the avowed inspiration of certain of Marx and Engels' most significant early works. Yet, in his 1859 *Preface*, Marx speaks of the *German Ideology* (1845) as an attempt by himself and Engels 'to settle accounts with our former philosophical conscience'.[3] This critique of 'post-Hegelian philosophy' includes an extended critique of the post-Hegelian Feuerbach, and therefore, by implication, their own Feuerbachian texts. If Feuerbach inverted Hegel, and Marx and Engels established their later positions from a critique of Feuerbach, then the relationship of Marx and Engels to Hegel *cannot* be adequately summed up as the 'inversion' of Hegel. Since neither the 'empiricist' selection of quotations nor reference to the retrospective comments of Marx and Engels themselves can be decisive for Althusser's thesis of the 'epistemological break', all that is left is for us to attempt to follow Althusser in 'unearthing' the problematics – the hidden, often unreflected and unarticulated presupposition and conceptual determinants – of the texts of Marx and Engels.

Hegel and the 'Young Hegelians'

The idealist philosophy of history whose greatest exponent was G.W.F. Hegel must (despite its immense difficulty) be the starting point for this analysis. Hegel's declared philosophical project was to restore and 'complete' the speculative metaphysical philosophy whose pretensions to a knowledge higher than and beyond the reach of sensory experience had been deflated by the eighteenth century philosopher, Immanuel Kant. According to Kant, knowledge, properly speaking, takes as its objects only what belongs to the domain of 'phenomena' or appearances: the domain of what can be experienced by the human senses, and to which alone can be properly applied the basic categories of experience, common sense and science (space, time, causality, necessity and possibility, substance and attribute, and so on). Knowledge of 'things-in-themselves' is beyond our reach and the objectivity of concepts such as freedom, God and immortality, which are necessary for our moral life, is a matter of faith, rather than positive knowledge.

Whereas Kant had attempted to demonstrate this by, amongst other things, showing that thinking falls into inextricable contradictions when it claims knowledge of the nature of things-in-themselves, beyond the bounds of possible sensory experience, Hegel embraces this argument and turns it into its opposite: the contradictory character of thought about things-in-themselves evidences only their contradictory character and their potential transcendence into a higher unity. The ultimate, underlying reality of the world, for Hegel, is spiritual in character: 'Absolute Spirit'. The world of our everyday experience: the world of particular things and people, of the difference between mind and matter, the world 'known' in science and common sense, is, indeed a world of mere appearances. It is a world in which Absolute Spirit is alienated from, or exists in contradiction to, itself. Through the development of religion and philosophical understanding (culminating in Idealist philosophy itself), the contradictions of this alienated form of existence are superseded, or 'transcended' into a higher dialectical unity, in which, ultimately, self-realisation of Absolute Spirit is achieved.

By 'self-realisation' here is meant both 'making real' in the sense of the achievement in reality of a potentiality, the overcoming of self-alienation, and also 'self-realisation' in the sense of the acquisition of self-understanding, a coming to full self-consciousness on the part of Absolute Spirit, but since 'Absolute Spirit' is conceived on the model of the human consciousness, these different senses of 'self-realisation' turn out to be the same.

This rise, through successive stages of self-alienation, or self-negation, by means of dialectical transcendence, to ultimate self-realisation in Absolute Spirit is played out in historical time. But since Hegel's Idealist metaphysics tells us that the Absolute Spirit which is realised through historical time is also the ultimate, self-subsistent ground and precondition of the historical process and, indeed, time itself, it follows that the historical process itself must be relegated to the realm of mere appearances.

As Marx recalls in the above-quoted passage from the Afterword to Volume 1 of *Capital*, the idealist dialectic of Hegel attracted the adherence of young radical intellectuals – among them Marx and Engels – in the 1830s and 1840s in Germany, since it seemed to be 'in its essence' critical and revolutionary. It seemed to expose every existing state of affairs as inherently contradictory, and so in the process of transcendence into a higher and better state: nothing was to be fixed and eternal. But in its use by Hegel, especially in his political philosophy, dialectical thought had somehow been divested of this critical capacity, and was instead used for the glorification of the reactionary and militaristic Prussian state of that period: for Hegel, the contradictory and irrational character of 'civil society', the realm of individual needs and self-interest was transcended in the authoritarian state's rational reconciliation of the particular to the general interest.

The task of the Young Hegelians had been to restore to itself the essential critical and revolutionary character of the dialectic, but, as Marx later pointed out, this was impossible whilst they remained trapped within the premises (the 'problematic') of the Hegelian system itself.

What appears to have been the starting-point for Marx and Engels in their abandonment of that problematic was the 'materialist inversion' of Hegel's idealist philosophy conducted by their fellow Young Hegelian, Ludwig Feuerbach, especially in his *Essence of Christianity* and critiques of Hegel's philosophy. The metaphor of 'inversion' fits perfectly: whereas for Hegel the 'subject' of the historical process had been Absolute Spirit (consciousness), and material life a mere 'predicate', or 'appearance', for Feuerbach, it is human beings, in their material life, who are the subjects of history, whilst spiritual, conscious life is itself a product of the historical evolution of matter. The inversion of subject and predicate, essence and appearance in Hegel's idealist philosophy produces a 'materialist' philosophy of history in which, now, it is 'man' as a 'species being' who undergoes successive phases of self-alienation and transcendence towards an ultimate goal of self-realisation.

From the standpoint of Feuerbach's 'materialist inversion', it is now speculative philosophy and religion which appears as human self-alienation. Denied fulfilment of their potentialities (their true essence) in social practice, human beings project their essential character onto an imaginary being (Absolute Spirit, God) set over and above themselves. This religious and philosophical self-alienation needs to be subjected to critique, in order for the human species to restore to itself its true essence – its 'species being' – in a democratic, republican state.

Feuerbach and Marx

The inversion of Hegel's metaphysics, and the retention of the forms of Hegel's historical dialectic (essence and appearance, contradiction, alienation, negation and self-realisation) constitute the premises of Marx's famous *Economic and Philosophical Manuscripts* of 1844.[4] But whereas Feuerbach is centrally concerned with the application of his materialist critique to religious and philosophical ideology, Marx extends the application of Feuerbach's method and premises to political economy and to political theory. The laws of classical political economy are shown to be a consequence of private property, itself both cause and effect of alienated labour. The alienation of labour (labour in which the labourer is separated from the product of labour, from his own labour and so from himself and other labourers) can itself be superseded only by the abolition of private property and the introduction of a communist form of economic life in which labour becomes the free, creative and collective 'appropriation' and humanisation of the world. The Hegelian synthesis of contradictions in a higher *spiritual* unity has its mirror image in Marx's synthesis of the contradictions between man and man, labour and the labourer, and man and nature, in a communist vision of the future material life of human beings.

But as early as 1845 Marx was to say, in his sixth Thesis on Feuerbach: 'Feuerbach resolves the essence of religion into the essence of *man*. But the human essence is no abstraction inherent in each single individual. In its reality it is ensemble of the social relations.'[5] This is a puzzling critical remark as it bears upon Feuerbach, since in the latter's concept of 'man' as a species being is contained a rejection of those seventeenth and eighteenth century philosophies which attempted to establish conceptions of human nature ('natural man') in abstraction from any specification of the social and historical situation of the individual. For Feuerbach the 'species life' of 'man' is essentially a form of collective, *social* practice, but in Marx's third sentence is revealed a decisive break from the premises of both Feuerbachian and Hegelian philosophy. To locate the 'reality' of the human essence in the 'ensemble of the social relations', is, in effect, to do away with the concept of human essence as such. The human essence provides the underlying dynamic (contradiction between alienated existence and essence or potentiality) and the ultimate goal (realisation of essence, transcendence of alienation) of the human historical process in both Feuerbach and the Marx of 1844. An 'essence' which is the underlying dynamic and ultimate goal of the historical process cannot be the *same thing* as the 'essence' which is merely the historically fleeting 'ensemble of social relations' in any phase of history. The *structure* of the Feuerbachian dialectical conception of history has been 'ruptured' in this phrase.

In the course of their critique of Feuerbach in the *German Ideology*, Marx and Engels repeatedly establish their distance from this philosophical scheme for thinking about the phases of human history:

> The individuals, who are no longer subject to the division of labour, have been conceived by the philosophers as an ideal, under the name 'Man'. They have conceived the whole process which we have outlined as the evolutionary process of 'Man', so that at every historical stage 'Man' was substituted for the individual and shown as the motive force of history. The whole process was thus conceived as a process of the self-estrangement of 'Man' ... Through this inversion ... it was possible to transform the whole of history into an evolutionary process of consciousness.[6]

Althusser uses such passages as these to argue that they are based on premises quite incompatible with the 'problematic' of the 1844 *Manuscripts*, which is to say, that of Feuerbach's 'inversion' of Hegel. On these passages, and the later work of Marx and Engels in founding the discipline of historical materialism, are based Althusser's provocative claims that Marxism is 'anti-humanist' and 'anti-historicist'. Neither 'historicism' nor 'humanism' are given clear or explicit definitions by Althusser, but the core of his usage of the terms can be 'extracted' readily enough. 'Historicism' consists in the attempt to impose upon 'concrete' historical processes a philosophical scheme such that, potentialities present in germ at the origins of the process, pre-figure and set in motion a process of transformation whose end result or goal is self-realisation. Historical teleology (the idea that history has a goal or end state) is, then, central to historicism, as is the idea of a linear series of stages through which the process must pass. In this sense, Hegel, certainly as Althusser reads him, is a historicist. In so far as the Hegelian pattern of dialectical motion in history is taken over by Feuerbach and the early Marx, notwithstanding their inversion of the *elements* in that pattern, then so far is their work governed by a historicist problematic. To merely *invert* Hegel is to remain trapped within Hegel's problematic, which is a historicist problematic.

'Humanism' is a theoretical ideology intimately linked to historicism in Feuerbach and the early Marx, in that what is, for them, the 'subject' of the historical process and its end point is the 'human essence' – human self-realisation. Marx's critique of Feuerbach (and also of his own earlier work – the *German Ideology* was a work of 'self-clarification') includes a critique of humanism in this sense. Marx seems to reject as a basis for historical analysis *both* philosophical conceptions of the human individual ('subject') abstracted from the necessarily socially and historically *located* character of human individuals *and* conceptions of the 'human essence', even conceived in Feuerbach's terms as a form of collective life, which are formed in abstraction from the concretely observable and historically transitory forms of actual social life. In terms which often border on the empiricist Marx here distances himself from any 'philosophical schema' which seeks to *impose* itself upon real historical developments, failing to respect their concrete specificity, their independent reality as objects of study. One such philosophical schema, the conclusion seems inescapable, is the historicist and humanist conception of the 1844 *Manuscripts*.

Very much later, in his letter of November 1877 to the editorial board of the Russian journal *Otechestvennije Zapiski*,[7] Marx accuses a Russian critic of metamorphosing his 'historical sketch of the genesis of capitalism in Western Europe into a historico-philosophic theory of the general path every people is fated to tread, whatever the historical circumstances in which it finds itself, in order that it may ultimately arrive at the form of economy which ensures, together with the greatest expansion of the productive powers of social labour, the most complete development of man'.

Comparing the expropriation of the plebeians of ancient Rome with the process of 'primitive accumulation' in early modern Europe, Marx continues:

> Thus events strikingly analogous but taking place in different historical surroundings led to totally different results. By studying each of these forms of evolution separately and then comparing them one can easily find the clue to this phenomenon, but one will never arrive there by using as one's master key a general historico–philosophical theory, the supreme virtue of which consists in being super-historical.[8]

Marx is again, in this text, rejecting any interpretation of historical materialism as a general philosophical theory, and, specifically, opposing views of history as a developmental process of 'man', or as a process whose outcome is pre-given, independently of concrete historical circumstances (humanism and historicism).

For Althusser, Marx's later critique of his own earlier work, and that of Feuerbach amounts to the rejection of it as a form of philosophical idealism (this is, indeed, explicit in the quotation from the *German Ideology* given above). The imposition of a philosophical schema onto the historical process, the neglect of the contribution to the determination of that process by specific historical contexts and circumstances, is only plausible on condition that the historical process is itself understood as a product of, or as ultimately identical with a process of thought, or consciousness.

The specificity of the Marxist dialectic

The inversion of Hegel is materialist only in appearance, since the retention of the terms and structures of Hegelian dialectics imprisons both Feuerbach and the early Marx within Hegel's idealist problematic. This is argued most convincingly in Althusser's major essays on the nature and specificity of the Marxist dialectic, 'Contradiction and Overdetermination' and 'On the Materialist Dialectic'.[9] A common formulation of the distinction between the Marxist and Hegelian dialectics, derived from Engels' later work, centres the distinction on the difference in the *object* to which a common *method* (dialectics) is applied: Hegel discovered the method, whereas Marxism's materialist inversion of the *object* of study now enables that method to be applied in the production of scientific results. But, argues Althusser, if Marxism goes beyond the mere 'inversion' of Hegel's idealism, discovering, independently, new structures and mechanisms in the real historical process, how can a method which served the purposes of Hegel's idealist philosophy possibly be appropriate to this new object of study? For example, the essence of civil society is located in the state for Hegel, whereas in Marx, the 'anatomy of civil society' is sought in political economy, whilst the Hegelian conception of the state as embodying the general interest is replaced by the idea of the state as a mechanism of the dominant class. But not only the *terms* of the relationship have changed, so has the relationship itself: there is no simple inversion of the essence–appearance relationship, but rather, the idea of an asymmetrical relationship of mutual determination is introduced (relative autonomy of the superstructures, determination in the last instance by the economic).

Althusser draws from these considerations two conclusions about the distinctive character of the Marxist dialectic. First, the conception of the nature of the *totality* upon which the dialectic is supposed to operate is quite different in Hegel and Marx. The Hegelian notion of totality is what Althusser calls 'expressive', in the sense that each specific element or 'moment' of a *seemingly* complex whole is interpreted as 'expressing' in its own particular way some general or essential character of the whole: the appearance of complexity is reduced by the Hegelian philosophical method to an *essential* simplicity. By contrast, the respect for the independent and specific reality of the concrete objects of study imposed by Marxist materialism commits historical materialism to a recognition of the irreducible complexity of social totalities: ideological forms, particular forms of the state, and so on, do not 'reflect' or 'express' any inner principle through which the whole can be grasped, but rather must be first analysed in their specificity, and only then explained in general terms.

Althusser uses historical texts by Marx, Lenin and Mao to show that in these writings, in which they distil their own experience of revolutionary practice, each of these Marxist thinkers emphasises the complexity of each situation, and the importance to its transformation of a recognition of the specificity of its circumstances. The distinct practices which make up a social formation at a particular moment in its history must each be assigned their own distinctive type and degree of autonomy and co-determination within the overall structure. Althusser attempts to defend this conception of the social totality from the charge of empiricism, or 'pluralism' in the claim that, though Marxism has as yet no adequate theorisation of the general character of social totalities, there are, at least, a number of preliminary specifications. The distinction between economic foundation and ideological–political superstructures, and the notions of the determination in the last instance by the economic, and the relative autonomy of the superstructures are, for Althusser, the most important of these. They aren't adequate, they locate only the site of problems for further analysis, but at least they are theoretical indicators that Marxism *does* have a general conception of the relationship between the elements in social totalities, and also that this conception is not that of the 'expressive totality'. Althusser's term for this conception is that of a de-centred 'structure in dominance'.

Althusser's second conclusion is intimately linked with this first one. It is that, to analyse complex 'structures in dominance' and their forms of motion and change, a new conception of 'contradiction' is required. Here, again, the main difference between Marxist and Hegelian concepts of contradiction centres on the *complexity* of the former. Lenin's notebooks reveal his analysis of the revolutionary situation in Russia as a synthesis of numerous distinct contradictions: the presence of both feudal and the most advanced capitalist relations, an imperialist country subject itself to imperialist domination, a simultaneous peasant revolt against landlords, and a workers' revolution. Borrowing terms from Lacanian psychoanalysis, Althusser comments that the Marxist conception of contradiction is not a simple one, in which apparently diverse contradictions are manifestations of a single underlying one (capital versus labour), but one in which a multiplicity of co-existing contradictions *overdetermine* one another, the *condensation* of these determinations producing a revolutionary rupture. Mao's distinctions, too, between principal and secondary contradictions, and principal and secondary aspects of a contradiction, are used to show that the classic writers of Marxism have always explicitly or implicitly recognised the complexity of the Marxian concept of contradiction, a complexity indicated in Althusser's term 'overdetermined contradiction'.

Structural causality

In his contribution to *Reading Capital*,[10] Althusser returns to this
problem of registering theoretically the distinctive character of the
Marxist conception of social totalities and also of 'the dialectic',
especially the concept of contradiction. The idea that the elements
and sub-structures of a complex structure enter into reciprocal but
asymmetrical relations of causality, the idea that there is a hierarchy
of dominance and subordination between social practices in a social
formation, between the elements of those practices themselves, and
between the contradictions and aspects of contradictions which
animate the structures, requires, if it is to be adequately expressed, a
new conception of causality. The idea of linear or 'transitive'
causality which Althusser associates with Galileo and Descartes,
and the concept of 'expressive' causality (proper to the idea of
expressive totality, originating in Leibrig, and adopted by Hegel)
were the sole concepts of causality available to Marx. Accordingly
Marx frequently presents his accounts of the relations between
elements and their structural determinants in terms of these concepts of causality (for example, the use of the essence–appearance
relationship to specify the relationship between capitalist production relations and the wage form).

There are, however, texts in which, according to Althusser, Marx
transcends these conceptions of causality to produce a new conception anticipated only by the philosopher, Baruch Spinoza. This
conception, 'structural causality', is irreducible to the other two,
and through it Althusser proposes to conceptualise 'the determination of the elements of a structure, and the structural relations
between those elements, and all the effects of those relations by the
effectivity of that structure'.[11] Though the provision of concepts
with which to think the effectivity of a 'structure' on its elements and
subordinate structures and all their effects is presented by Althusser
as a *problem*, it is hard to see in his attempt to resolve it any more
than a restatement of the question. The outcome of Althusser's
prolonged and laboured discussion is that the structure of the
totality is *nothing other than* its effects, it is, in Spinoza's sense, a
cause 'immanent in its effects' (just as, in Spinoza's philosophy, God
is a cause immanent in His creation: God and Nature are identical).

Althusser recognises that his problem is not specific to the science
of societies: psychoanalysis, linguistics, biology and even physics

have had to confront the question of systemic totalities which are irreducible to their elements, but he goes no further in eliciting analogies, or in comparing theoretical solutions between disciplines. All we have are the allusive references to psychoanalytic concepts in the earlier essays in *For Marx*. It remains open to question, then, precisely what theoretical problems are supposed to be solved in his conception of structural causality. Is it the means whereby an asymmetrical, hierarchical set of relations of causal determinacy is established between elements (or sub-structures)? If so, it is hard to see how the notion of a structure 'present in its effects' helps us with this. Or is the problem one of theorising the relationships between structural determinants and their appropriation in the consciousness of agents (this is at least one of the functions of Marx's essence–appearance distinction)? If so, then the earlier notion of overdetermination, derived from Freud's own attempt to think the relationship between transferences of energy and relations of meaning, seems much more helpful. Finally, is the problem one of explaining the capacity of a set of social relations to maintain its integrity, to persist and reproduce itself? If so, and if the reference to Spinoza is to be taken seriously, then the concept of structural causality is if anything *far too* effective. Spinoza's 'cause immanent in its effects' is, as a self-generating and self-sustaining totality, eternal. If Althusser is to be taken strictly at his word, then a central feature of the Marxist project – the fluid, the essentially transient and transformable character of the social world – is abandoned.

We shall, in later chapters, allude to Althusser's criticism of his own use of this concept, and his reference to Spinoza, as well as to critics for whom Althusser's 'Marxism' is represented as irreparably faulted in its dependence on Spinoza. For the moment, however, it is necessary to press on to a closer look at what is left of Marx's view of history if it is to be purged, following Althusser's periodisation and epistemological critique, of the concepts and presuppositions of the early works.

4

The Basic Concepts of Historical Materialism

The preoccupations of Althusser's writing during this early period remain philosophical: the elaboration of conceptions of knowledge, of science and its contrast with ideology, of dialectics, totality and historical causality. These philosophical ideas and themes are, as we have seen, set to work in an attempted periodisation of Marx's work. This periodisation represents Marx's work as divided by an 'epistemological break' through which a scientific approach to historical analysis emerges from the critical rejection of an earlier historicist and humanist philosophical perspective.

Althusser himself rarely moves beyond the provision of textual analyses which supposedly demonstrate this break, and the incompatibility of the concepts of the later with those of the earlier texts. The positive labour of elucidating the conceptual structure of the 'mature' and supposedly scientific conception of history established from the break is not directly engaged in by Althusser. This task was left to Althusser's then-collaborator, Etienne Balibar, whose text 'The Basic Concepts of Historical Materialism'[1] was the most systematic attempt at that time to provide an account of the Marxist conception of history, purged of all historicist and human assumptions, and I shall use it as the basis of my discussion in this chapter.

Balibar's essay is a complex, uneven and sometimes inconsistent one, but it is full of interest and originality. Much of the essay is devoted to multiplying the examples and expounding the implications of Althusser's thesis that Marxism is not an historicism, that the Marxian conception of the social totality is that of a complex 'structure in dominance' (and not a 'pluralistic' concatenation of elements, nor the manifold of the phenomena of some simple inner essence or principle), and that the specific forms of human individuality can only be understood as effects of social relations: human agents are 'bearers' of social relations, not their source, as in 'humanism'. But in developing these themes at a lower level of abstraction than is usually attempted by Althusser, Balibar provides new (not always, of course, *preferable*) interpretations of some of the central concepts of historical materialism.

Mode of production

First, and quite centrally, the concept of 'mode of production'. For Balibar this concept has two distinct functions in the Marxist science of history: as a principle of historical periodisation, and as the conceptual means of thinking the relationship between the levels or 'instances' of a social formation. In its latter, 'synchronic' role, the concept of mode of production is the concept of that (relatively) autonomous domain which assigns to its place in a hierarchy of dominance and subordination each of the other elements in the social formation.

That the articulation of the non-economic elements or levels (ideology, politics) of a social formation is to be explained by the mode of (economic) production is a thesis given by Marx in this well-known passage:

> The specific form, in which unpaid surplus labour is pumped out of direct producers, determines the relationship of rulers and ruled, as it grows directly out of production itself and, in turn, reacts upon it as a determining element . . . It is always the direct relationship of the owners of the conditions of production to the direct producers – a relation always naturally corresponding to a definite stage in the development of the methods of labour and thereby its social productivity – which reveals the innermost secret, the hidden basis of the entire social structural, and with it the political form of the relation of sovereignty and dependence, in short, the corresponding specific form of the state.[2]

Within the mode of economic production, according to Marx, it is the relationship of the 'owners of the conditions of production' to the 'direct producers' which is the key, and he also mentions a 'correspondence' between this relationship and a definite stage in the development of 'the methods of labour'.

This, together with other passages scattered through Marx's works, provides Balibar with the basis for his analysis of the concept of modes of production as specific combinations, specific 'states of variation', of certain invariant 'elements'. These elements are five in number: two distinct relations ('connexions') between three terms, or elements. The terms which are related are: the labourer ('direct producer'), the means of production (including both the 'object of labour', what is transformed in the labour process, and also the instruments of labour, or 'means of production' in the narrow sense), and a non-labourer who appropriates a surplus (for example, feudal landowner and capitalist). On the question of the relations or 'connexions' by which these invariant elements may be combined to form the various 'modes of production' (Asiatic, Ancient, Feudal, Capitalist, Communist....) of which Marx speaks there is some considerable shift away from Althusser's silences and ambiguities in his earlier definition of 'practices'. Whereas Althusser seems hesitant about the inclusion of social relations of production in the concept of 'practice', and even then sees the 'labour process' in the narrow sense (the setting in motion by the labourer of the technical means of production to produce a specific product) as the 'determinant moment', Balibar is at least clear on two points: first, there is a two-fold set of relations binding together the three terms, what Balibar terms a 'property connexion' and a 'material-appropriation connexion' and second, that the 'property connexion', which Marx's famous 1859 'Preface'[3] takes to be the same thing as the social relations of production, is the dominant relationship in the characterisation and in the transformation of the 'mode of production' in the full sense.

However, where Balibar is much less clear is in his characterisation of what distinguishes the property and material-appropriation connexions. The latter relation is one sometimes referred to by Marx as the 'appropriation of nature by man'. It is the relation characterising the labour process, in the narrow sense, as a combination of labourer, means of production and object of labour in the transformation of that object. Balibar, having specified the 'material-appropriation connexion' in this way, goes on to connect it with the 'technical' division of labour, but also, surprisingly, with the function of the capitalist as 'organiser of production', which, he says, is a 'technically indispensable moment of the labour process'[4] (this, of course, concerns the *capitalist* mode of production, as one 'state of variation' of the historically invariant elements). Now, the thesis that control over and organisation of the labour process is a 'technically indispensable' function of the capitalist is not only a surprising one for a Marxist, but it has the consequence of drastically attenuating the conception of the 'property' connexion with which the technical relations of production are contrasted. If that aspect of property as powers of 'disposal over' the conditions of production is abstracted from it and conferred on the technical relations of production, then what is left? Merely a power of appropriation of the surplus product from the direct producer: in the case of the capitalist mode of production, the appropriation of surplus value.

This attenuated conception brings Balibar dangerously close, despite his own intentions, to a technological determinist conception of production relations, on the one hand, and a conception of class relations as relations of distribution, on the other. This latter point is extremely damaging to Balibar's claims as an expositor of Marx's distinctive categories, since it is precisely this conception of classes as constituted on the basis of the sources of their revenues (the so-called 'trinity formula' of wages, profits, and rent) which was held by the Classical Political Economy, which Marx was supposed to displace, and which Marx explicitly opposes in his final, unfinished chapter on 'Classes', in *Capital* Volume III.[5] This conception of classes as functions of the social relations of *distribution*, rather than *production*, is also a major demarcation between contemporary Marxist conceptions of class and sociological conceptions of stratification. However, that Balibar's position here is not a consistent or settled one is indicated by his later insistence that 'technical' relations are, of course, also *social* relations, and also that relations of distribution include the distribution of means of production, not just of individual consumption.[6]

Balibar's discussion of that 'state of variation' of the invariant elements, the 'capitalist mode of production' takes its point of departure from Althusser's own work on Marx's critique of Classical Political Economy. The site of Marx's revolutionary discoveries is the recognition that the category 'value of labour' has no strict meaning. Marx's predecessors had conceptualised the wage relation between capitalist and labourer as simply an exchange relation in which there is an exchange of equivalents: a certain quantum of labour against the equivalent value in the commodities which can be bought with the wage. But what this fails to explain is the basis upon which this purchase is the means by which both the total social wealth is expanded, and the wealth of the capitalist is also expanded, whilst the worker remains impoverished. Marx's analysis of the capital–labour relation does not depart from the assumption of an exchange of equivalents, but it radically alters the conception of what is exchanged. For Marx, what the labourer sells is labour power, a capacity to work. The value of this labour power is taken to be equivalent to the 'bundles of commodities' necessary to ensure the reproduction of that labour power, and the appearance of the labourer at the factory-gate the following day: this 'bundle of commodities', the subsistence requirement of the worker, is purchased with the wage.

But underlying, and determining the form of this *exchange* relation between capitalist and worker is a *production* relation. The labour power purchased by the capitalist is set to work in the labour process for the duration of the working-day, in which time the *exercise* of labour power, its *consumption* by the capitalist in the form of labouring activity on the capitalist's means of production, has the result of *creating* a value greater than the value of the labour power itself (which equals the value of the wage, that is the cost of reproducing the worker). This is the distinctive characteristic of labour power (its consumption yields a value greater than its own value) and it underlies the expansion, under capitalist relations, of the total social wealth, and also explains the peculiar pattern of distribution of the product such that, on the basis of an exchange of equivalents the capitalist becomes richer, whilst the worker remains subject to the necessity to continually repeat the cycle: sale of labour power → production for the capitalist → purchase of means of consumption.

Capitalism and 'relative autonomy'

Now, the relations of exploitation – the means of appropriation of a surplus by the owners of the conditions of production – are central to all class societies. But what distinguishes capitalist exploitation relations, according to Balibar, is that the appropriation of an economic surplus occurs wholly within the sphere of economic relations, without the intervention of any 'extra-economic' coercion. What makes this possible is the coincidence in time and space of the labour process, as the process whereby specific, useful products are produced, and the process of production of surplus value, through which exploitation is achieved. There is, in other words, no detectable moment in the working day beyond which the worker is working, *not* to replace the value of his or her own consumption, but producing a surplus which will be appropriated by the capitalist. This coincidence is what enables the exploitation relation to be masked beneath the appearance of a relation of exchange of equivalents, and is a consequence of the dual character of the separation of the labourer from the means of production in the capitalist mode of production: separation in the sense of 'non-ownership' but also in the sense of 'non-access' except through the wage contract.

Balibar contrasts this aspect of the capitalist with the feudal mode of production, in which there is a clear separation between 'necessary' and 'surplus' labour time, for example, where a feudal serf works on his 'own' plot of land to meet his own subsistence needs, but also has to pay rent in the form of labour services on the lord's land. This is a consequence of the non-coincidence of relations of 'possession', or 'access' and of 'property' in the feudal mode of production. On this contrast Balibar bases his account of the different articulation and hierarchy of dominance of the levels or 'instances' of the two modes of production. In the capitalist mode, the extraction of a surplus and the constitution of social classes within the economic level determine a relative autonomy of the other levels or instances of the social formation. By contrast, the clear division of labour time into that which meets the subsistence needs of the direct labourer, and that which is appropriated by the landowner in the feudal mode, necessitates extra-economic coercion if the surplus is to be extracted. This, supposedly, explains why class relations under Feudalism are 'directly and indissolubly political and economic', and so why politics plays, in social formations of this type, the 'determinant' part.

Balibar's discussion is terminologically inconsistent, and, in several respects, confused, but what he appears to be arguing is that economic relations, centrally those between owners and direct producers, are always determinant (in the last instance) with respect to the other levels or 'instances' in a society, and with respect to the configuration of society as a whole, but that this determination by the economic structure takes the rather indirect form of assigning to the other, non-economic levels, their place in a hierarchy of *dominance* with respect to one another, and the *kind* of articulation between them. Confusingly, Balibar sometimes uses the term 'determinant' to refer to both types of causality, and also intertwines the whole discussion with a treatment of the *ideological forms* corresponding to the structure of each mode of production, so that it is not always clear whether he is arguing that a specific type of economic structure assigns a dominant role to ideology (or politics), or necessitates a specific type of ideological misrecognition of social relations on the part of agents (sometimes, even, it seems that he is presenting a thesis concerning the relations of dominance as between the sub-regions of ideology itself – economic ideology, religious ideology, and so on).

The confusion is further compounded by a brief suggestion that the specific type of unity of economics and politics necessitated in feudal social formations is not merely a matter of the binding together of two distinct levels, or 'instances' but, rather, a question of the *conceptual inseparability* of these levels with respect to Feudalism.[7] What this, in turn, seems to suggest is that the concepts of the levels – political, ideological, economic, and so on – are not, after all, trans-historical concepts of historical materialism, but have to be constructed (if, indeed they are required at all) in forming the concept of each epoch in the history of human society. As we shall see this relativisation of the concepts of historical materialism, undermining, as it must, the very concept of mode of production itself as a general concept, radically subverts the whole project of a 'science of history' as Balibar has so far conceived it.

Mode of production and social formation

A further area of terminological confusion concerns Balibar's (and Althusser's) usage of the mode of production – social formation contrast, and, underlying the terminological confusion, a serious conceptual and epistemological one. There are, broadly, three quite distinct contrasts which are made with this terminological opposition, in different (and sometimes the same) places in the text. These are : first, a distinction between the concept of the economic level and the concept of the society as a whole (an articulated structure of economic, ideological and political levels); second, a distinction between the concept of the social unity comprising economic, ideological and political levels, on the one hand, and the concept of the possible *articulation* of several such provisional social unities within a single whole society; and, third, a distinction between social forms as *theoretical objects* (as the internal objects of knowledge) and real, concrete societies at specific historical conjunctures. The first two contrasts concern different levels of abstraction or concreteness *within* theorisation of social reality, whilst the latter concerns the *application* of theory to historical reality.

The first distinction, that between a mode of production, in the strict sense, and the set of ideological and political relations with which it is thought of as combined is well established within Marxism, but, as we have seen, Balibar's fleeting suggestion about the unity of the levels in feudal societies renders problematic the conceptualisation in general terms of the distinct levels. This is something, at least for the non-economic levels, which Althusser designated as a primary task for the future development of historical materialism,[8] and which Balibar does not, in this essay at least, take on. Another respect in which Balibar, remaining within the epistemological 'problematic' of Althusser, departs from most of the Marxist classics is in his treatment of the non-economic levels of the mode of production and their relations by *conceptual derivations* from the definition of each mode of production as a particular state of variation of invariant elements. This is, of course, required by the epistemological characterisation of the mode of production as a *conceptual* object (*Capital*, for example, doesn't present a description of the English economy, or the German or French, for that matter, but, *in abstraction from* any *specific* national economy constructs a concept and theory of the capitalist mode of production as such),[9] but also makes Balibar susceptible to the criticism that what he offers is an *a priori* structuralist formalism, rather than an historical science.

The second distinction, between the unity comprising a mode of production and its associated ideological and political forms, on the one hand, and other modes of production with which it may be combined in a social totality is already to be found in Althusser's work, and is connected with the thesis of the complexity of the social totality and the necessary overdetermination of contradictions. Complexity and overdetermination may derive not only from the relative autonomy of the ideological and political practices *vis-à-vis* the economic, but also from the combination of *several* modes of production, together with their ideological and political conditions of existence in a single social formation.[10] This idea has been a remarkably fruitful one for subsequent Marxist research in such fields as sociology of development and under-development, and the analysis of the sexual division of labour in society (in the idea, for example, of a domestic mode of production in articulation with the capitalist mode, which, whatever its intrinsic problems, has helped in the clarification of contemporary sexual divisions). Further, as we shall see, this concept of social formations as involving a multiplicity of modes of production in combination has profound implications for the Marxist conception of class struggle and revolutionary politics (the theory of 'transition', as Balibar delicately puts it). In particular, revolutions can no longer be conceived as effects, mediate or immediate of the auto-genesis and 'maturation' of the contradictions in a single mode of production.

The third distinction which Balibar sometimes marks terminologically by the mode of production – social formation contrast is that between social forms ('modes of production') considered as conceptual objects and particular historical societies at definite conjunctures ('social formations') on the other. Now, this distinction has a very dubious status, given the Althusserian epistemological separation of the 'real–concrete' which remains forever external to thought, and the 'concrete in thought' which is its 'cognitive appropriation'. In the strict terms allowed by this epistemology, even the most concrete level of analysis – the analysis of specific societies at specific moments in their history – must be regarded as nevertheless 'within thought', so that the relationship between, say, the concept of 'mode of production' in the strict sense, and the analysis of British society in 1982 is simply one of different *levels of abstraction* within theory, and not a question of the relationship between theory and reality. Nevertheless, Balibar *does* pose the question of the 'application' of theory to historical reality, only to abolish it again as an 'empiricist' question: to accept it would be to fall into the empiricist interpretation of for example, Marx's *Capital* as providing an abstract 'model' of capitalist economies, which show varying degrees of empirical divergence from this model, or 'ideal type'. But no matter how much Balibar attempts to suppress the question, it nevertheless reasserts itself (Althusserian epistemology insists on the *theoretically constructed* character of knowledge, but never quite rids itself of the realist – materialist assumption that knowledge is, after all, *knowledge of* something extrinsic to knowledge). The problem of the application of knowledge to historical reality is

already present as one element of Althusser's treatment of over
determination, since the *necessity* of complexity and overdetermination in Althusser derives not merely from the relative autonomy
of the levels of a social formation and the combination of modes of
production, but from the necessity that in their real existence (in
which state they are the object of political practice – hence Althusser's reliance on texts by Lenin and Mao which directly relate to
questions of political strategy) social practices and contradictions
are always present in their particularity as qualified by innumerable
specific circumstances, conditions and antecedents.

Historical transitions

The reappearance of this question of the relation of theory to reality
in Balibar's text occurs in his tortuous concluding sections on
'transition'[11], and it is to these that I shall now turn. So far we have
been concerned centrally with the nature and relationship of social
structures 'synchronically' – that is to say, without regard to their
persistence, or transformation, through time. But Balibar has already introduced us to the view that the concept 'mode of production' has a place in the historical practice of periodisation: of
dividing up human history, or the histories of specific societies into
epochs. Clearly a procedure which involves reference to considerations of temporal succession and persistence, and so, seemingly, one
which, to follow Balibar's structuralist terminology, involves 'diachronic' analysis. But the situation is more complex than this. On the
face of it, Marx offers a new principle of periodisation – historical
epochs are demarcated according to the mode of production and
reproduction of material life conducted within them, rather than by
their ideological or cultural forms (Reformation, Renaissance, and
so on) by the lineage of their sovereigns (Tudor, Victorian, and so
on) or whatever. But, argues Balibar, this 'overlooks' the revolution
which Marx wrought in historical science, a revolution which consists not in finding new answers to old questions, but in exploding
the very questions. The traditional historians' practice of periodisation presupposes 'linear' time, and so reduces history to a continuous series within this linear time. By contrast, the complexity of the
social totality, as disclosed by Marx, implies that each social practice
has its own inner cycles and rhythms of development and change, in

short, its own 'time', so that the unity and linearity of the traditional historians' conception of time is shattered, and the problem of periodisation, at least in its traditional form, disappears.

Nevertheless, certain central concepts of *Capital* do entail a reference to the persistence of the capitalist mode of production through time, as well as its future dissolution. According to Marx it is an erroneous abstraction to conceive production independently of 'reproduction': the process of production is necessarily and simultaneously a process of reproduction of the conditions and relations of subsequent productive activity. We have already seen this in the cyclical relationship between the sale of labour power, value-producing labour, and the consumption of means of production by the labourer under Capitalism. Comparable considerations apply to the replacement of means of production and raw materials as they are used up, worn out, and so on, in the production process, and also to the relations of production themselves. Marx distinguishes 'simple' reproduction, in which production in the branches or 'departments' of production is thought of as in balance, so that a given phase of production simply replicates the conditions for its repetition on the same scale, from 'expanded' reproduction in which the conditions are provided for a global expansion of productive activity.

As Balibar emphasises, the concept of reproduction, including that of reproduction on an expanded scale, presupposes that what is reproduced *by* capitalist social relations *is* those very capitalist relations, so that of itself the concept of reproduction only teases out further theoretical implications of the initial conception of the capitalist mode of production, and does not yield a theory of its dissolution, much less replacement by *other* relations. The same applies to other seemingly diachronic concepts in *Capital*, such as the famous (and subsequently highly controversial) law of the tendency of the rate of profit to fall. A law of tendency is *surely* diachronic? Only, says Balibar, if one thinks of the counter-influences to the law as merely an assemblage of contingently occurring 'obstacles' to the operation of the law. But this is not how Marx conceives them. The tendency of the rate of profit to fall is derived by Marx from another tendency – that of the 'organic composition of capital' (very roughly equivalent to the productivity of labour) to rise. But the tendency of the rate of profit to fall can legitimately be derived from the tendency of the organic composition of capital to rise only on condition that the rate of exploitation of labour is assumed not to rise, and yet a rise in the rate of exploitation of labour can also be expected to follow from the increasing organic composition of capital. In short, both the tendency, and its principal counter-tendency are rooted in one and the same underlying cause, itself governed by the structure of the capitalist mode of production.

In the laws of tendency, and in the associated concept of reproduction, Marx is only drawing out the implications of his conceptualisation of the capitalist mode of production: he is not inscribing these cyclical and developmental patterns onto the real historical time of particular societies. Balibar marks this difference by referring to the 'time' of the theoretically derived cycles, tendencies and so on of the capitalist mode of production as a matter of the 'dynamics' of the system, and not its 'diachrony'. But in this very distinction has reappeared the problematic (for Balibar) opposition of theory and the historical reality to which it is applied. The problem now takes the form, 'how does each of these times, for example, the time of the 'tendency' of the mode of production, *become* a historical time?' At this point, Balibar doesn't suppress the question, but instead relegates it to the field of epistemology.[12]

Again, though, the question will not go away so easily. If the inner dynamics of a mode of production, considered in abstraction from real historical processes, cannot of themselves demonstrate the mechanism of transition to new modes of production, and yet such transitions are of fundamental importance both intellectually and politically, to Marxism, then some form of return from theoretical exposition to real historical analysis must be required. Without seeming to explicitly recognise it, this is precisely the path Balibar follows. Periods of transition, he argues, cannot be understood *either* as chaotic and structureless, *or* as self-induced transformations of pre-existing modes of production. The inner tendencies of a mode of production always operate within limits set by the mode of production itself (the Marxist theory of crises seems to suggest this – the outcome of a crisis is the restoration of an economic equilibrium, not transition to a new form of society). The rhythms, cycles, and therefore 'crises' and dislocations of the different levels of a social formation, and the forms of development of the different modes of production in articulation have no necessary relationships of coincidence or co-temporality. Revolutionary transitions, it follows, cannot be thought of in terms of the Hegelian dialectic of supersession and transcendence. Nor can they be thought of in terms of a 'simple' class struggle in which a subordinate class defeats its dominant class to become, in turn, a new dominant class.

So how can revolution, or 'transition' be conceptualised? If the thesis of the determinancy of social structures over 'elements' is to be retained, even for periods of transition, it seems that revolution must be conceptualised, as Althusser himself seems to, as a more or less fortuitous, and certainly not deliberately achievable, 'condensation' or 'fusion' of contradictions at different levels and in the different practices, which occurs 'over the heads', or 'behind the backs' of historical actors. If, on the other hand, this structural determinism is weakened, as it must be if any serious conception of political practice as *transformative* practice is to have a place, then space is opened up in the theory for a conception of revolutionary politics as involving *alliances* between social classes formed on the basis of the different, articulated modes of production, and which takes as its *object*, the combining and synthesis of contradictions and antagonisms sited at the different levels in the social formation. Such a conception of politics is not explicitly developed in Balibar, but is implicit in some of Althusser's discussion of Lenin and Mao, and was developed further most notably by the late Nicos Poulantzas, a brilliant young political theorist who was strongly influenced by Althusser.[13]

Balibar's own treatment of 'transition' is somewhat hesitant and confused, confining itself to specifying certain general characteristics of periods of transition. One innovation in this discussion is the introduction of a concept of 'transitional modes of production' in which relations of production do not correspond to forces of production, and so become means of transforming those forces of production: the manufacturing phase of the capitalist mode of production is given as an example. But as well as being only dubiously consistent with Balibar's earlier definition of the concept of mode of production, such a concept is clearly no solution to the problem as Balibar has set it up: what is to be said about the transitions *between* transitional modes and the predecessor – successor modes? The theory either leads to an indefinite regress or to a re-establishment of a 'continuist', or evolutionary conception of historical change.

As if in recognition of this, Balibar adds several other elements to

his account. One such element is the idea that the inner development of the central contradiction of one mode of production may, at
a certain point generate a displacement in the relations of dominance between levels, on the basis of which the economic may be
transformed by an intervention from the newly dominant political
level. This brief and cryptic suggestion appears to be a restatement,
in structuralist terms, of an aspect of Lenin's political theory:
'spontaneous' transition from Capitalism to Socialism through the
auto-development of the former is impossible, so that decisive
political intervention is required to effect the transition. But unless
some form of retreat into political voluntarism is to be contemp-
lated, this political intervention must be thought of as one 'mutation
of the structures' alongside others. The second additional feature of
transitional periods (though earlier, as we have seen, Balibar has
mentioned it as a general feature of social formations) is the
co-presence, in relations of dominance and subordination, of a
multiplicity of modes of production. Presumably, political intervention is to be thought of as acting upon the relations of dominance
and subordination of disappearing, advancing, and transitional
modes.

But still the question of the conditions of emergence of radically
new forms is unanswered. The closest Balibar gets to this is his
discussion of Marx's treatment of 'primitive accumulation': the
provision, in pre-capitalist societies of the essential pre-conditions
(disposable wealth and 'free' labour) for capitalist production.
Marx, as Balibar reports, conceptualises the emergence of these
pre-conditions, not teleologically, as an aspect of the self-
transcendence of the pre-capitalist mode into the capitalist mode,
but rather as *one historical route amongst other possible routes* by
which what are necessary presuppositions of capitalist production
are *in fact* satisfied. This distinction between the theoretically-
derived 'presuppositions' of a given mode of production and the
different ways in which they may or, indeed, may *not* be satisfied in
real history is an important one, and its recognition carries with it
the implication that historical change must be thought of not as a
linear, evolutionary process towards some pre-given end point, but
rather as a contingent and open process, whose interpretation must
involve the use of theoretical means in the analysis of empirical
materials. If there can, indeed, be a general theory of the capitalist
mode of production, there cannot be a general theory of transitions,

or even of the transition from Capitalism to Socialism. This is a conclusion for which the premises are already to be found in Balibar's text, but he didn't reach it until some time later, as we shall see.

5

Self-criticism and Revision

The year 1967 marks the beginning of a period of self-critical activity in which Althusser takes his distance from some, though not all, of the concepts and theses of his essays of the early and mid – sixties. In the course of these self-criticisms, new theoretical positions emerge. As we shall see, these 'new' positions sometimes are genuinely new, but there is also some justification in the view of those commentators who have seen the later positions as a retreat – as a termination, in effect, of 'Althusserianism' as a distinct tendency of thought in Marxism.[1] As Althusser himself comments, his self-critical work is not generated wholly 'within theory' – it has its 'external sources' in politics. Undoubtedly these external sources were, principally, the radical student movement of the late 1960s, culminating in the mass strikes and factory occupations of May 1968, and, connectedly, the Chinese 'Great Proletarian Cultural Revolution'. For the students, and for many of the working class militants of the period, the response of the PCF to the 'events' of May '68 exposed it as not just incapable of offering revolutionary leadership but as an essentially conservative apparatus of control and containment of mass struggles. In the face of this assessment of the role of the PCF, and with the example of the Chinese cultural revolution in mind, some of Althusser's former students and colleagues on the left of the PCF broke with the Party and were active in the formation of several small 'Maoist' groups and parties. From these former colleagues – especially from Jacques Rancière[2] – come some of the most radical denunciations of Althusser's 'revisionism', and there is little doubt that these denunciations played some part in prompting Althusser's own shifts of position.

The most fundamental departures from Althusser's earlier positions are contained in his revision of the earlier conception of philosophy as the 'Theory of theoretical practice' and in his remarkable essay on ideology and the state apparatuses.[3] Both the new conception of philosophy and the later work on ideology pose in an acute way a problem denied explicit recognition in the 'structural' terminology of the earlier essays: the question of the role and nature of agency in social transformation. Increasingly, in the post-1967 work of Althusser the concepts of class struggles and of politics acquire a new prominence. It would be to oversimplify, but not to seriously misrepresent this shift, to say that whereas, in Althusser's earlier works, it was the structures of social formations which 'made history', in his later works it is 'the masses who make history'. As we shall see, Althusser is able to maintain that both conceptions retain the anti-humanism and anti-historicism of the earlier work, but a profound theoretical shift has nonetheless taken place. Finally, this new priority for the politics of class struggle in Althusser's theoretical 'problematic' is associated with a series of more directly and explicitly political writings in the seventies.

Philosophical self-criticism

Althusser's criticism of the earlier definition of philosophy is first signalled in a foreword to the Italian edition of *Reading Capital*: 'To define philosophy in a unilateral way as the Theory of theoretical practices (and in consequence as a Theory of the differences between the practices) is a formulation that could not help but induce either "speculative" or "positivist" theoretical effects and echoes.'[4] And in his introductory remarks 'To my English Readers' (October, 1967) in *For Marx*, Althusser concedes that whilst he dealt with the 'unity of theory and practice' within theoretical practice in his earlier essays, he had failed to pose the question of the most important union of all – the fusion of Marxist theory and practice within *political* practice: the political practice of the organisations of the working-class movement.[5] These comments from 1967 are developed and consolidated in a number of later essays and interviews, some collected together in *Lenin and Philosophy and other Essays* and others in *Essays in Self-Criticism*.[6] In broad outline, the argument is that the earlier conception of philosophy misconceives the relationship between philosophy and science, and that this is partly due to a one-sided emphasis on the relationship between philosophy and science at the expense of the relationship between philosophy (and, of course, science itself) and politics. A new conception (and practice) of philosophy is needed to rectify these errors.

To take, first, Althusser's criticism of his earlier conception of the relationship between philosophy and science, we can distinguish a critique of the earlier *definition* of philosophy from an implicit critique, also, of the earlier *practice* of philosophy. The two are not identical. As we have seen, the earlier *definition* of philosophy as 'Theory' seems little removed from a dogmatised 'dialectical materialism', which Althusser takes from Mao's essay 'On Contradiction'.[7] As a supposedly 'scientific' theory of the difference between science (truth) and ideology (error, distortion, misrecognition) this conception of philosophy shares the logical difficulties (circularity or infinite regress) of the classical epistemological theories (philosophies of guarantees). Secondly, a proclaimed general theory of all theoretical practices which contains the key to knowledge of all practices and so to 'the development of things in general' cannot but be an objective idealist metaphysics. This, presumably, is what Althusser later recognises as the source of 'speculative theoretical effects'!

But the earlier *practice* of philosophy doesn't always conform to this definition. Althusser also manages to incorporate into his theory of 'knowledge as production' a recognition of the force of the conventionalist critique of classical epistemology and its assertion of the historical character of cognitive practices. Each theoretical practice produces its own criteria of validity and notion of what constitutes a proof. Mathematics, for example, doesn't await the development of physics for an external source of 'guarantees' of its own procedures of validation. Any attempt to provide such 'guarantees' would itself come up against the requirement to demonstrate the source of the validity of its *own* judgement. If the work of philosophy is conceived as rendering explicit, or giving theoretical form to, the internal criteria of validity produced *in practice* in the constitution of a theoretical discipline, then one can make sense of a number of Althusser's rather bald assertions: for example, that a revolution in science is always, simultaneously, a revolution in philosophy, but that the birth of the philosophy is always delayed. On this view, the new science establishes, with its new 'problematic', new criteria of validity and forms of proof. These are a new philosophy, but in its practical state. Only later are the means produced for representing these criteria in their theoretical form – the birth of the new philosophy as a distinct theoretical discipline. Now, whatever the merits of this revitalised and 'historicised' (as distinct from 'historicist'!) conception of philosophy, it is quite inadequate to the task set by the *political* objective of Althusser's philosophical interventions. Since *any* theoretical practice – astrology, phrenology, alchemy, and even humanist Marxism will have its own inner criteria of validity and forms of proof, a philosophy which merely articulates those inner criteria will simply reproduce the cognitive claims made by those disciplines, and so cannot acquire the external critical purchase which is required if 'theoretical ideologies' are to be distinguished from 'genuine' sciences. This is why Althusser's earlier texts are littered with oscillations between these two radically different conceptions and practices of philosophy.

A further difficulty inherent in this second interpretation of the conception of philosophy in Althusser's earlier work is that, at best, Marxism's theory of knowledge can give us knowledge of the nature and history of certain social practices ('cognitive practices') alongside others. Since social formations are complex combinations of different practices – ideological, political, theoretical and economic – historical materialism, which is the science of social formations and their history will have within it 'regional' theories of the different practices and their histories. If the Marxist theory of knowledge gives us 'scientific' knowledge of one of these forms of practice – theoretical practice – then it is merely a 'regional' theory within historical materialism. In short, Marxist philosophy has been 'reduced' to the status of an element *within* historical materialism, and Althusser's claim to recommence the development of Marxist philosophy falls.

This may, indeed, be what Althusser's later self-criticism registers as a 'positivist' theoretical effect of the earlier conception of philosophy. But if it is, then the later revisions only compound the 'positivism', without resolving the inner tensions of the earlier philosophical position. In his 'Elements of Self-Criticism', for example, Althusser argues that his earlier conception of the epistemological break reduces it to a 'speculative' opposition between science and ideology as 'truth' and 'error' without adequately registering its social, political, ideological *and* theoretical dimensions. Of course, what is scientific in Marxism had to be established on the basis of struggle against ideological obstacles, but the speculative opposition of science and ideology *in general* had prevented Althusser from recognising that in Marx and Engels that struggle was against a *specific* ideology, that of the bourgeoisie. It had also prevented him from recognising that a condition of possibility of historical materialism itself was yet another specific ideology, that of the emerging proletarian movement. Marx's epistemological break was possible only 'because he took inspiration from the basic ideas of proletarian ideology, and from the first class struggles of the proletariat, in which this ideology became flesh and blood'.[8] The epistemological break, then, is in one sense, a historical 'fact', to be explained, like other historical facts, as the result of a complex, overdetermined conjuncture of ideological, political and economic conditions. Among these conditions, Marx's and Engels' taking up proletarian political positions in the class struggles of 1840–8, and, on that basis, adopting proletarian *philosophical* ('class – theoretical') positions, was decisive.

Though they give specific recognition to extra-theoretical determinants in the constitution of the 'epistemological break', and assign a new role to philosophy as *condition of possibility* of a new science, these remarks are in fact quite continuous with one aspect of Althusser's earlier philosophical practice: the borrowings from historical epistemology. Interesting as these new positions are, they tend to consolidate the status of such concepts as epistemological break, problematic, and theoretical practice as concepts belonging to a regional theory of historical materialism (theory of cognitive practices) and not as specifically *philosophical* concepts.[9] Moreover, the critical, evaluative work required of Marxist philosophy still remains to be done. Althusser is quite emphatic that his self-criticism does not entail withdrawal of the claim to scientific status on behalf of *historical* materialism. The latter is still to be regarded as objective knowledge, and the 'epistemological break' is a historical fact also in the *extraordinary* sense that it establishes a recognition of the 'errors' of its prehistory. The problem therefore still remains that it is open to *any* 'theoretical practice' to *claim* scientific status and to expose the 'errors' of its prehistory and Marxist philosophy is without any means of evaluating and criticising such conflicting and competing claims.

On the other hand, there is no doubt that Althusser has significantly changed the terms in which such questions may now be posed. Marxism is a science, but at the same time a 'revolutionary science' whose emergence effects a shift in the meaning of the term 'science' itself. At the same time, posing the question of the differential cognitive value of sciences and ideologies as *specific* alternative theoretical formations in historical contexts suggests ways of resolving it without recourse to a universal philosophical theory of the difference between science and ideology as such. It is true, then, that Althusser has registered a significant theoretical shift, *vis-à-vis* his earlier positions, but important philosophical issues remain unresolved.

For Althusser himself, however, it seems that these philosophical issues, in so far as they are recognised at all, are to be resolved by way of a rectification of the 'unilateral' earlier conception of philosophy. Albeit in a tentative and ambiguous way, Althusser suggests that the question of the verification of Marxist theory is to be answered in the domain of political practice. Sometimes, it seems, Marxist politics is the analogue of experiment in the natural sciences, whilst elsewhere Althusser speaks of verification as occurring in *both* scientific and political practice.[10] There are well-known objections to the analogy of politics with experimentation, but the notion is especially problematic for Althusser, given his commitment to theory as a 'relatively autonomous' practice in its own right. The specificity of theory is immediately abandoned of it requires another practice for the verification of its results.

The new conception of philosophy

This question is part of the wider one of Althusser's conception of the relationships between politics and theoretical work. Whereas the earlier conception of philosophy had remained more or less silent on these relationships, the new conception centres on them to the point of abandoning what was of value in the earlier: the specificity and autonomy of theoretical work *vis-à-vis* the political practices it informs. As we have already seen, this conception of the autonomy of theory, whatever its intrinsic merits, does pose problems in Althusser's early essays. In particular it renders the specific historical and political conditions of Marx's 'scientific discovery' unthinkable. The self-criticism, as we have seen, takes up this problem by way of a conception of philosophy as an extension, or 'representation' of proletarian class struggle in the domain of theory. Philosophy is a mediating link through which politics makes itself felt in the constitution of scientific theories. But this is only half the story. The earlier conception of the autonomy of theory also posed in an acute way the problem of the relationship between theory and politics in the reverse direction: the problem of how Marxist theory was to become a historical force in the thought and practice of organised workers. Again, philosophy to the rescue! Philosophy relays the requirements of scientificity in the domain of politics, so that 'scientific' politics may be distinguished from 'deviations' of a leftist or rightist tendency. Philosophy, then, in its new conception, is a two-way intervention, in theory on behalf of politics and in politics on behalf of theory.

Philosophy represents politics in the domain of theory

In its role as representative of politics in the domain of theory, philosophy must abandon the cognitive status formerly accorded it. Philosophy is still required to make an intervention in theory to draw a dividing line between science and invasive ideological obstacles within scientific discourse. But the basis for this boundary-drawing is no longer a scientific 'meta-theory', but rather the unprovable 'tendency' of a class position. Making (rather tendentious) use of Lenin's philosophical text *Materialism and Empirio-Criticism*,[11] Althusser emphasises the difference between science, with its 'concepts', on the one hand, and philosophy, with its 'categories', on the other. Lenin had argued against the followers of Ernst Mach that a change in the *scientific concept* of matter need not affect the status of the *philosophical category* of matter. Similarly, Althusser argues, philosophical materialism is not bound up with any specific 'modalities' or characteristics of matter, other than existence as an objective reality. Since the categories with which philosophy works are the most basic, and therefore all-inclusive concepts, the question of defining them (in terms of *more* extensive concepts) cannot arise, and, likewise, neither can the question of 'proving' fundamental philosophical tendencies. Philosophy is, then, at root, a matter of partisanship, for or against, one or another tendency.

Following Lenin, Althusser reduces the whole history of philosophy to a tendency struggle between materialism and idealism, a reduction which, as Althusser admits, amounts to a denial that philosophy has any real history. This lack of any real history derives from philosophy's lack of an 'object', in the sense in which sciences have an 'object'. Whereas a science may revise and transform its conception of its object as knowledge advances, philosophy, having no 'object' in this sense is confined to an endless repetition of its opposed tendencies. Althusser allows one minor qualification, here, in his 'Elements of Self-Criticism': the opposed – materialist and idealist – philosophical tendencies do not occur in actual philosophical debate as a 'pure' opposition. Instead, elements of idealism and materialism are combined in particular philosophical positions. Althusser's own earlier texts are such a combination, though in them the materialism is primary, the idealism a secondary 'deviation'.

Two questions immediately arise in connection with this view of philosophy. First, in what sense is this tendency struggle 'political', and second, how can it provide reliable criteria for distinguishing science and ideology? A hint as to the answer to the first question has already been given in the thesis of the unprovability of philosophical tendencies, and therefore of the essentially partisan character of philosophy. The rest of the answer is given in Althusser's claim that the materialist tendency in philosophy is the theoretical 'representation' of the world-view of the proletariat, whilst the idealist tendency represents that of the bourgeoisie. 'In the last instance' at stake in this tendency struggle is the hegemony of one or other of the world-views in contestation in the contemporary political class struggle. The second question is answered, in so far as it is answered at all, in the form of an assertion about the 'spontaneous materialism' of scientists themselves.[12] If the sole characteristic of matter to which materialism as a philosophical tendency is committed is its existence as an objective reality, then the scientists' strict respect for the reality of their objects of study is a spontaneous materialism. The spontaneous materialism of the proletariat, then, represented in the form of materialist philosophical categories serves to defend the spontaneous materialism of the scientists against the incursion of idealist philosophical ideologies which introduce error and distortion into science.

But these answers serve only to pose further problems, and one in particular: what is the source of the spontaneous materialism of the proletariat (and the complementary idealism of the bourgeoisie)? The only hint at an answer to this question which Althusser gives is the familiar thesis of historicist Marxism, that historical materialism reveals the exploitation and oppression inherent in class societies, and so is unbearable to the bourgeoisie who cannot admit to themselves its truth. The working class, on the other hand, has an interest in knowing this truth, so that the materialist respect for the reality of Marxism's object of knowledge (society) can be expected to be its spontaneous attitude.[13]

In some respects this very abstract and schematic conception of philosophy as a mediating link between politics and science involves, not an advance beyond the achievements of Althusser's earlier work, but, rather, a retreat. The supposed essential link between the proletariat and materialism is susceptible to two decisive types of objection. One is that in order to explain why it is that the proletariat has an interest in the truth, and the bourgeoisie in its suppression, Althusser has to *use* the concepts of historical materialism (exploitation, oppression, and so on), whereas this device is supposed to provide a means of establishing the validity of historical materialism. The argument is clearly circular. It seems that the only means available to Althusser to avoid this implication is to extend the 'unprovable tendency' thesis to historical materialism itself. To do this would be, of course, to effect a complete retreat into historicism. It would mean the abandonment of the idea of the specificity of theoretical practice, and the abandonment of the claims to objectivity and cognitive validity on the part of Marxism, except in so far as these claims could be made good in terms of the class position and historical role of the working class. In fact Althusser does stop short of this wholescale retreat, continuing to refer to historical materialism as a science, though he remains without adequate philosophical means to defend the claim.

The second type of objection to this supposed link between the class position of the proletariat and materialist philosophy is the 'empirical' one that no such universal connection in fact exists. First, and most obviously, the philosophical opposition between idealism and materialism long pre-dates the emergence of the class struggle of proletariat and bourgeoisie instituted with modern capitalism. This objection could be countered by a revision of the thesis to apply to the spontaneous outlooks of the dominant and subordinate classes of all class societies, not just to bourgeoisie and proletariat. But this wouldn't defend the thesis against the reality of the contemporary world that the Communist movement itself is internationally divided, and internally fragmented ideologically (this is, indeed, the raw material of Althusser's problem, so how can it be his *solution*? – only by denying the reality of the problem, it seems), whilst the working-class movement is divided in its ideological allegiances into anarchist, communist, socialist, social democratic, Catholic, populist and other tendencies. How can any one of these tendencies be accorded a privileged status as 'the' spontaneous tendency of the working class without begging the central question at issue? Both of these types of objection to Althusser's new conception of philosophy as a solution to the question of the 'union' of theory and practice were already familiar as objections to the humanist and historicist methods of solution to the same problem (albeit posed in different terms), and this adds strength to the claim that, in this respect at least, Althusser has retreated theoretically onto the 'terrain' or 'problematic' of his theoretical opponents.

But this is not all. If what was at stake in Althusser's earlier philosophical work was the necessity for theoretical work to be conducted independently of political control by the party leadership, then his later philosophical work implies a significant compromise on that question. The defence of 'scientificity' within science is now assigned to a philosophy which represents working-class politics in the domain of theory. Of course, this philosophy is supposed to serve only to establish the proper scientific respect for reality, and not to decide between *specific* scientific propositions or theories (for or against the theory of state monopoly capitalism, for example). Althusser continues to polemicise vigorously against the latter type of political intervention in the domain of theory by the PCF leadership,[14] but in practice the distinction may be harder to sustain than Althusser supposes. For someone who accepts the truth of, for example, the theory of state monopoly capitalism, opposition to it might easily look like an unscientific lack of respect for reality.

It seems to me that Althusser's earlier insistence that theoretical work can only be of use to politics on condition that it is conducted independently of political requirements and constraints was right. His partial withdrawal on this point, then, is an unwarranted retreat. The retreat is still more regrettable in that it is not, in fact, required to overcome the 'unilateralism' of the earlier conception of philosophy. Notwithstanding the views of some of his critics,[15] there clearly is room in Althusser's earlier conception of theoretical practice for the pertinence of politics to theoretical work to be taken into account. Class struggles and the ideas through which they are fought constitute the object and raw materials, respectively, of historical science. If this latter is recognised to be a theoretical reflection upon, among other things, the conditions and outcomes of historical class struggles, then the supposed 'autonomy' of theoretical practice clearly does *not* entail its divorce from political concerns.

Philosophy represents science in the domain of politics

Comparable problems arise from a consideration of philosophy's intervention in the 'opposite direction': its role as representative of science in the domain of politics. Here Althusser is very schematic and seriously ambiguous. The distinctive character of Marxism–Leninism as a political tradition is its claim to be guided by the science of historical materialism. Marxist philosophy is to be the means whereby the results of scientific work are inserted into the class struggles of the working class and its allies, 'correct' politics defended, and 'deviations' exposed. At least two very important distinctions are suppressed here, and Althusser's silence on the questions they pose is indicative of a partial failure to break from the assumptions of the 'orthodox' tradition of Marxism. Not surprisingly, these turn out to be questions on which Stalin really is rooted in Lenin himself. The first distinction has to do with the cognitive status of science itself. Althusser has defended a conception of science such that scientific theories are subject to revision, to complete 'recasting' of their problematics, and, consequently, to a degree of internal unevenness and contradiction. The self-criticism makes this explicit: there can be no direct correspondence between the science–ideology opposition and the opposition of truth to falsehood. If this view of science is combined with the abandonment of a cognitive role for philosophy, then it follows that philosophy's interventions in politics on behalf of science *cannot but* reflect the unevenness, contradictoriness and *provisional* character of current scientific debate. There is absolutely no basis here, even accepting, for the moment, the idea of a 'scientific' politics, for a distinction between 'correctness' and 'deviation' in politics. This latter distinction can be seen only as a surviving residue of that familiar dogmatic conception of 'science' – which really has nothing at all to do with science – as a body of universally applicable 'truths', embodied in a sacred tradition which renders them immune from revision.

Althusser's new conception of philosophy as a theoretical intervention in politics is, then, ambiguous between these two conceptions of science. It is also importantly ambiguous in its conception of
the applicability of science in politics. On the one hand, 'scientific
politics' may be seen as an application of science to politics in the
sense that strategic and programmatic positions in politics are
uniquely and exclusively determined by scientific analysis of the
conjuncture. Calculations of the probable consequences of alternative courses of action, given the current configuration and tendencies of the conditions of action, can lead directly to a political choice
of instrumentally preferable means. This conception of 'scientific
politics' requires not only the dogmatic conception of science
mentioned above, but also a technocratic and 'positivist' conception
of politics itself. It implies a fusion of cognitive powers with political
authority of a kind that may serve to legitimate a 'Stalinist' political
practice of authoritarian domination by a technocratically defined
élite.

But scientific analysis can guide and inform political practice in
other ways. The provisional, contradictory and uneven character of
scientific work alone is enough to undermine any technocratic view
of the relationship of science to politics. But still more importantly,
politics itself cannot be reduced to the calculation of tendencies and
probabilities. Choice of both means and objectives in political
struggle is irreducibly evaluative. Even if the results of analysis were
able to show a given course of action to be the most likely means of
achieving a given objective, it would not follow that it should be
adopted. A socialist movement has to have an eye to the moral
consistency of its means of struggle with its objectives, and has also
to allow for the objectives of struggle themselves to be constituted
by the participants in the struggle. This suggests a conception of
'scientific socialism' in which scientific analyses inform political
debate in the sense that they provide resources for democratic
debate about means and objectives, indicating, for example, what
are and what are not real possibilities for action in a given situation.

The shift from a view of science as an indispensable resource for a
democratic movement to a view of scientific authority as an *alternative* to democratic decision-making is a technocratic ideology,
increasingly influential as a mystification of power, East and West.
It can and has led, in the organisations of the labour movement, to
forms of cynical moral opportunism no less damaging than the

forms of opportunism which are made possible by an insufficient development of theory. In view of subsequent political critiques of Althusserianism, however, it is important to recognise at this stage that these adverse consequences do not flow from the idea of science as a guide to politics as such. Only if science and politics are conceived in dogmatic and technocratic ways does their conjunction lead to authoritarian, dogmatic and technocratic politics.

But amid the abstraction, the silences, and the retreats of this later conception of philosophy it does seem to me that there are some, albeit limited, advances. First, the critical rejection of the 'speculative' and 'positivist' aspects of the earlier conception is itself a positive achievement, if one for which Althusser doesn't get the sole credit. Second, the problem, which Althusser had earlier on, of accounting for the epistemological break which inaugurated histori- cal materialism except through according exceptional personal qualities to a certain 'subject', Karl Marx, is genuinely resolved. The thesis that theoretical revolutions in science have their extra- scientific, including political, conditions of possibility as well as their purely theoretical ones, whilst it takes away some of the autonomy attributed to science, also makes it possible to think theoretically about the concrete *relationships* between sciences and other social practices.

In the specific case of the theoretical revolution which inaugu- rated historical materialism, we have seen how Althusser's revised view of the 'epistemological break' allows it to be seen as condition- al upon 'the basic ideas of proletarian ideology'.[16] This is an important innovation for Althusser, in view of persistent criticism that his theory of ideology as a universal 'instance' in the social formation leaves no room for a conception of independent working- class ideologies. Clearly, if Althusser's theory of ideology were capable of sustaining such an idea then not only would it help in the explaining of the historical conditions of emergence of Marxism but it would also substantially alter the terms of the problem of the relationship between Marxist theory and the politics of the working class and other oppressed or exploited groups. Instead of an *opposi- tion* between science and ideology, we now have, instead, a (prob- lematic) relationship between a specific theoretical discourse (Marxism) and specific 'forms of social consciousness' (class prac- tices and cultural forms).

I have elsewhere attempted to show how Engels' later

philosophical writings can be understood as a kind of 'mediating discourse' through which concepts drawn from historical materialism are linked with a theory of science, and with ethical and political precepts, to constitute a 'world outlook'.[17] Such mediating discourses have been a typical means of appropriating scientific knowledge within popular cultural and political practices. Comtean positivism and the various forms of social Darwinism are other examples. This is, it seems to me, one useful way of developing Althusser's conception of philosophy as a mediating link between science and politics. But there can be no question of accepting Althusser's own way of making this link. In particular, a specific intellectual labour of theoretical transformation and construction is involved in these popular appropriations of scientific ideas. Philosophy in this sense most decidedly does have a history, and there is no reason to suppose that different scientific popularisations may not be compared and evaluated in terms of their cognitive content. Moreover, the idea of an independent working class, and/or popular culture, upon which such links between science and popular culture rely, remains inconsistent with all of Althusser's systematic theoretical writing on ideology. It is to a consideration of Althusser's later writings on this topic that I now turn.

Ideology and the ideological state apparatuses

Alongside and connected with the revision in the conception of philosophy, other shifts were occurring in Althusser's work. The 1960s saw student unrest and struggles for educational reform in many parts of the world, and France was no exception. The revolutionary events of May 1968 in France, in which a student uprising was combined with widespread mass strikes of workers and factory occupations, served to give a new seriousness to revolutionary socialist politics in the advanced Capitalist countries. At the same time, these events challenged the credentials of the Communist Parties, most especially in France, as the leading force for socialist advance. One important source of the inspiration, slogans and tactics of these student campaigns, especially in France, was the 'Great Proletarian Cultural Revolution' then taking place in China.

Althusser's position on, and part in, these great events is unclear. He appears to have been absent from the scene during the disturbances, remained a member of the broadly pro-Soviet PCF (whilst some of his former students and collaborators broke organisationally from the PCF and associated themselves with the smaller Maoist groupings and parties which emerged at this time), and continued to hold his academic post. From the perspective of some of his radicalised former associates, his earlier use of the science–ideology opposition, his failure to consider the social relations of theoretical work, and his structuralist conception of social change came to be seen as themselves ideological supports for academic élitism, Stalinist politics, or both.

On the other hand, it has been said that Althusser's practical involvement in politics, like that of many intellectuals, was always sporadic, idiosyncratic and naive.[18] In the light of this it might not be surprising to find him missing out on the most important political events of a generation. It should also be said that, before May 1968, Althusser was already introducing concepts and perspectives from Chinese Communism, and especially from the works of Mao into his writings, and he also clearly had some form of oppositional role *vis-à-vis* the PCF leadership, however indirectly and naively conceived. Crucial aspects of the later conception of philosophy, too, can be understood, at least in part, as showing an ability to learn from the political events surrounding him: the thesis that philosophy represents class struggle in theory, that Marxist philosophy is a 'revolutionary weapon', and, in general, the shift towards a recognition of the importance of political conjunctures and class positions in the development of theoretical work.

Althusser's first major piece of writing after 1968 also, in its theoretical concerns, as well as in some of its terminology, displays the impact of the struggles and issues of the late 1960s. Like the student campaigns themselves, Althusser's 'Ideology and Ideological State Apparatuses' (January to April, 1969) bears the unmistakable imprint of the themes of the Chinese Cultural Revolution. The 'Decision of the Central Committee of the Chinese Communist Party Concerning the Great Proletarian Cultural Revolution' (8 August, 1966) declares:

Although the bourgeoisie has been overthrown, it is still trying to use the old ideas, culture, customs and habits of the exploiting classes to corrupt the masses, capture their minds and endeavour to stage a come-back. The proletariat must do the exact opposite: it must meet head-on every challenge of the bourgeoisie in the ideological field and use the new ideas, culture, customs and habits of the proletariat to change the mental outlook of the whole of society. At present, our objective is to struggle against and overthrow those persons in authority who are taking the capitalist road, to criticise and repudiate the reactionary bourgeois academic 'authorities' and the ideology of the bourgeoisie and all other exploiting classes and to transform education, literature and art and all other parts of the superstructure not in correspondence with the socialist economic base, so as to facilitate the consolidation and development of the socialist system.[19]

In its advocacy of the necessity of struggle – class struggle – in the 'superstructural' fields of culture and education, this text clearly assigns 'real existence' and hence a degree of autonomy to these elements of the superstructure. Though China has a socialist economic base, persistence into post-revolutionary China of the 'ideas, culture, customs and habits' of the previous ruling classes despite their political overthrow, and the ending of their *economic* dominance, is evident. There are, consequently, areas of 'non-correspondence' between the socialist economic base and 'parts of the superstructure'. That the superstructures are not a mere 'epiphenomenon' of the economic structure, but have their own specific 'relative autonomy', and that ideology, in particular, is a reality in its own right, not reducible to the 'ideas and beliefs' of individual subjects are characteristically Althusser's themes. But in the earlier works of Althusser the political implications, clearly drawn in this statement by the Chinese CP, are given no prominence. If the fields of ideology and 'culture' have their own autonomy and reality, then these domains must be both the *site* of, and, in part, what is *at stake* in, the political class struggle. As we have seen, the new conception of philosophy, in an abstract and schematic way, recognises this. But what remains wholly inimical to this perspective is the conception of ideology, and its contrast with science, which is a central feature of the 'problematic' of the writings of the early 1960s.

Reproduction and the ISAs

The 'Ideology and Ideological State Apparatuses' essay can best be understood as a rigorous attempt by Althusser to rectify the earlier conception of ideology in this new theoretical and political conjuncture. How far this is achieved, we shall see. The 'topographical' metaphor through which Marxism has always attempted to conceptualise the relationship between economics and the various non-economic practices as the 'base–superstructures' relationship, is, Althusser argues, merely 'descriptive' and requires theoretical development. The analysis Althusser procedes to give of the relationship is a functionalist one, which gives central place to the concept of 'reproduction', already the subject of Balibar's contribution to *Reading Capital.* The persistence of a social formation depends on the reproduction of the conditions of production. This must include not only the replacement of instruments of production (the task of 'Department I' of the economy), but also the replacement of labour power, day by day and generation by generation, and the reproduction of the *relationships* within which production takes place, too.

The material means for reproducing their labour power are purchased by workers from their wages, and this is, of course, for Marxism not a matter of biological subsistence, but an historically variable minimum standard of life, established, as Althusser comments, through class struggle. But the reproduction of labour power in a specific social formation at a specific moment in its history must mean reproduction of that labour power in a definite quantity, distributed in requisite proportions with respect to skills, aptitudes and so on, and provided with appropriate ideological accomplishments and dispositions. Increasingly, skills and dispositions are provided not 'on the job', but outside the sphere of production as such, in the family and, primarily, in the schools, where skills are inculcated 'in and under forms of ideological subjection'.[20]

Important aspects of the reproduction of labour power then, cannot be explained if consideration is given exclusively to processes within the sphere of the economic structure. The same is true of the reproduction of the social relations of production. For both of these 'elements' of the economic structure, the conditions of their reproduction are secured by extra-economic practices and processes: the superstructures. Althusser's argument leads him, then, to a consideration of the nature and functioning of these superstructures. Beginning, as usual, with the Marxist–Leninist classics, Althusser repeats their central doctrines concerning the capitalist state: the state is not 'neutral' and 'above' society, but is a machine of class domination. A distinction must be made between the state apparatus (essentially: police, courts, prisons, army, head of state, central administration) and state power. State power is the principal objective of the class struggle of the working class, which it establishes by simultaneously destroying the Capitalist state apparatus and establishing its own proletarian state apparatus, through which it proceeds to expropriate the capitalist class, and build socialism. In a subsequent phase, the proletarian state, too, will wither away as a classless society is established.

This classical statement of the Marxist theory of the state is quite incompatible with any kind of reformist or 'gradualist' conception of the transformation of society by a governing party or coalition of the Left adapting the machinery of the capitalist state for this purpose. In particular it is incompatible, on the face of things, at least, with those 'Eurocommunist' tendencies which gained strength in a number of European Communist Parties in the 1970s. Althusser's position in relation to this classical Leninist conception of the state is quite clear. The state is 'a force of repressive execution and intervention "in the interests of the ruling classes" in the class struggle conducted by the bourgeoisie and its allies against the proletariat', and 'not for one moment can there be any question of rejecting the fact that this really is the essential point'.[21]

Despite its essential correctness, though, this classical Marxist–Leninist conception requires supplementation. Althusser begins by doing no more than recognising what many modern Marxists before him (most notably, as is acknowledged by Althusser, Antonio Gramsci) had also recognised: that modern capitalist societies, characterised as many of them are, by parliamentary political systems of one sort or another, rest principally on securing the active consent of the subordinate classes to the existing form of society and their assigned place in it. If bayonets and prisons ever were the principal means whereby the subordinate classes were kept in their place, this is no longer true for many of the more 'advanced' of the world's capitalist countries. At least for most of the time, and with respect to the majority of their indigenous populations, the place of physical repression has been taken by vastly superior means of ideological and cultural subordination.

Althusser, drawing upon Gramsci's distinction between state and civil society, argues that the ideological dominance of the ruling class is, like its political dominance, secured in and through definite institutional forms and practices: the ideological apparatuses of the state, or 'ISAs', as Althusser calls them. The schools, the churches, the family, communications media, literary, cultural and sporting organisations, the trades unions and political parties (including, one is tempted to ask, the Communist Party?) are all ISAs, superstructural formations which function by ideology rather than by violence, as do the apparatuses of the state more narrowly defined (the repressive state apparatuses, or RSAs). The RSAs, operating under the 'commanding unity' of the political representatives of the ruling class(es), secure by 'force' the political conditions of the reproduction of the relations of production (relations of exploitation) but they also contribute to their own reproduction, and provide the 'political conditions', or act as the 'shield' behind which the ISAs operate. It is the ISAs which play the major part in the reproduction of the relations of production, behind this 'shield' inculcating skills and aptitudes under the dominant ideology, and in the requisite proportions and variant forms. Althusser goes on to advance the hypothesis that, under Capitalism, the dominant ISAs are the 'school–family couple', whereas in feudal society the reproduction of the relations of production, in its ideological aspects, was secured by the 'church–family couple'. This reconceptualisation of ideology and of the base–superstructure relationship through the concept of reproduction is complemented by a new account, drawing upon elements of Lacanian psychoanalysis, of the mechanisms through which overall reproductive requirements of the social formation are inscribed in the subjective world of individual social actors.

First, though, it is necessary to consider some objections to Althusser's broadly functionalist account of the relationship between the ISAs and the economic structure. Two of these objections are foreseen by Althusser himself. First, there is no absolute institutional separation of 'coercion' and 'persuasion'. The ISAs have their own internal coercive practices (for example, forms of punishment in schools), and the RSAs secure their internal unity and their wider social authority significantly through ideology (for example, traditional and charismatic legitimations of leadership in the armed forces, the guarantee of security against lawless elements in the ideology of 'law and order', and ideologies of patriotism and national integrity). For Althusser, the distinction between RSAs and ISAs is a matter of degree, a matter of whether force or ideology predominates in the functioning of the apparatuses. This is, in fact, a less sophisticated treatment of the relation of coercion and consent than that offered by Gramsci. For the latter, the mechanism of hegemonic domination is a specific *combination* of consent and coercion, the two being understood as inseparable aspects of a single process.

The second obvious objection to Althusser's conception of the ISAs is that they are a diverse and seemingly 'empirical' list, in the main belonging to the private domain. What grounds are there for classifying them *together*, and as part of the *state*? Althusser argues that the distinction between private and public is valid within bourgeois law, and the state is above the law, so that these categories have no necessary validity when applied to it. This argument seems to me to be not only based on false premises, but quite unnecessary to Althusser. He could more effectively argue that the distinction, in this sphere, belongs to legal ideology and therefore has no validity for a historical materialist analysis. This is, in effect, the position adopted by Althusser, since he goes on to argue that the unity of the ISAs, and the justification of their classification together with the RSAs in the theory of the state is given by an analysis of their *functions*: presumably, ISAs and RSAs are alike in being non-economic instances which contribute to the reproduction of the relations of production, but are distinguishable by the different parts they play in this reproduction.

A further contrast between the ISAs and RSAs, which follows from their different functions, is that a definite structure of command unifies the RSAs, whereas the ISAs have of necessity a diverse, uneven, and internally contradictory unity, provided by the dominant ideology under and through which, but in different variant forms, they all operate. This latter feature of the ISAs, which is necessary to their functioning (that is, they prepare and distribute agents to *different positions* in the social relations of production, and do so, at least with the *illusion* of free choice and consent), simultaneously ensures that the effects of the class struggles of the subordinate classes cannot be excluded from the ISAs: 'the Ideological State Apparatuses may be not only the *stake*, but also the *site* of class struggle, and often of bitter forms of class struggle'.[22] Here, then, is a theme from the struggles of the revolutionary students of the 1960s, and from the Chinese Cultural Revolution: ideological class struggle. We shall have to return very shortly to ask whether Althusser has the means to integrate such a theme into his broader political perspective.

But first it is necessary to look at several other problems with Althusser's conception of the state as so far presented. First, the list of ISAs is not at all homogeneous, as Althusser recognises, but it is, in fact, much more radically heterogeneous than he seems to suggest. In particular, the trades unions and the political parties cannot all be assimilated so easily to the 'reproduction' perspective. Althusser's attempt to do this can only be interpreted as either an oblique leftist critique of PCF and Communist union federation as agencies of the bourgeoisie, or as a very odd instance of theoretical 'forgetfulness'. If the former interpretation is the correct one, then it is very difficult to see what could possibly justify Althusser's remaining within the PCF, where his former colleagues, adopting precisely this perspective, abandoned it. For a practice of continuing oppositional struggle within a mass organisation like the PCF, or an openly reformist one like the British Labour Party to make sense at all, it must be assumed that its role *vis-à-vis* the oppressed and exploited classes is at worst contradictory, if not actually beneficial to their interests.

Secondly, Althusser's conception of the school and family as the dominant ISAs under Capitalism rests on their supposed function in the reproduction of labour power. Since under Capitalism, labour power is a commodity, it may be argued that the domestic and educational labour which reproduces it may properly be regarded as productive of value, so that the status of the school and family as non-economic institutions is rendered doubtful. As we shall see,[23] these problems gave rise to an extensive and inconclusive debate, especially about the status of domestic labour, and with it the sexual division of labour. It is a further pertinent criticism of Althusser's conception of the ISAs that the social distribution of agents is treated exclusively with regard to class and occupational distribution, neglecting the constitution of, and allocation to, the sexual division of labour.

And still more difficulties could be raised. Is Althusser justified in dismissing the distinction between public and private so quickly? Like other ideological distinctions might this one also allude, in its own way, to a real difference in the mutual 'articulation' of the different institutional forms? There clearly is, for example, an important difference between a fully corporate state structure in which the unions *are* primarily an arm of those who control the state apparatus, and forms of state in which unions operate independently of the state, on the basis of policies determined by the membership but circumscribed by labour law. Of course, there are no 'pure forms' of either paradigm but some of the central struggles of the contemporary labour movement are rendered entirely unintelligible by a theory which would obliterate the distinction. Similar considerations apply to the family – the locus of 'privacy', *par excellence*. Though a degree of regulation of family life is attempted by state policy and legislation, direct intervention is generally avoided. Again, it could be effectively argued that Althusser's nonchalance with respect to the distinction between the public and the private is a further obstacle in the way of an adequate analysis of the constitution of the sexual division of labour and the specific forms of oppression of women.

Further, the functional perspective on the ISAs, that they reproduce the relations of production, has more than a ring of 'economism' about it: the economy sets up requirements which are 'met' by the superstructures. Althusser does mention in passing that the ISAs and RSAs reproduce themselves, and also, in a footnote, that the relations of production 'are first reproduced by the materiality of the processes of production and circulation.[24] He also appears to suggest that, in the ISAs, the inculcation of ruling ideology meets resistance so that, presumably, the processes of social reproduction do not run smoothly or without obstacles, but none of these qualifications to the basic 'economistic' functionalism is fully theorised. Balibar's self-criticism goes much further in this respect, arguing that reproduction must be understood first and foremost from the perspective of the *totality* of social relations which are, in turn, to be thought of as relations of class struggle.[25]

But here Balibar forces a confrontation with the whole conception of ideology so far developed by Althusser. This confrontation is, indeed, implicit in Althusser's own recognition of the existence of 'ideological class struggle' in the ISAs. If there is ideological class struggle, waged by the subordinate classes, then what are the *means* whereby this struggle is waged? Certainly among the means, the 'weapons' of the struggle will be Marxist philosophy, and the science of historical materialism, but since 'man is an ideological animal'[26] who 'lives' his struggles, as a 'subject' in the element or 'medium' of ideology, then these theoretical weapons must somehow be woven into a discourse and a practice which is quite other than science or philosophy: an *ideological* practice of transforming consciousnesses.

But the conception Althusser has so far advanced, of ideology as a universal social reality, whose universality and necessity derive from the universality of a functional requirement – that agents are distributed to different places in the division of labour (in order for the relations of production to be reproduced), leaves no theoretical room for a discourse and practice of ideology which *resists and opposes* this very process of ideological social reproduction. So, at the very best, what Althusser has done is to identify and begin to theorise the nature and mechanisms of the *ruling ideology*, but to represent this as a theory of ideology as such and in general.

Ideology and interpellation

That this criticism is well-founded is confirmed by Althusser's extended discussion of the concept of ideology in the latter part of 'Ideology and Ideological State Apparatuses'. To a considerable extent, this discussion repeats and extends the earlier treatment of ideology in the 'Marxism and Humanism' essay in *For Marx*. Here, too, ideology is an 'imaginary' or 'lived' relation (or representation of that relation) of individuals to their real conditions of existence, and here, too, ideology is held to have 'no history' – that is, to be an 'omni-historical' reality. But Althusser is careful, now, to qualify the generality of scope of this thesis: for the moment, at least, Althusser is confining himself to the history of *class* societies. The provocative question of ideology as a social necessity even in socialist society is at least verbally shelved.

There are, in addition, two significantly new 'theses' on ideology. One, already implicit in the earlier essay, but now given more thorough exposition, is the thesis of the 'materiality' of ideology. In what Althusser rejects as the prevailing 'ideology of ideology', the actions of individual subjects are understood as flowing from freely chosen ideas and beliefs. Althusser's thesis of the materiality of ideology inverts this causal sequence: the 'material' ideological apparatuses govern 'material' practices and rituals into which are inserted the 'material' actions which *are* the ideas and beliefs of the subject. It is in our daily participation in the practices and rituals of the family, school, party, union, and so on, that we come to 'live' our relation to our conditions of existence under the symbolic and conceptual forms provided by ideology, as it is 'materialised' in these practices.

Though Althusser is evasive as to the precise meaning of the word 'material' in this exposition (matter exists, he says, in many 'modalities'), the thesis has much to recommend it. Ideology has its own reality, it is not reducible to 'consciousness', which may be 'true' or 'false', so that ideological struggle may now be thought of as itself a 'real' struggle to transform institutional structures and social practices, rather than as an exercise in the 'correction of illusions'.

But what, exactly, is the mechanism whereby the individual is, through participation in these 'material' practices, incorporated into ideology? Althusser's treatment of this question is obscure and condensed, but in essence it consists in an attempt to appropriate and generalise the concept of the 'mirror-phase' from Lacan's psychoanalysis so as to show that in the process of acquiring self identity individuals necessarily acquire a conception of themselves as subject, but *freely* subject, to a 'super-Subject', with a capital 'S'. Althusser concludes his article with an attempt to illustrate this process – the process of 'interpellation' – in the case of religious ideology.

What is required is a theory which will help to explain the constitution of human 'individuals' as conscious 'subjects' who voluntarily submit to the requirements of the social system. Lacan's 'mirror-phase' gives Althusser a means of conceptualising the entry of the human infant into conscious life. The child's ability to recognise itself in a mirror-image is an indication of its formation of a conception of self and recognition of the 'self-hood' of others. The constitution of individuals as 'subjects', then, is bound up with their recognition of other 'subjects'. But since the conscious life within which this mutual recognition occurs is only a portion of psychic life (that is, the greater part of psychic life is *un*conscious), and since subject-hood is consciously lived as the *source* of 'free' initiatives and self-transparency, we must conclude that this sphere within which conscious subjects recognise one another has a peculiar status: it is the domain of the 'imaginary', and of 'imaginary' relations to real conditions of existence. Finally, according to Freud's Oedipal phase, the constitution of gendered subjectivity depends upon the infants' subjection to patriarchal authority, which is equivalent, in Lacanian psychoanalysis, to submission to the prevailing symbolic order. Though Althusser, again rather tellingly, does not develop the significance of *gendered* subjectivity as the outcome of the process of 'interpellation' of subjects, we can, at least, see how Lacanian psychoanalysis does provide a suggestive way of linking the constitution of subjectivity with the ideological constitution of *subjection*.

But, again, Althusser's position is not unproblematic. As P. Q. Hirst has argued,[27] this whole theory of the *constitution* of subjects actually *presupposes* that the human infants who are 'interpellated' are already possessed of the capacities of subjects: they 'perceive', 'recognise', 'desire' and so on. Secondly, the concept of 'interpellation' is no advance over the conception of socialisation offered by functionalist sociology, in that in the context of Althusser's identification of 'ideology' with 'ruling ideology' there is no basis for 'interpellations' of oppositional forms of subjectivity. Individual human subjects can be no more than willing 'dupes' of the social system. As we shall see,[28] several of the more fundamental critiques of Althusser's approach start from a recognition of this difficulty in the theory of ideology.

Part II

Althusserian Marxism: Towards a New Orthodoxy?

6
Mode of Production, Articulation and Social Formation

The Althusserian project of rigorous problematisation and reconstruction of some of the most basic concepts and propositions of historical materialism was bound to have enormously wide-ranging implications. In fields of debate where Marxist positions were already well established, in conflict both among themselves and against rival theories, the impact of structural Marxism was to undermine the established terms of debate, to pose new questions, and to re-shape the pattern of alliance and opposition between the established traditions: anthropology, the sociologies of development and underdevelopment, the debate over the nature of the Soviet Union and the other societies of Eastern Europe, theories of the state and the class structure of the advanced capitalist societies, and a number of other fields of enquiry were all affected in this way.

In other fields, where Marxist positions were underdeveloped or almost wholly non-existent, Althusser's work made possible several major advances which retain their historical importance even where they have been superceded. In this context, the Althusserian attempt to theorise ideological and theoretical practices as distinct and relatively autonomous instances in the social formation made it possible for Marxists to analyse literary texts and other cultural products in a way that did not implicitly or explicitly reduce their specificity to class outlook or economic conditions of production. Of course, the best of Marxist writers on literature and the arts had always managed to avoid this reductionism, and some (such as Sartre) had attempted, long before Althusser, to reconstruct Marxist categories in such a way as to theoretically underpin a non-reductionist criticism. Where Althusserianism differs from most of this previous work is in its attempt to avoid reductionism without recourse to any individualist theory of the cultural product as an expression of subjective meaning. For Althusser and his followers, the specificity of the cultural object is a result of the complexity of its structural determinants, operating both upon and within the cultural practice of which it is the product (the materials it employs, the relationships it involves, the practices it includes and excludes and so on).

Structural Marxism was also an important source for new ways of theorising the sexual division of labour in society, and the relationship between class domination and the oppression of women, fields of inquiry which had been scandalously undeveloped within Marxism, as within other traditions of social theory. As we shall see, several different elements of Althusserian theory have been taken up in the attempt to develop a feminist theory compatible with Marxism, with results not always either internally consistent, or consistent with one another. Finally, and relatedly, Althusser made possible new ways of integrating Marxism with psychology through the concept of the function of ideology in the 'interpellation of individuals as subjects'. Althusser's attempt to use certain elements of Lacan's reading of Freud in the development of this idea was the starting point for a new series of attempts to align and articulate Marxism with psychoanalysis.

I have neither the space nor the ability to cover the whole range of Althusserian influences in these areas. What I shall do instead is, first, to say something in very general terms about the kinds of critical encounter with alternative traditions of thought which Althusserianism made possible, and, secondly, to evaluate the effects of Althusserian work in a small number of selected fields of controversy: fields selected, that is, on the grounds that they seem to me to be areas of importance both for the viability of historical materialism in social science, and for social theory as such.

Althusserian criticism

First, the Althusserian practice of critique. The key critical concepts deployed by Althusserians against alternative approaches in the various disciplines engaged are by now a familiar repertoire: 'empiricism', 'humanism', 'reductionism', 'teleology', 'problematic'. Texts which work with concepts supposedly drawn from, and corresponding directly to, empirical findings are guilty of empiricism, as are texts purporting to emanate from the Marxist tradition, which interpret the basic concepts and statements of historical materialism as having directly empirical referents. Theoretical approaches which refer to actors' volition (whether individual or collective), subjective meaning, or rational choice as ultimate explanatory principles are guilty of 'humanism'. Texts which fail to accord specificity and autonomy to the various non-economic 'instances' or 'practices' making up the social formation are guilty of 'reductionism'. Accounts of historical processes which represent them as either the outcome of an underlying rational agency (for example, Hegelian Marxisms) or as the temporal 'working out' of inner necessities inscribed in social forms from their inception (evolutionist theories of history of various kinds, 'Marxist' and non-Marxist) are rejected as relying upon epistemologically suspect teleological concepts of causality. Finally, an Althusserian critique may be bound together through the epistemological concept of 'problematic', according to which the basic concepts of a theory structure what may or may not be asked, and the answers which may and may not be given within that specific theoretical discourse.

Now, these critical tools *can* be, and often have been, set to work in the following way: a text or theoretical tradition is analysed in such a way as to uncover the basic concepts (the problematic) which govern its empirical appearance, in the form of connected sentences, texts, and debates. These basic concepts are then examined for any sign of teleology, humanism, reductionism, and so on, whose status as 'error' has already been established independently of the specific intellectual encounter. Should these errors be discovered at the level of the theoretical problematic, then the critic is home and dry – no need to examine the detail of the text, no need to confront its specificity with the available evidence. The text is governed by its problematic, and so simply reproduces the errors of its founding concepts. The truly labour-saving character of this mode of critique may even be complemented by a version of the Althusserian critique of empiricism according to which any appeal to evidence which has its source outside the domain of discourse is in any case necessarily misconceived.

Such a mode of critique can offer no more than a sterile confrontation of theoretical paradigms, but is it the best Althusserian Marxism has to offer? Interestingly, Althusser's own approach to the concept of critique, in *Reading Capital*, attempts to explain

Marx's 'theoretical revolution' in political economy as itself an effect of a critique of the classical political economy of Smith and Ricardo. Althusser claims to distinguish two principles of 'reading' in Marx's critique of classical political economy – one which views their texts through the 'grid' of Marx's own theoretical position, and points out presences and absences: recognitions and failures of vision in the writers criticised. But alongside this is a second principle of reading, one which understands the *link* between the specific pattern of recognitions and oversights, as something internal to the text. Here, classical theory is not compared 'with anything *except itself*, its non-vision with its vision'.[1] Classical political economy treats labour as a commodity, and so for labour as for other commodities, asks the question 'What is the value of *this* commodity?' The answer given by classical theory is 'the value of the subsistence goods necessary for the maintenance and reproduction of labour'. But this answer strictly makes no sense. If the final term were replaced by 'labourer' sense might appear to be restored, but with the cost that there is now a 'clash' between the question and its answer: the labourer and his labour are quite different things, as different as a machine and its operation. What Marx shows is that the discourse of classical economics produces the answer to a question *it is not able to pose*. Marx provides that question through the distinction between labour and labour power. What is exchanged between capitalist and labourer is labour power, a capacity to labour, for a sum of money equivalent in value to the commodities necessary for the maintenance and reproduction of the *capacity* to labour. The exercise of labour power, that is to say, its productive consumption in the capitalist labour process, produces a value greater than the value of these subsistence goods, and this is the source of surplus value. In the provision of the question to which classical economics had already provided the answer, Marx explodes the whole structure of classical economic discourse with his concepts of labour power, constant and variable capital, surplus value and exploitation.

The point here is that, for Althusser, Marx's critique of classical political economy is not a sterile confrontation between two incompatible systems of thought. It is, rather, only through a painstaking and rigorous analysis of the inner contradictions and unresolved problems of that discourse that Marx finds *already produced in it* the conditions of possibility for his own 'immense theoretical revolution'. On this model, an Althusserian critique would begin by analysing the internal contradictions and unevennesses of the texts or discourses to be criticised, without presupposing from the beginning that these contradictions must have their source in the errors of historicism, humanism, and so on. The resources of the non-historicist, non-humanist conceptual apparatus provided by Althusser and his colleagues would then have to be tested anew with each theoretical project by their capacity to advance debate within that domain of enquiry.[2] While it is no doubt true that a good deal of avowedly Althusserian critical activity degenerated towards the caricature I drew earlier, it is still the case that there were creditable exceptions, some of which I shall discuss later in this chapter.

The Althusserian alternative

So much for Althusserian criticism. I shall now turn to a consideration of some of the new directions in social and historical enquiry proposed by leading structural Marxists. We saw, in Chapter 4, how Balibar's essay in *Reading Capital*, together with several of Althusser's own essays, began to move away from specifically philosophical concerns towards the elaboration of the historical concepts belonging to the Marxist tradition in line with the new 'reading' of Marx's work. Those essays left an uneven legacy of partial achievements, gestural solutions to half-posed questions, and a number of what turned out to be intractable theoretical problems.

Perhaps the most striking feature of Balibar's essay is the scope of the project it announces: 'Marx's "historical materialism" gives us not only *elements* of scientific historical knowledge (for example, elements restricted to the history of "bourgeois" society, in its economic and political aspects), but, in principle, a true theoretical science, and therefore an abstract science.'[3] Central to this claim of classical Marxism, now revived by Althusser and Balibar, is the commitment to an interpretation of such concepts as 'mode of production', 'social formation', 'determination in the last instance by the economic', and even the concepts of the 'levels' or instances of the social formation themselves (ideology, politics, and so on) as trans-historical and cross-cultural concepts. That is to say, some, if not all, of these concepts must be universal in the sense that they must be applicable in the analysis of the radically different forms of social existence which are represented through human history and pre-history, and which are, in any historical period, distributed through the world. This project of an 'abstract science' must be distinguished from an 'historical schema': the different forms of society identified by the basic concepts need not be thought of as constituting a linear series or hierarchy, or as being linked by necessary mechanisms of transition and supersession. Nor is it argued that the basic, and universal concepts are of themselves and *without addition* capable of providing adequate theoretical analyses of *specific* social forms, or of phases in their temporal existence.

Still, the claim of universal applicability, even of a mere fistful of concepts, is a strong claim. In the past this claim on behalf of classical Marxism had come up against major obstacles and challenges. Among the most important of these are:

1. A range of problems connected with the analysis of 'pre-capitalist' societies. Marx's own indications were peripheral to his main concerns, and very schematic. Can a rigorous typology of pre-capitalist economic forms (modes of production) be produced which is both consistent with the main propositions of Marxist theory and capable of providing illuminating analysis of the rich empirical data field of anthropology and cognate disciplines? Can the Marxist thesis of determination by the economic be sustained against the apparently overwhelming importance of such institutions as kinship, religion and the state in pre-capitalist formations?

2. A nexus of questions concerned with the Marxist conception of the social totality: how should the supposed determination by the economic of the other 'levels' of society be conceived, and how can this determination be reconciled with an autonomy on the part of the non-economic levels? Can the distinctions between the levels even be sustained, and are they unequivocally the same distinctions when they are applied to radically different forms of society?

3. A range of questions having to do with the explanation of historical change. Short of a schematic philosophy of history, can anything be said in abstract theoretical terms about the possibility of, and the forms of transition from one socio–economic formation to another? Can such a theory avoid teleological or 'historicist' modes of explanation? Can, in particular, the transi-

tion from Feudalism to Capitalism in the West be explained in terms consistent with the basic concepts and propositions of historical materialism? And what of the transformation of Capitalism itself? Does Marxism have a coherent theory of socialism as a socio–economic form, and its historical conditions of possibility? How can the prevailing socio–economic forms of Eastern Europe be conceptualised using historical materialist categories?

4. Given that Marxist theory conceptualises a number of distinct actual or possible socio–economic forms, how does it theorise their relationships of co-existence? Colonialism, imperialism and war are all examples of phenomena of the inter-relation of different socio–economic formations for which classical Marxism offered explanations. What do the Althusserian reconstructions of classical Marxist concepts have to offer in response to the difficulties encountered by these attempts at explanation?

The work of Althusser and Balibar gave rise immediately to new directions of inquiry and new terms of debate surrounding almost all of these questions. What was at first principally a French debate very rapidly became international. The work of the French Marxist anthropologist, Claude Meillasoux was the subject of a seminal critical discussion by Emmanuel Terray, under the direct influence of Balibar's indications on pre-capitalist formations and the debate was joined by P. P. Rey and others. Very much rooted in this French debate was an influential subsequent English theoretical work, *Pre-Capitalist Modes of Production*, by Barry Hindess and Paul Hirst. This work was itself the subject of strong critical reaction from within Structural Marxism and was also shortly afterwards critically rejected by its authors from a rather different perspective. The question of the European transition to Capitalism was taken up by Perry Anderson, whose work was also the subject of a critical response from Hirst. The problem of historical transition, posed as a general theoretical problem by Balibar, and confronted also by Hindess and Hirst, further provided the basis of an original approach to the question of the nature of Soviet society in the work, strongly influenced by Althusser and Balibar, of Charles Bettleheim. As we have seen, the absence of an adequate historical materialist account of Soviet society was an important element in the formation of Althusser's whole philosophical project and had an obvious bearing on the development of socialist political strategy.

The idea, advanced in Althusser and Balibar, of the complexity of the social formation, and the possible articulation within a single formation of a plurality of modes of production, proved to be of use in advancing debate in several of these fields of enquiry. It was employed in the analysis of the feudal–capitalist transition in the West, the 'transitional' formations of Eastern Europe, and the nature and dynamics of capitalist penetration of non-capitalist formations in the 'third world': the ideas of complex combinations of modes of production or elements of them, together with associated non-economic levels or instances, made possible new approaches to the sociology of development and underdevelopment, as well as restructuring the relationship between these disciplines and anthropology. The idea of articulation of modes of production was also used in the search for a theory of the relationship between domestic and wage labour, and the connected sexual division of labour in capitalist formations. But, alongside this were two other types of feminist use of the Althusserian 'corpus' of concepts: analyses of the relation of the family to the state and its role in the reproduction of capitalist social relations (an approach deriving from Althusser's ISAs essay), and attempts to integrate the Lacanian reading of Freud, and through it the concept of 'patriarchy', with structural Marxism. Juliet Mitchell's work was central to this development, which has subsequently largely abandoned its Marxist origins.

Pre-capitalist societies[4]

Returning, now, to a more detailed consideration of some of these elaborations and extensions of the work of Althusser and Balibar, I shall begin with the debate about the identification and analysis of the 'pre-capitalist' modes. The starting point for this debate is Claude Meillasoux's *L'Anthropologie Economique des Gouro d'Côte d'Ivoire*,[5] which attempts to apply the categories of historical materialism to a specific 'primitive' society, that of the Gouro of West Africa. Meillasoux's objectives were to provide a characterisation of the mode of production of lineage-based societies, but also to analyse the basis for a transition to commercial agriculture under colonial rule. It is typical of lineage societies that their principal social activities are organised through relationships of descent (actual or fictional) and kinship. In the case of Gouro society, the allocation of individuals and instruments of production to production units, the redistribution of the product, and the circulation of women in exchange for a 'bride price' paid in élite goods are all generally organised through kinship relations, the 'locus' of these distributions and allocations resting with the elders of the lineage. Meillasoux's work is developed and reconceptualised by Emmanuel Terray,[16] drawing explicitly on the definition of the concept of mode of production given by Balibar. Like Balibar, Terray thinks of the economic base of a mode of production as a two-fold combination of labourer, object of labour and instruments of labour. These elements are combined through forms of co-operation which arise out of the technical necessities of transforming nature, and through social relations which have to do with the social allocation of the elements of the labour process, and the social appropriation of the product. The mode of production itself is to be thought of as a three-level combination of this economic base with an ideological, and a juridico–political superstructure.

The question is, can these concepts be employed in the analysis of lineage-based societies, such as the Gouro? Terray rightly sees this as a decisive question. According to the structuralist anthropology[7] of Claude Levi-Strauss, the dominance of kinship and marriage relationships in 'primitive' societies is such that the analysis of kinship is the key to their fundamental structures, in much the same way that analysis of the economic infrastructure is the key to the social structure of contemporary capitalist societies. Terray's argument on this question is that kinship relations are not dominant in all primitive societies, that they do not structure all activities even where they are dominant, and that in different societies kinship and marriage rules function in quite different ways: 'the unity of the entity "kinship" can no longer be thought of as given and has to be proved'.[8] The secondary character of kinship relations is further demonstrated through a re-working of Meillasoux's material. As Meillasoux argues:

> Life and death act as disturbances and tend to break down the natural family. Economic imperatives, among others, contribute to the creation of new units whose members are tied by relations of production and consumption. The biological family cannot

stay within its narrow genealogical framework and is replaced by functional families whose members are associated by consanguinity. Under such a dynamic, the bonds of kinship have to be sufficiently elastic to adapt to such modifications.[9]

Kinship as a system of social relationships does not correspond to genealogy: it is genealogy modified by the requirements of production and reproduction, so that, in Terray's terms 'relations of production can be "realised" within it'. For Terray, the Althusserian concept of overdetermination provides the key to an analysis of the place of kinship relations in the 'primitive' social formation: comparably with class relations in more advanced formations, kinship relations cannot be identified with one or other 'level' of the mode of production, but are the effect of a *synthesis of determinations* by the economic base, and its ideological and juridico-political superstructures. It is in this sense that kinship relations 'realise' economic, political and ideological relations: they are the form of appearance taken by these relations in lineage-based societies.

The difficulty here is that the category of the economic structure of the mode of production (and, indeed, the other levels) is removed to the status of an analytical abstraction, whose referent (the economic structure itself) has *detectable effects*, but which is not empirically present. This poses rather obvious problems for the project of analysing actual economic forms and processes in lineage societies. Terray himself argues that the existence and characterisation of modes of production in primitive societies has to begin with the identification and enumeration of indicators: these indicators are the various labour processes involved in agriculture, hunting and gathering, craftwork, and so on. The assumption is that these labour processes, forms of appropriation of nature, are both empirically detectable and distinguishable. Once this task is complete, the Marxist thesis of the correspondence of forces and relations of production allows the identification of the social relations of production (that is, the relations of social appropriation of the product) which correspond in each case to the inventory of labour processes.

Application of these analytical procedures to Meillasoux's ethnography allows Terray to draw two significant conclusions. The first of these is that Gouro society comprises two modes of production in articulation. One, based on the 'complex co-operation' required for hunting, has the tribal-village organisation as the 'realisation' of its relations of production, whilst the other, based on 'simple co-operation' in agriculture and domestic production realises its social relations in the lineage. The second conclusion is that the 'lineage mode of production' so identified in Gouro society is a mode with no social division into classes.

The British Althusserians, Barry Hindess and Paul Q. Hirst, in their commentary[10] on the work of Meillasoux and Terray, criticised both for what they described as a 'technicist' concept of mode of production. Modes of production, they argued, cannot be identified and distinguished on the basis of inventories of different labour processes, but only on the basis of a previously elaborated conception of the mode of production in question as an 'articulated combination'. The provision of such concepts, by theoretical derivation from the fundamental concepts and propositions of historical materialism, and in *abstraction from their empirical instantiation*, was the declared object of Hindess and Hirst's own work.[11] However, it is precisely *because* they define their project in this way that Hindess and Hirst fail to recognise that Terray does, indeed, begin with an elaborated conception of the mode of production, one closely similar to the one employed by Hindess and Hirst themselves. The problem which Terray addresses is, however, of quite a different order: it is the problem of utilising this concept in the analysis of a specific body of empirical ethnographic materials.

Terray's second conclusion, that the lineage modes is not divided into social classes is also, in the view of Hindess and Hirst, an effect of the 'technicist' concept of mode of production. The role of the elders in the co-ordination of production, and in the circulation of women through exchanges with élite goods, is made to appear as a technical necessity arising from the labour process, and so as a non-exploitative appropriation of surplus labour. Two French critics of Terray, P. P. Rey and G. Dupré,[12] reached the opposite conclusion from Terray (that is, they held that there *is* exploitation and therefore class antagonism between juniors and elders) but according to Hindess and Hirst they reached this conclusion on the basis of an error comparable with Terray's: they begin with the analysis of elements in the mode of production in isolation from a consideration of its overall structure. Terray's response to his critics is quite different: it is conceded that the elders appropriate a portion of the surplus produced by the juniors, but this does not necessarily constitute exploitation. In fact most of the surplus appropriated returns to the juniors in the form of a wife, who is a means to the future emancipation of the junior. Moreover, the élite goods, possession of which is the basis of the elder's control over the circulation of women, are not in the main products of the labour of the juniors, as would be required for the relation between them to be one of exploitation. For Dupré and Rey, on the other hand, the elders are a social category who control the circulation of surplus product in such a way as to reproduce their own domination over direct producers, the juniors of the lineage.

Despite the neatness of their critique of all participants to this debate, Hindess and Hirst themselves fail to resolve it. For them, lineage-based societies can be analysed through the concept of the primitive communist mode of production, which has two variant forms, according to whether the collective appropriation of surplus product is through 'simple' or 'complex' redistribution – that is, through redistribution according to shifting and temporary relationships, as in hunting and gathering bands, or according to settled, and often quite extensive kinship and marriage relationships. Quite rightly, Hindess and Hirst argue that all modes of production must necessarily involve some form of extraction of a surplus from direct producers, over and above their immediate subsistence needs if social relations are to be reproduced day by day and generation by generation. So what distinguishes those modes in which appropriation of the surplus is exploitative and constitutive of class oppositions from those in which it is not?

According to their first definition,[13] the primitive communist mode is characterised by Hindess and Hirst as classless on account of the *communal* character of the appropriation of the surplus: surplus is not appropriated by a distinct group of non-labourers. But in the course of their discussion of Gouro society Hindess and Hirst concede that the elders 'perform little or no productive labour'.[14] If they are non-labourers, do they also appropriate the surplus labour of others? There is no clear answer to this in Hindess and Hirst. We are told only that the complex division of labour in Gouro society requires a distinct function of co-ordination and direction. Kinship relations 'allow for' this direction to be carried out by adults and elders in a double mechanism of co-ordination on the one hand, and extraction of the surplus, on the other. It follows that a necessary condition of economic reproduction is reproduction of the kinship system, and this, in turn, requires a social mechanism: 'the elders must also regulate marriage exchanges'.[15] Thus the position of the elders is such that 'they do not necessarily constitute a class'.[16] Of course, if lineage societies *do* correspond to the primitive communist mode, as Hindess and Hirst claim, then this won't do: the elders *cannot* constitute a class. It appears, then, that Hindess and Hirst must concur with Terray's conclusion that these are classless societies, while dissociating themselves from his 'technicist' method of demonstrating this. Notwithstanding this disclaimer, it can readily be seen that the argument given by Hindess and Hirst is equally technicist: the position of the elders follows, by way of some dubious logical steps, from the complex division of labour in Gouro society.

The confusion inherent in this debate seems to me to result from several unresolved questions concerning the concept of a mode of production and its applicability to 'primitive' societies. First, Althusser's and Balibar's original formulations of the general concept of mode of production were clearly designed to deal primarily with class societies, and included a reference to 'non-labourers' who were to be combined with the other elements in the mode of production through the 'property connection'. Secondly, this 'property connection' is sometimes interpreted by Balibar as simply a relation of extraction of a surplus. In this, he is followed by Hindess and Hirst, and, generally by Terray also. The attenuation of the concept of the 'property connection' (the relations of production, properly speaking) to the process of extraction of the surplus has the effect of relegating powers of disposal, and control over conditions of production and reproduction to the level of technical relations of necessity, and of reducing production relations to relations of *distribution* of the product: Hindess and Hirst's 'simple' and 'complex redistribution'.

Now, if the extraction of a surplus is performed by the elders, then this extraction implies a *power* to extract it. That power, like any other power, must derive from material or social resources: according to Meillasoux's ethnography, the control by the elders over the exchange of women, the 'instruments of reproduction' is decisive in this respect. In general, control over conditions of production and reproduction is the basis for the power of extraction of the surplus, and is thus also the basis both for the system of distribution and for the formation of economic classes. By failing to pose the question of the relations of production of lineage society as anything but *technical* necessities, Hindess, Hirst and Terray all manage to preserve intact their *assumption* that these relations are communal in the face of considerable evidence of important differences between categories of economic agents in their access to conditions of production and reproduction.

My purpose here is not, in fact, to challenge the conclusion that in the pre-colonial period Gouro society was classless. The point is rather to show that the contending Althusserian conceptualisations of Gouro society did not have the means of deciding either way. Partly this is a question of conceptual confusion, but, more importantly, in the case of Hindess and Hirst it arises from commitment to a particular way of constructing concepts. For them, the concept of a primitive mode of production gets its validity and status from the basic concepts and protocols of the discourse to which it belongs, 'historical materialism': 'It is a valid concept if it is a possible mode of production, if it is constructed according to the concepts of the Marxist theory of modes of production.'[17] For Hindess and Hirst, both validity and theoretical argument flow, so to speak, in one direction, from the higher to the lower levels of abstraction. All theory involves *some* level of abstraction. This view of concept construction and validation was, as we shall see, the subject of a later 'autocritique', but its effects in this text are plain: the concept of primitive communism initially advanced is quite empty of content. In the absence of any attempt to specify, in terms of available ethnographic material, precisely what is and what is not 'communal' appropriation, there are no theoretical decision procedures to settle such questions as the class character of lineage-based societies. In fact, of course, the necessity to engage with the work of Terray, Meillasoux and others forces Hindess and Hirst to contradict their own project and test the resources of their conception at the much lower level of abstraction involved in the interpretation of ethnographic evidence. The result is an *ad hoc* and descriptive selection of that material to suit their own theoretical assumptions. These, as Asad and Wolpe argue,[18] merely reproduce the work of Morgan and Engels.

Two further confusions in the debate need to be mentioned. First, the whole project of conceptualising 'primitive' societies in terms of of historical materialism requires that the economic level, or 'instance' can be distinguished in these societies, and that its 'determination in the last instance' is demonstrable. Terray approaches this problem through a use of the concepts of overdetermination and structural causality: kinship 'realises' the multiple determinations of each of the levels, which are themselves not empirically present. 'Determination in the last instance' is demonstrable through the modifications it imposes on the operation of the kinship system, but since the relations of production cannot be identified independently on the kinship system, this 'demonstration' has a dubious status. For Hindess and Hirst, kinship relations are ideological relations, so their direction of the extraction of surplus labour is an example of the intervention of ideology into the economic structure.

Balibar, as we saw, argued that all pre-capitalist modes involve coercion of a non-economic kind in the extraction of surplus labour, and therefore a quite different 'articulation' of the levels of their social formations. But it is one thing to argue that in some social formations, reproduction of the economic relations requires an intervention into the economic on the part of non-economic social practices, and quite another to argue (as Balibar *sometimes* seems to do) that in these formations, the relations of production are in fact *constituted* through this non-economic intervention. The effect of this argument is to concede the inapplicability of the distinction between economic and ideological in the pre-capitalist formations, and so to abandon the Althusserian project of a science of history. Without seeming to recognise its significance, this is in fact the route taken by Hindess and Hirst in the case of the 'primitive communist' mode: having identified the relations of production with the mechanism of redistribution, they go on to say that the relationships constituting this mechanism (kinship relations) are ideological, and 'not *economic* in the sense of being derived from the purchase of labour-power or of labourers'.[19] If, indeed, we are to use 'economic' in this sense, then its use must be restricted to those modes characterised by commodity production and the market. These and related problems were effectively analysed, and related to the still partially descriptive character of the Althusserian conception of the mode of production and its levels, by Ernesto Laclau in his 'The Specificity of the Political'.[20]

A second area of confusion in the anthropological debate relates more directly to questions of an ideological and political nature. As we have seen, the distinction between 'production' and 'reproduction' occurs repeatedly in the debate, but is nowhere treated in a rigorous way. Sometimes 'reproduction' refers to the process of overall social reproduction: the maintenance of kinship and other social relations through time, the replacing of means and conditions of production, the allocation of agents to tasks, the allocation of means of consumption, and the biological reproduction of human agents themselves. Elsewhere, however, and sometimes with the scanty theoretical justification that human energy is the main source of power used at this low level of development of the productive forces, 'reproduction' is treated as more or less identical with biological reproduction, so that, for example, control over the mechanism which regulates this (circulation of women) is refered to as 'control over reproduction' on the part of the elders. This tendency to functionally differentiate 'production' and 'reproduction' and to represent them as belonging to distinct institutional spheres is another instance of a failure to think through critically the 'received' tradition of Engels and Morgan. Moreover, it has the effect, through the implicit identification of women with 'reproduction' to marginalise recognition of the role of women in 'production' (and, of course, in 'reproduction' in the wider sense). This 'androcentrism' was brilliantly exposed by Maxine Molyneux, writing in the journal *Critique of Anthropology*.[21] Molyneux demonstrates that whereas the criteria employed by Terray in demonstrating that juniors are *not* an exploited class can be used directly to show that women *are*, neither Terray nor his critics even consider that there might be exploitative relationships in Gouro society between men and/or elders on the one hand, and women on the other. The point here is, in fact, not to argue that women are, after all, an exploited class, but that the social division of labour, and especially the sexual division of labour, together with the relations of domination and subordination they institute had yet to be adequately theorised in the literature.

Transition and articulation of modes of production

If the concept of mode of production is central to the Marxist theory of history, the concept of social transformation, of transition from one social form to another, is no less central. The Marxist thesis of the determination 'in the last instance' by economic practice implies the centrality of the concept of mode of production (or of its economic level, if 'mode of production' is to include specification of its ideological and juridico–political conditions of existence) in the theorisation of historical change, of 'transition'. We saw, in Chapter 4, some of the difficulties faced by Balibar in theorising 'transition' in terms of the Althusserian 'anti-historicist' and 'anti-empiricist' methodological requirements. In particular, 'transition' had to be thought of in terms which:

1. Avoided the 'teleology' and/or 'historicism' of much previous Marxist work on this problem, and which represented transition as a necessary effect of the working out of inner tendencies of the mode of production itself. The ultimate self-dissolution and supersession of a mode is already given in its moment of constitution as a mode. Avoidance of teleology in this sense is already built into Balibar's concept of mode of production.

2. Avoidance, at the opposite extreme, of a conception of transition as a chaotic 'hiatus' between periods, in which successive dominant modes coherently reproduce themselves and their conditions of existence. Since transition may be a more or less extended historical period, then it is clear that production and the reproduction of the conditions of production must continue to take place, though in transformed forms. However these forms are theorised, avoidance of historicism requires that the outcome of a period of transition is open: it may or may not result in the dominance of a new mode of production.

3. Although Balibar vacillates on this question, it is an implication of Althusser's epistemology that the *object* of a theory of transition, as of any other theory, is not the concrete reality of specific historical processes, but, rather, a constructed 'thought-object' which constitutes the 'appropriation in thought' of the real object. The difficulties of theorising transition with the theoretical means available to Balibar led to a tendency on his part to think of periods of transition as the sole instances of real, concrete history, the timelessness of the concept of a mode of production and its reproduction seeming to evacuate from the concept any power of interpretation of real history in non-transitional periods: the Althusserian *epistemological* opposition between the abstract and theoretical, and the concrete and real, was transposed onto an opposition between the periods of history.

In their *Pre-Capitalist Modes of Production*, Hindess and Hirst followed their attempts to construct, within the problematic of historical materialism, the concepts of the various pre-capitalist modes with a chapter on transition from Feudalism to Capitalism. In fact, however, the chapter and the debate to which it led is much more concerned with the general question of how historical transformations are to be dealt with in Marxist theory. In opposition to Balibar (though, in a way, reproducing his transposition of the abstract – concrete opposition) Hindess and Hirst maintain that there can be no general theory of transition, nor even any theory of transitions from one mode to another (for example, from Feudalism to Capitalism, or Capitalism to Socialism). Paradoxically, Hindess and Hirst continued to share with Balibar the three Althusserian methodological requirements listed above, so that in particular they were committed both to the denial that transition is to be thought of as an untheorisable chaotic hiatus *and* to the assertion that there can be no theory of transition.

Their argument against Balibar is this: Balibar's conception of transitional modes contradicts the 'anti-teleology' methodological requirement. For Balibar a transitional mode is characterised by non-correspondence between forces and relations of production, such that the reproduction of the relations transforms the forces. This transformation of the forces is written into the concept of the transitional mode as an inner tendency to self-dissolution and supersession and so indicates a teleology in the concept. Moreover, even allowing teleological explanation, the transitional mode could explain only the ending of a period of transition, and not its onset. So why did Balibar have to resort to teleology in explaining transition? The answer, according to Hindess and Hirst, is that Balibar's concept of a non-transitional mode satisfies the anti-teleology requirement at the price of conceiving of such modes as necessarily self-reproducing 'eternities'. The concept of structural causality common to Althusser and Balibar, and derived by them from Spinoza, is applied in such a way that 'the structure' has, as its effects, the provision of its own conditions of existence. Such a 'being' is subject to no external causality, but is the self-subsistent cause of its own continuation. This is a concept of mode of production with its associated form of causality, then, which not only rules out necessary self-transcendence, but also excludes even the *possibility* of transcendence. Balibar's concept of mode of production and the problem of transition are quite incompatible, hence the 'invention' of teleological 'transitional modes'. Balibar's position is finally reduced by Hindess and Hirst to its opposite, through a demonstration that the 'structural' causality of the mode of production, and the 'teleological causality' of the transitional mode are, after all, only variant forms of the very 'expressive' causality to which structural causality was supposed to be the antidote.

This last step in the argument is achieved by the device of a formal substitution of the words 'structure' for 'essence' in sentences taken from Balibar. This 'formalist' method of argument, as John Taylor[22] has called it, both obliterates the content of the problem to which the concept of structural causality was addressed and also obstructs any serious critical discussion of this concept's adequacy in relation to that problem. If we recall the context of the formation of the concept structural causality as a means of thinking the form of causality operative in complex, 'decentred' totalities, and if we also recall that Althusser treats such totalities as characterised by an overdetermination of *contradictions*, such that a 'fusion' of contradictions may (but need not necessarily) issue in a revolutionary conjuncture,[23] the link between structural causality and the 'eternity' of a structure is not so evident as Hindess and Hirst's argument implies. Undoubtedly there is a basis for their argument in the repeated references to Spinoza,[24] but precisely what is avoided by Hindess and Hirst is any serious encounter with the inner problems and contradictions of the texts they criticise. Instead, the texts are reduced by one-sided abstraction to a caricature of themselves, and the categories of an Althusserian epistemological critique of the first kind (see above pp.112–15) imposed upon them.

In fact, Balibar's approach to the problem of transition, as we have seen, cannot be reduced to the idea of a transitional mode. Alongside this idea are several other concepts and half-developed arguments. First, there is a discussion of Marx's famous 'tendencies' of the capitalist mode – the rising organic composition of capital, and the falling rate of profit. Balibar rightly argues that these 'tendencies' are not to be thought of as predictions in Marx as to empirical developments in the chronology of specific capitalist economies.[25] The tendencies and the counteracting influences to which they are subject are derivations from Marx's *concept* of the capitalist mode of production. All that can be theorised on this basis is the possible effects on, say, the accumulation of capital, of specific combinations of tendencies and counteracting influences, and what strategies might be open to capital to restore a given rate of accumulation. Such considerations refer to the *dynamics* of the capitalist mode, and are not, directly at least, historical concepts. Balibar also introduces discussion of what has been termed the '*genealogy*' of a mode: that is to say, the conception of those conditions (for example, separation of the labourer from the means of production, accumulation of money capital and the existence of a commodity market in the case of the capitalist mode) which must necessarily be present if that mode is to emerge. Balibar clearly poses this question non-teleologically: the conditions of possibility of a mode can be derived from its concept, but *whether* those conditions are satisfied, and the form of the historical processes *whereby* in fact they *are* satisfied, are not so derivable. This concept of genealogy is important, then, in breaking away from the conception of history as a linear succession between modes: the question may be posed of an emergence of the capitalist mode, for example, not just from the feudal mode as 'predecessor', but from some other non-capitalist mode or combination.

A third important concept in Balibar, a specific application of Althusser's idea of the complexity of the social formation, is that of the articulation of two or more modes of production in a single social formation. If such articulation is indeed possible, then transition may be thought of as a shift in the relations of dominance and subordination between the articulated modes. This way of conceptualising historical transition, if it can be sustained, has several advantages. First, it allows for the possibility that transitions may be open to theoretical analysis without any necessary commitment to a general theory of 'transitions'; that is, depending on the modes which are articulated, their dynamics, and the form of articulation, a variety of actual historical cases and possible outcomes may be theoretically comprehended. Secondly, the concept of an articulation of modes allows for the possibility that economic and social reproduction may be continued throughout more or less extended historical periods of transition. The only alternatives to such a conception are: 1. transition as 'chaotic hiatus' or 2. transition as a momentary, spasmodic dissolution and re-structuring of the social totality. All parties to the debate are committed to avoiding the first, but Hindess and Hirst are, in fact, committed to the second by two features of their theoretical position. The first is their insistence that the protocols of Marxist theory allow validity to a concept of a mode of production only if the 'articulation' between its forces and relations of production is such that the former can be *deduced from* the latter.[26] Taken strictly, this must entail the denial that the relations of production in every mode are compatible with more than one form of the labour process, and therefore exclude the possibility of variant forms, of dynamics of modes, and also the notion of relations as 'forms of development' of the forces. The concept of mode is reduced to an entirely static inventory of the elements and their combination. In practice, of course, Hindess and Hirst relax this requirement, but in an *ad hoc* way that reduces the original protocol to the more or less empty requirement that relations set *some* limit to the range of possible labour processes.

The second element in Hindess and Hirst's position which necessitates a conception of transition as a momentary and total rupture, not as a more or less extended historical period, is their arbitrary pronouncement that the conditions of reproduction of one mode must exclude the reproduction of any other: that is, that the articulation of modes within a single formation is impossible. The transition from a social formation characterised by one mode to one characterised by another must entail the *simultaneous* disappearance of the elements of the first (since they are united by a *necessary* correspondence) and their conditions of existence, and *instantaneous* replacement by the next and its conditions of existence (since any intervening period would be governed by no structure at all, and would therefore be a 'chaotic hiatus').

On the other hand, the concept of articulation of modes is not without its own problems. First, to be applicable, the concept requires some conception of the 'dynamics' of the articulated modes not simply as theoretical possibilities, but as realised tendencies which provide conditions of possibility for the different articulations (for example, an explanation of imperialism as an 'articulation' between capitalist and non-capitalist modes requires that the conditions of this articulation are present in real tendencies of each mode: problems of accumulation arising from the falling rate of profit being offset by exports of capital to non-capitalist formations where, however, such conditions as free labour and a commodity market have already emerged from, or have been imposed upon, the non-capitalist mode). This problem can only be solved if epistemological problems related to the Althusserian critique of empiricism can be resolved.

Secondly, the concept of articulation of modes renders problematic the concept of 'reproduction'. Generally, the Althusserian debate theorised reproduction as reproduction of the elements and relations of a single mode of production. What the concept of articulation requires is that the practices whereby one mode is reproduced also have as an effect the provision of conditions of existence of another mode (the emergence of free labour and accumulations of money capital as an effect of the reproduction of feudal relations at a certain point would be an example).

Beyond the provision of those conditions constituting the genealogy of a new mode, the reproductive practices of the old mode may continue to have the effect of reproducing the relations of the new mode, whilst that mode may become self-reproducing to the extent that its expanded reproduction tends to dissolve the relations of the older mode (this is, of course, no more than a schematic possibility, and in no sense the beginning of a theory of transition). The central theoretical point is this: there is absolutely no theoretical necessity that the practices which reproduce one mode may not also have effects which contribute to the reproduction of another. Co-existing modes may contribute to one another's preservation or dissolution, depending on the specific features of the articulation and its dynamics.

A third set of problems with the idea of articulation of modes of production also has to do with the concept of reproduction. Social reproduction can, as we have seen, easily be confused with reproduction of human individuals, and allocated to a set of institutions distinct from production, but serving a complementary function (the family, kinship relations). Althusser's 'Ideology and Ideological State Apparatuses' at least avoids *this* problem. Reproduction is not artifically abstracted from production, and it is recognised that in some respects the conditions of production are secured in the production process itself (for example, reproduction of means of production is allocated to a distinct 'department' of the economy), but the reproduction of labour power and of the relations of production is secured by the state apparatuses, some of which operate mainly through coercion, others through ideological 'interpellations'. So, social reproduction is *not* reduced to biological reproduction, though the absence of any adequate theorisation of oppositional ideologies, or of class struggles in the state apparatuses continues to pull Althusser's theory towards a form of functionalism. Specific functional requirements are deduced from the concept of the mode of production and institutional complexes in the state are identified with the fulfilment of those functional requirements. Only a conception of reproduction as the site of political and cultural struggles which are both rooted in the relations of production and reproduction and have determinate effects on them (that is, affecting the scale upon which reproduction is secured, and the specific institutional forms in which it is secured), only such a conception can avoid the collapse of the theory into a form of functionalism.

The bearing of this on the concept of articulation of modes is that the various ways in which securing the reproduction of one mode has effects on the conditions of existence and reproduction of the other(s) have to be thought of as provisional outcomes of complex political and cultural struggles rooted, not in isolated modes, but in their complex combination. Where we think primarily of class struggle, for example, then the class structure of a society in transition will be more complex than one dominated by a single mode of production. Shifts in relations of dominance between modes may then be thought of as mediated effects of particular patterns of class alliance and associated political strategies. But if even Althusser's later work on the state and ideology fails to adequately theorise class struggles over social reproduction, then it does not even *begin* to pose questions about the conditions of possibility of other social oppositions and forms of political struggle (such as those related to gender and race) which 'overdetermine' the forms of class struggle. The concept of social reproduction is the site of these difficulties, too.

The concepts of the dynamics and genealogy of modes of production, and most especially the concept of articulation have had immense consequences for fields of analysis as diverse as the characterisation of the Soviet Union and the Eastern European societies (transitional between Capitalism and Socialism),[27] the analysis of successive forms of capitalist penetration of the non-capitalist countries (unequal trade, colonialism and imperialism as dynamically related but distinct forms of capitalist and non-capitalist articulation) and the associated critiques of the sociologies of development and underdevelopment,[28] the formation of political strategy in the West (transition to socialism) and the analysis of the sexual division of labour.

Althusserian Marxism and feminism

I have no space to consider the advances and problems involved in the various Althusserian and post-Althusserian developments in all these fields but there is one area in which the concept of reproduction again becomes the site of problems, and which is of decisive political importance. This is the use of structural Marxist categories to analyse the sexual division of labour and the forms of oppression of women. In terms both of theoretical analysis and political practice, Marxism has earned a justified hostility from a large part of the feminist movement. This hostility derives in part from the combination of Marxism's status as both the pre-eminent political force on the Left and the principal intellectual resource for movements of social and political emancipation: it leads to high expectations. In view of this, the relative paucity of its political and theoretical achievements in relation to the emancipation of women is inescapable. And, so far as the classics of Marxist theory are concerned, this is not simply (though it is also this) a matter of the underdevelopment of Marxist theory in this domain; it is rather that the categories of the dominant traditions of Marxist theory have actually obstructed the formation of a theoretical analysis adequate to the requirements of feminists.

Three aspects are crucial here. First, the centrality in classical Marxism of class exploitation and class struggle. The subjects of class exploitation are genderless. The forms of domination and subordination which work through gender differences are untheorisable in these terms, and are both theoretically and politically marginalised. Second, and, of course, closely related, is the economic reductionism of a good deal of Marxism. This not only sustains the centrality of class, but also necessitates the relegation of such questions as sexuality, the constitution of gender identity, and the sexual division of labour to the domain of ideology and therefore to an inherently secondary significance in relation to the central dynamics of the society.

In some respects Althusser's reconstruction of Marxist categories involved a break with elements in Marxist theory which had previously obstructed its development in a feminist direction. Out of this situation emerged a number of important theoretical developments in feminist theory which were able to make use of structural Marxism. This is not to say, of course, that such uses of Althusser were unproblematic. Neither Althusser nor Balibar, nor indeed, the participants to the debates we have so far discussed, themselves confronted the key questions concerning the analysis of women's oppression. For example, as we shall see,[29] Althusser's political interventions include a reference to the women's movement as one element (along with the radicalism of youth, the ecology movement and so on) in a radically new strategic situation to be taken account of by the PCF, only elsewhere to be discounted as a 'peripheral' question.

Three aspects of the Althusserian framework seem to me to have been of significance for the subsequent development of feminist uses of Marxism. First, the attempt to rigorously define the Marxist concept of mode of production in relation to the reproduction of its conditions of existence, and the identification of the distinction between labour and labour power as central to Marx's critique of classical political economy. Recognition that labour power was produced and reproduced under relations (in the family) quite different from those between capital and labour under which the other factors of production (means of production, raw materials) were produced and reproduced, immediately called into question the failure of the Marxist tradition to theorise the production and reproduction of labour power as an economic phenomenon. This was particularly important in displacing the previous tendency to relegate the family to the sphere of consumption, in so far as it was assigned any economic role at all.

The ensuing debate centred on the proper economic designation of the 'domestic labour' performed in the family and which resulted in the production and reproduction of labour power, day to day and generation by generation. The very existence of domestic labour implies that the labour time necessary for the production and reproduction of labour power cannot simply be equated with the labour time embodied in the 'bundle of commodities' purchased with the wage. The equivalence assumed by Marx, then, between the value of labour power and the value of this 'bundle of commodities' is immediately rendered problematic, and some of the most basic concepts in Marx's economic theory, surplus value, and exploitation, for example, are rendered problematic along with it. This cannot be resolved by the simple device of adding together the value of subsistence goods (measured in terms of the labour time socially necessary to their production) with the domestic labour time necessary for their utilisation in the reproduction of labour power (that is, labour time expended on such tasks as shopping, cooking, cleaning, child-bearing and child-rearing, and so on), since the market relationships through which the labour time of wage-workers is standardised do not enter the sphere of the family.

Despite the apparently subversive implications of some of these considerations for the categories of Marxist economics, a number of attempts were nevertheless made to adjust definitions, or add distinctions so as to provide a theory of the economic relations between domestic labour and capital. Several options were attempted: one possibility is to treat domestic labour as commodity-producing labour (the commodity produced is labour power). On this basis the family as an economic unit can be interpreted as characterised by internal 'exploitation' in which husbands appropriate the surplus labour of their wives through forms of non-economic coercion: the marriage contract and patriarchal or other ideological forms.[30] One difficulty (amongst others) faced by this approach is that it seems to have the implication that children, too, exploit the labour of their mothers. A second variant of this approach is to see domestic labour and the economic relations of the family as a form of petty commodity production,[31] within which 'exploitation' in the Marxist sense does not occur, though surplus labour may be appropriated indirectly from the domestic labourer by the capitalist through the purchase of labour power at below its value.

An alternative way of conceptualising domestic labour is to deny that it is commodity-producing labour. Instead it may be argued that domestic labour transforms commodities into a consumable form and in so doing produces utilities, 'use values', but is not productive of 'exchange value' in the Marxist sense.[32] The Marxist theory value is not applicable, on this view, to domestic labour, which is therefore not commensurable with labour performed under capitalist production relations. This approach may leave intact the theory of exploitation of wage-work in Marxist economics, but renders problematic the economic relationship between capitalism and the family. Although it is clear that the economic reproduction of any capitalist society rests on a division of the total available labour time between wage labour conducted under capitalist relations and domestic labour conducted under familial relations, the thesis of the incommensurability of the two labour times renders the mechanisms through which this allocation occurs unanalysable except in purely qualitative terms. An element of arbitrariness is also involved in the posing of such questions as whether domestic labour is subject to exploitation, and, if so, whether principally by the presumably male head of household or principally by an indirect appropriation by capital.

Some of these ways of theorising domestic labour and the family as an economic unit have also made use of the idea of an articulation of modes of production. The family may itself be seen as a distinct mode – the domestic mode – which at the same time contributes to the reproduction of the capitalist mode with which it is articulated,[33] and there is sometimes also an explicit analogy between the contribution made by the family to the reproduction of capital in the advanced capitalist societies, and the contribution made by a rural non-capitalist sector to the reproduction of industrial capital in third-world formations, and in some racially divided societies such as South Africa.[34]

Subsequent criticism[35] has exposed a number of deficiencies in the terms of this debate as a whole, however, and, most of these technical problems remain unresolved. Two principal failings were identified. First, as an attempt to analyse the economic foundation of women's oppression it fails, since identification of the opposition of domestic labour and wage labour as the site of the problem simply *assumed* what it was supposed to be explaining (that is, the sexual division of labour). At the very least, this economic debate needed to be supplemented by a theory of the differential allocation of gendered subjects to these different economic tasks. But even the assumptions made about the sexual division of labour could be seen to be defective: in the advanced capitalist countries a very large proportion of the wage-labour force is composed of female labour. It can be argued that the social division of labour between men and women in wage work can only be understood in terms of the division of labour within the household, and *vice-versa*, so that *both* aspects of the sexual division of labour are in fact obscured by the assumed association of men with wage work and women with domestic labour.

But if the general problem here is that the debate employs economic categories which are, like the concepts of traditional Marxist analyses, 'gender blind', then this economic analysis can explain nothing about the sexual division of labour unless it is supplemented by a theory of the social mechanisms whereby individuals are constituted as 'gendered subjects' and socially allocated to positions in society on this basis. This is, in fact, the basis of the second major criticism of the domestic labour debate: in its failure to adequately conceptualise ideological and psychological aspects of women's oppression it simply continues the errors of 'economistic' Marxism. Here again, though, structural Marxism might be seen to have something to offer: it, too, is a rebuttal of economistic Marxism. In so far as Althusser presents a conception of the social formation in which the ideological 'level is a relatively autonomous domain, then it seems that the possibility arises for a theory of gender constitution and the specific forms of gender-related subordination as more or less autonomous processes *vis-à-vis* the economically rooted constitution of individuals as class subjects.

Two broad lines of analysis are possible at this point. The first deals with Althusserian attempts to classify the family among those apparatuses of the state which function to reproduce the relations of production, and which do so principally through ideological 'interpellations'. The point here is that the reproduction of the labour force (in the case of working-class families) is not simply a question of the reproduction of labourers as physical beings capable of work, but also involves the inculcation of a form of subjectivity in which the disposition to accept the disciplines and types of subordination required by a life of labour in capitalist enterprises is ingrained. It is argued that the family, the school, and the other ideological apparatuses incorporate individuals into social practices which have this effect. For this general line of argument to help with the analysis of gender divisions it has to be rendered more sophisticated with the recognition that what is reproduced in the family, school, and so on, is not just a labour force, but a gender-divided labour force, and, beyond this that the social divisions established in the family, school and other apparatuses themselves have to be reproduced, and in ways which are gender related. In this perspective, valuable work has been done in analysing both the form and content of school curricula, and forms of organisation and discipline, and also on the ways in which family relationships constitute gender identities.[36]

There are two dangers in this 'reproduction' approach, however. One is that the functionalist tendency of Althusser's original essay can easily re-emerge in the absence of any theory of the constitution of subjects which allows for the possibility of *oppositional* subjects. As we saw, this is a difficulty for Althusser's theory of ideology even for class subjects. There is not even a beginning in that theory of an explanation of the constitution of oppositional *gendered* subjectivity. The second danger is that the assumption of a 'relative autonomy' of the ideological level can lead to an analysis of the ideological effects of familial relations and practices in abstraction from their economic effects (especially as these have so far not been adequately theorised).

The second line of argument from Althusser's theory of ideology operates not at the level of overall functional relationships between institutions and practices, but at the level of individual psychology. The locus in Althusser for this development is the concept of 'interpellation' or 'hailing' of individuals as subjects. In order to conceptualise this process as the defining feature of ideology, Althusser drew on the work of Lacan, and especially his conception of the 'mirror-phase'. As we saw, for Althusser, the acquisition of subjectivity and subjection to authority are simultaneously achieved through ideological interpellation. Through this concept, Althusser brought into alignment (albeit in a highly problematic way) psychoanalytic theory (in its Lacanian version) and Marxism. This development within Marxism coincided with attempts on the part of some feminists, most notably Juliet Mitchell,[37] to overcome the general feminist hostility to Freud's work. The aim was to utilise his theories of sexuality and the unconscious as a way of thinking through the social constitution of gendered subjectivity that would be helpful for feminism. According to Mitchell, Freud's patriarchal attitudes have to be distinguished from the scientifically valuable analysis of the mechanisms whereby patriarchy is established and reproduced. Freud's use of the Oedipus myth to theorise the entry of humankind into civilisation, and the repetition of this entry into civilisation by every individual subject through the 'Oedipal phase' is linked by Mitchell with the Althusserian theory of ideology to produce the result that patriarchy is the universal form (ideology in Althusser, and the unconscious in Freud are trans-historical realities) under which the subjection of subjects in ideology is accomplished.

These theoretical realignments have been enormously influential, and do seem to offer a way of situating the constitution of gender difference at the level of the individual psyche within a general theory of the social practices which operate upon, transform and consolidate gender identities. Here, too, though, there are unresolved problems and associated dangers.[38] First, the original assumption of the scientific status of psychoanalysis is questionable, as is its availability, unmodified, for feminist use. Second, the question of the generality of the Freudian theory of sexuality emerges here with special force. If patriarchy really is the universal form of the ideological subjection of subjects, and ideology is, as Althusser argues, an omni-historical reality, then can struggles against patriarchy ever be successful? Third, the identification of ideological subjection with patriarchy, and of patriarchy with the rule of the father in the family implies a segregation of emancipat ory struggles: a feminist struggle against ideological subjection in the family, and an economic struggle for socialism. This seems to neglect the prevalence of patriarchal forms of authority in wage-work, and also the existence of non-patriarchal forms of ideological subjection, and so fails to see important relationships between these struggles.

Finally, and relatedly, this approach shares with the 'reproduction' approach the danger that the 'relative autonomy' of the ideological domain comes to be taken to be *de facto* absolute autonomy, through an abandonment of the project of theorising the economic, political or other conditions of existence of specific types of 'interpellation' of gendered subjects. More recent work in this area tends to follow this course, and, in effect, detaches the psychoanalytic theory of gender constitution from the articulation with Marxist theory which was established in Juliet Mitchell's work. This detachment finds an epistemological justification in the later work of Hindess and Hirst which establishes a decisive break not only with Althusser but with the Marxist tradition itself. I shall return to this work and its implications in Chapter 8.

7

Class, State and Politics

In this chapter I shall be discussing some of the new directions in political theory and analysis which have been made possible by Althusser's work. Obviously the scope here is potentially enormous, so again I shall be very selective. The main criterion of selection I shall use will be the bearing of Althusserian political theory on the prospects for socialist strategy in the advanced capitalist countries, and especially in Europe. Especially useful in this respect is the debate surrounding and following the decision to abandon the concept of 'dictatorship of the proletariat', which was taken by the Twenty-second Congress of the French Communist Party in 1976. A number of the leading participants in this debate, including Nicos Poulantzas and Etienne Balibar (not to mention Althusser himself) employed broadly Althusserian ideas in an attempt to think through a viable socialist strategy for France. Though there are very significant differences between them, what they have in common is, on the one hand, a recognition of the necessity to obliterate the remains of Stalinism in PCF organisational practices and strategic precepts, but, on the other, an opposition to any headlong rush into what they see as reformism, or right-wing opportunism.

Before looking in more detail at this debate, however, it will be necessary to present, very briefly, some of the new work in political analysis which was stimulated by Althusser's re-structuring of Marxist theory. Absolutely decisive in this respect was Althusser's opposition to 'economism'. Politics cannot be 'reduced' to economics, and, especially, political conflict is not reducible to the class struggle between capital and labour. This is established by means of two related theoretical devices. First, the idea of the 'relative autonomy' of ideology and of the juridico–political superstructure within the overall 'determination in the last instance' by the economic level. Political and ideological structures play a more or less independent part in defining the form and dynamic of political conflict, which is therefore not in any straightforward sense an 'expression' of conflicts and interests established at the level of economic practices. Secondly, the complex and overdetermined character of a social formation is a result, not simply of this 'relative autonomy' of the non-economic levels, but also of the combination, or 'articulation' of a multiplicity of forms and modes of production within a single formation. This is important in that even in an 'advanced' capitalist society the presence of subordinate modes and forms, the remnants of previously dominant modes, and so on adds a complexity to the class structure not recognised in alternative versions of Marxism. Capitalists and workers are joined by small businessmen, petty commodity producers, perhaps the remnants of an old feudal class, and, significantly, social and political groupings formed out of or in the interstices of the articulation itself. This complexity in the pattern of political alliances and oppositions in capitalist societies is, of course, recognised at the level of 'concrete' political and historical analysis by Marx himself (the *Eighteenth Brumaire*[1] is a magnificent example of this) and, as Althusser shows in the essay 'Contradiction and Overdetermination',[2] by Lenin and Mao. What is substantially new is Althusser's attempt to develop concepts of Marxist theory in such a way as to show the 'mediating links' between these 'concrete analyses' and basic concepts of historical materialism.

A second area of Althusser's work also suggests new lines of investigation for Marxist political analysis. This is the later work on ideology and the state apparatuses. As we have seen, Althusser's analysis of the role of these non-economic 'instances' gives a central place to the concept of reproduction, and especially the reproduction of the labour force. There is an inherent instability in this perspective in that, on the one hand, analysis of the state and ideology in terms of their functioning *vis-à-vis* the reproductive requirements of the economy, runs the risk of a collapse not just into structural functionalism, but into an economic reductionist version of this perspective. On the other hand, emphasis on the 'relative autonomy' of state and ideology, and the 'real existence' of ideology as 'materialised' in the relations and practices of the ISAs cannot be taken seriously if, in the end, these relations come down simply to the non-economic correlates of economic requirements. Althusser himself re-introduces the idea of effective class struggle, both within and upon the superstructures, as a means of avoiding collapse into economic reductionism but, as we have seen, this conception of class struggle is not integrated into the reproduction perspective. It seems, for example, to be inconsistent with Althusser's use of the concept of interpellation and his associated identification of ideology in general with ruling ideology.

What Althusser offers for political theory and analysis, then, is a series of provocative and often illuminating ways of looking at some old questions whilst avoiding old and threadbare solutions. But the new perspectives are by no means offered without problems and contradictions of their own. The problems are compounded when it is recalled that Althusser's programme in the field of political analysis is to recover and continue the work of Lenin. Althusser's retention of Lenin's conception of the state as a 'machine of class domination' has important effects on his strategic thinking, which nevertheless does, in a contradictory way, go beyond the limits imposed by Lenin's idea. And, perhaps still more significantly, the basic outlines of Lenin's solution to the problem of the relation between Marxist theory and mass political action are left untouched. With no conception of the basis in capitalist societies for the formation of oppositional ideologies and forms of subjectivity, nor yet of real cognitive content in ideology, Althusser continues to think of the indispensable role of science for the socialist movement in terms of a specialist intellectual practice which is relayed to the mass movement through the apparatus of a 'vanguard' party.

Class and state

Class structure and class struggle

Let us briefly consider, then, some of the more significant developments of structural Marxist political theory and analysis. Above all this must be a consideration of the work of Nicos Poulantzas, both in the field of state-theory and in the class analysis of contemporary capitalist formations. For purposes of exposition, it is better to begin with Poulantzas's approach to class analysis.[3] Opposition to both economic reductionism and voluntarism is evident in this field, as elsewhere in Althusserianism. It is achieved by an analytical distinction between what is called 'the structural determination' of classes, and 'class position in the conjuncture'. The time-honoured distinction (which is both voluntaristic and economistic) between 'class in itself' and 'class for itself' is rejected in favour of a conception of class as *conceptually inseparable* from class struggle. In so far as classes exist at all, they relate through struggle at the various economic, ideological and political levels. Classes are not groupings of agents established on the basis of relationship to the means of economic production alone, but are effects on the 'field of social practices' of ideological, political and economic structural determinants. In accordance with the complexity of their structural determinants we find that social classes are not homogeneous 'collective subjects'. Fissures, oppositions and contradictions of various kinds exist, not just at the boundaries of classes but also within them. Poulantzas is able, on the basis of the idea of ideological, political and economic 'structural determinants' of classes, to present an elementary typology of such inter- and intra-class divisions. Where a class suffers divisions arising from economic differentiations (for example, between financial, industrial and commercial capital) Poulantzas proposes to speak of 'class fractions', whereas divisions arising from ideological or political structural determinants (for example, the mental/manual division, or the division between supervisory and direct labour, and so on) are refered to as constituting strata (for example, the labour aristocracy, as a stratum within the working class). Finally, there may be 'social categories' (a state bureaucracy would be an example of this) in which agents drawn from quite different social classes are bound together in a unity of *function*.

It is important, I think, to recognise the immense advantages that these conceptual differentiations give for Marxist class analysis, by comparison with the main alternatives. In particular, they enable a theoretically informed (as distinct from merely 'empirical') recognition of the multiplicity of the forces operative in political conflict, which assimilates these forces to a form of class analysis without dissolving away the specificity of any of them into the homogeneous 'real' or 'objective' interests of the basic classes. It means that, for example, divisions within the working class, often dissolved away in Marxist analysis in terms of economic bribery practised by the ruling class or in terms of a 'false consciousness' induced by the ruling ideology, now have to be understood as deriving from real structural determinants which cannot be abolished by mere propaganda, nor by coercive means.

Another consequence for Poulantzas' approach is that for him, as for Althusser, class struggle is not reducible to the conflicts between capital and labour. The co-presence of other modes and forms of production implies a complex pattern of opposed classes and class fractions, such that, first, the economically dominant class does not establish its political rule independently, but through alliances with other dominant classes and fractions, and, second, that the subordinate classes must also form alliances to wage effective struggle against the 'power bloc'. It is here that Poulantzas has to move closer to an analysis of the specific class configuration of contemporary Europe, and France in particular. One effect of Poulantzas' way of combining ideological and political with economic criteria in defining classes is that the working class is then defined as a rather narrow segment of the population, and not as wage earners in general, as many of them are 'unproductive', or are supervisory or 'intellectual' workers and so should be differentiated from the working class, strictly defined. This generates for Poulantzas in an acute form a problem which has long haunted Marxist class analysis: that is, the 'status' of that increasingly large proportion of the population in the advanced capitalist countries which appear to stand intermediately between the capitalist class and the proletariat as traditionally defined.

What Poulantzas takes to be distinctive of Marxism is the thesis that all social strata must be strata *of* some class or other: there are no strata standing above and outside classes. Whilst it is true that some of the problematic intermediate 'strata' may be analysed away as classes or class fractions associated with non-capitalist modes of production, there remains an uncomfortably large residue with clear affiliations to the capitalist mode. One obvious option, to allocate these heterogeneous strata to a new class, coming to prominence with the current phase of capitalist development, is also rejected by Poulantzas on the grounds of its incompatibility with the historical materialist problematic. A mode of production can found two classes only, established on the basis of opposed positions in the relations of production. To suppose the formation of a new class without a change in the mode of production would be to abandon this basic postulate. Poulantzas' alternative, though, is arguably still more 'unorthodox' than this. It is to represent the 'intermediate strata' as a class fraction (the 'new petty bourgeoisie'), linked with the traditional petty bourgeoisie (petty commodity producers, shopkeepers and the like) on the basis of the common ideological and political *effects* of their radically different economic situations.[4]

It seems likely that Poulantzas' attempt to conceptualise the 'intermediate strata' as a fraction of the petty bourgeoisie was dictated more by political than theoretical reasons. The object is, on the one hand, to avoid the political implications associated with theorists who claimed to find in supervisory and intellectual workers a 'new working class',[5] and, on the other, to insist on the independent interests of the 'intermediate strata' *vis-à-vis* the traditional working class. The purpose of this latter insistence has to do with Poulantzas' opposition to the PCF's policy on class alliances. If workers' organisations, the argument goes, think of the 'intermediate strata' as having no independent class interests, then when contradictions emerge within the popular alliance the way is open to coercive solutions on the grounds that all participants have a common 'real' interest.[8] This argument seems to me not only methodologically suspect, but also unsatisfactory in its own terms. It suggests a retreat on Poulantzas' part to an economistic conception of 'interests' such that only classes have them, and not other social forces. Conversely, in the example given by Poulantzas of the Stalinist suppression of the peasantry in the USSR, a coercive solution to 'contradictions among the people' was adopted precisely when the alliance *was* conceived as an alliance between distinct classes.

Beyond this, though the manifest difficulties in a conception of a social class, the petty bourgeoisie, with two fractions, each rooted in a different mode of production, soon led to some sharp criticism of Poulantzas' position. Perhaps the foremost of Poulantzas' critics was the American political analyst, Erik Olin Wright.[7] In addition to showing just how small a proportion of the US labour force (less than 20 per cent) fall within the working class, using Poulantzas' restrictive definition, Wright also argues very effectively that Poulantzas' allocations of groups to classes on the basis of ideological and political criteria is arbitrary and contradictory. Less successful, in my view, is Wright's argument that groups excluded by Poulantzas from the working class have common interests. This suggests that 'interests' can somehow be 'read-off' from objective social positions, independently of the culture and politics of the individual or groups concerned. I have criticised this idea elsewhere.[8]

Wright's own view is that not all positions in the social division of labour can be unequivocally allocated to one class or another. There

are, in short, what Wright calls 'contradictory class locations'. The
increasing size and changing social character of the 'intermediate
strata' is explained by Wright in terms of extended processes of
historical change in capitalist social relations. These include a
tendency for increasing loss of control by direct producers over the
labour process and the processes of concentration and centralisation of capital. The effects of these changes include a differentiation
of the functions of entrepreneurial capitalists and the establishment
of complex hierarchies of management and supervision of the
labour process and of the labour force, and of direction and control
of the allocation of resources and investment. It is the growth of
these differentiated hierarchies which accounts for the flourishing
of the 'intermediate strata' and the various positions defined by
them are contradictory class locations intermediate between
capitalist and working class. The analysis is saved from economic
reductionism in that ideological and political criteria are introduced
in defining class position according to the degree of contradictoriness of the position (for example, an exactly intermediate position
between 'pure' working class and 'pure' capitalist would be the most
contradictory, and therefore one in which ideological and political
relations played the largest part in determining class position).
Despite Wright's criticisms of Pourantzas, he shares a good deal
with the latter's theoretical perspective, and has made an important
and interesting contribution to the empirical interpretation of Althusserian concepts. He remains one of the few American scholars
to have drawn extensively from this area of European theoretical
debate.

Class struggle, state and urban conflict

We are now in a position to turn briefly to Poulantzas' contribution
to Marxist state-theory.[9] Here, Poulantzas' work follows the classics
of the Marxist tradition in defining the state in terms of classes and
class domination. For Poulantzas, in any class society the function
falls to the state of intervening at all levels of the social formation to
secure cohesion, and, by so doing, to maintain the conditions of
existence of the dominant mode of production and its associated
system of class domination. The theory of the specific nature of the
state in capitalist society is derived from the structural 'matrix' of
capitalism in a characteristically Althusserian way. Capitalism is

distinguished from other modes in that the extraction of an economic surplus occurs through exchange relations conducted at the economic level without necessity for extra-economic intervention, except to secure the external conditions for these economic processes. This is the structural condition determining the specific autonomy of the capitalist juridico–political system. In the field of class relations and practices, this means that the policies and interventions of the state are not reducible to the pursuit of the economic interests of the dominant class or class fractions but that, on the contrary, the function of the state as a global unifier of the social formation requires a degree of sacrifice of that economic interest for the sake of consolidating an alliance of dominant classes and fractions, the 'power bloc', at the political level. It is important to recognise that the 'hegemonic' class or fraction within this power bloc may not be the economically dominant class or class fraction. As well as acting as unifier of the power bloc, the state, especially in its legal and ideological aspects, serves to dissolve the unity of the dominated classes and to isolate individuals as 'juridical' subjects rather than as members of social classes.

I have insufficient space to give adequate attention to Poulantzas' important work on the 'exceptional' forms of the capitalist state (fascism and military dictatorships)[10] or to the important shifts which took place in his theoretical writings up to his early and tragic death. Readers who wish to follow up on Poulantzas' work are advised to read the excellent work by Bob Jessop in this series. However, several further developments need to be indicated if we are to understand the significance of Poulantzas' work for strategic debates. First, a problem which affects the early work of Poulantzas both on class and on the state, is his distinction between 'structural determinants' and 'social relations' or 'class practices'. Though sometimes presented as if it were an analytical distinction, it sometimes takes on an ontological dimension (for example, the 'social classes' article shifts between specifying ideological, political and economic 'structural determinants' of class and 'criteria' of class membership, as if these were equivalent) and so opens up Poulantzas' position to the criticism that it is a 'structural super-determinism',[11] leaving no room for structural change as a result of class struggle. Poulantzas' later work[12] gives primacy to class struggle in bringing about historical change, and tends to represent institutional structures of the state as 'crystallisations' or 'condensates' of a prevailing balance of class forces.

Secondly, it is important for an understanding of Poulantzas' contribution to strategic debates that, for him, the relative autonomy of the state, both as a feature of the structural matrix of capitalism and in relation to the field of class struggle (that is, the relative autonomy of state policy from the economic interests of the dominant class or class fraction) makes possible a distinctive kind of political domination in capitalist societies. This is conceptualised, following Gramsci, as hegemonic leadership, in which prominence is given to the organisation of an ideological and political unity among the classes and fractions of the power bloc, and to the securing of 'active consent' on the part of the dominated classes. Interpellation of the dominant ideology, especially through the operation of the ideological state apparatuses, coupled with the constitutional exercise of coercion (that is, the 'rule of law') and representative democracy are distinctive capitalist political forms. Significantly, this form of political domination achieves unity through an unstable balance of compromises, both among the fractions of the power bloc, and between it and the dominated classes. An essential condition of hegemonic domination over the dominated classes is that they, in turn, have ideological apparatuses, for example, trade unions and social democratic parties which pursue their interests and thereby achieve concessions. These concessions, however, are always of an 'economic–corporate' kind (that is, can be accommodated without a challenge to the prevailing system of class domination) and do not appear to modify Poulantzas' commitment to the proposition that state power always corresponds to the interests of the power bloc. In so far as the working class has a 'fundamental interest' in socialist transition and securing its own hegemonic domination, the capitalist state does not provide a viable means for this.

Poulantzas' later works give a more central place to a periodisation of capitalist development, and to associated changes in the structure and forms of intervention of the state. The shift from competitive capitalism, for which the liberal, non-interventionist state is the 'normal' form, to the monopoly–imperialist phase is accompanied by a decisive shift in the nature and function of the state.[13] Monopoly dominance requires an 'interventionist' state which is increasingly and directly involved in the production circuits of capital and in the reproduction of labour power (health care, education, housing, and so on). This shift from a state which is involved, principally, in securing the general social conditions for economic activity, to one which is directly involved in the creation and realisation of surplus value, is seen by Poulantzas as marking a shift in the structural matrix of capitalism from one in which the economic instance is both determinant and dominant, to one in which dominance shifts to the political instance.

Associated with these shifts in the relation between the functions of capital and the changing functions of the state arises a new 'normal' form of the state: 'authoritarian statism'. The increasing dominance of economic intervention in the overall activity of the state requires these interventions to be increasingly *ad hoc* and particularistic, as the state reacts to specific economic problems in different sectors. Increasingly, monopoly capital pursues its interests through direct influence on specific administrative arms of the state, rather than working through the party system. This form of the capitalist state is therefore characterised by a decline of parliamentary institutions, political parties, political liberties and the rule of law in favour of a strengthened executive and a tendency towards fusion of legislature, executive and judiciary. The development of a reserve repressive apparatus parallel to the main organs of the state consolidates the authoritarian character of this form of state into an 'intensified state control over every sphere of socio-economic life'.[14]

But the interventionist character of the state, in disrupting the rule of law and devaluing representative institutions, also disrupts the role of the state in organising hegemony, both within the power bloc and between it and dominated classes. The consequence is a generalised ideological and political crisis, in which fissures and contradictions within and between state apparatuses become more marked, and sections of the state personnel themselves become politically polarised leftwards. Simultaneously, state economic intervention, now indispensable, faces obstacles and limitations inherent in the very location of the state within a capitalist economy: its role is principally reactive, rather than initiatory, and its resources are themselves ultimately dependent on the profitability of capital.

Finally, very brief mention must be made of an important development of some of these ideas in the field of urban sociology, most notably by Manuel Castells.[15] The increasingly interventionist character of the state, and the Althusserian emphasis on the role of the state in social reproduction, especially in the reproduction of the labour force are related by Castells to the effects of the social structure on the organisation of physical space in the urban environment. Though Castells shares several of the difficulties of the tradition from which his work derives (a tendency to abstract 'structure' from 'practice', and to proliferate formal taxonomies which are then imposed on empirical reality in a frequently arbitrary way) he does make an important contribution to the analysis of urban social conflict. According to Castells, urban space is overdetermined by the ideological, political and economic levels, but in this overdetermination it is the securing of the reproduction of the labour force that preponderates. Castells follows Poulantzas in linking the scale of direct state intervention in this sphere of consumption with the monopoly phase of capitalist development. The correlate of the centralisation and concentration of productive capital into large units with a complex division of labour is urban concentration of the working population and a requirement for large scale provision of their means of consumption, housing, education, transport, health-care and other services. Either because of expected low rates of profit on investment, or because of other difficulties in providing some services in a commodity form, the state is increasingly involved in providing, financing and/or managing them, to the extent that this function has become the main item in urban policy. The state has become, without exaggeration, the main organiser of everyday life.

A direct consequence of state provision of means of 'collective consumption' is that consumption is rendered directly political, and becomes a site for class struggles. Housing, education, health and transport, then, acquire a new strategic importance as the object of a political struggle between state agencies and diverse 'urban social movements' which have a capacity to move beyond pressure for reforms to a demand for qualitative change in the urban structure. Castells has been criticised[16] on general theoretical and methodological grounds, but also in more specific terms, for the imprecision of his idea of 'collective consumption', for his one-sided abstraction and generalisation from certain particularities of the French scene, for his underestimation of the extent to which what he calls 'collective consumption' can be provided by the private sector, and for his assumption that state provision necessarily implies a greater level of conflict over provision. Castells's own position has changed, partly in response to these criticisms, but this has not prevented his work from influencing valuable and theoretically rigorous empirical work in several countries.[17]

Socialist strategy and the Party

Eurocommunism, reformism and Leninism

These and other developments in state and class theory and analysis stimulated, in their different ways, by the work of Althusser since the early 1960s can be seen as providing a diverse set of intellectual resources for thinking about politics, socialist politics in particular. By the early 1970s most of the European Communist Parties were engaged in internal theoretical conflicts over basic strategic orientation, and, in the French Party especially, structural Marxism presented a more or less distinct strategic line. In several of the European Communist Parties, a supposedly new strategic orientation was being actively canvassed. 'Eurocommunism' as it came to be called, was by no means a homogeneous tendency of thought, and it is debatable how far, like the 'revisionist' Marxism of the Second International, it was an attempt to give theoretical recognition to a political practice already adopted, untheorised.

Nevertheless, we can characterise the main outlines of Eurocommunist thinking fairly simply. The Leninist strategy of dual power, a frontal assault on the state apparatus, and consolidation of a 'dictatorship of the proletariat' is no longer appropriate to the conditions obtaining in Western Europe. Sometimes the argument proceeds by rooting the break with Lenin's 'formulae' in the differences of situation and prospects separating his time and place and our own. In this version, Eurocommunism may still be presented as Leninist, applying what is 'essential' to Lenin, Lenin's 'principles', to a new situation. For other Eurocommunists, the Leninist strategy in the Soviet Union is linked with the bureaucratic and authoritarian development of socialism in that country, so that an alternative model of socialism, 'advanced democracy' requires a decisive break with Leninism itself. Already, we can see that the Althusserian 'disruption' of the orthodox tradition is pertinent to Eurocommunism, too: How far is Stalinism rooted in Leninism? to what extent is Leninism a development and to what extent a betrayal of Marxism?

The alternative offered by Eurocommunism, often drawing, as had Althusser and Poulantzas, on the work of Gramsci, emphasises the significance of hegemonic leadership, especially in the advanced Western democracies. The 'Leninist' strategy of a frontal assault on the state apparatuses (the 'war of manoeuvre'), whatever its validity for the circumstances of Russia in 1917, cannot be appropriate for a form of class rule in which domination is achieved through the organisation of consent through moral and cultural leadership, combined with constitutional coercion. In the face of such a form of class domination, socialism cannot be built other than through struggles in every aspect of social life – in literature and the arts, in the educational system, in sporting and leisure time activities, as well as in the home and at work – to achieve a 'counter-hegemony' for socialist ideas and culture amongst the popular masses. Only if the great majority of the people can be won to these ideas, and to the prospect of living them in their daily lives, can socialism become a reality. The prolonged and dispersed character of such a struggle (a 'war of position') is contrasted with the spasmodic and highly concentrated assault on the central apparatuses of the state which is at the core of the Leninist strategy.

This Gramscian heritage enables Eurocommunism to put at the centre of its strategic proposals the idea of a more or less prolonged democratic struggle within the existing framework of political domination: in the parliamentary arena, and within what Althusser called the 'ideological state apparatuses'. The strategy of combining popular struggles in these institutions and struggles for democratic changes in the organisation of firms with parliamentary struggles, in alliance with other parties of the Left, opened up the prospect of a peaceful and democratic route to the socialism which would itself be democratic.

Though the *word* 'Eurocommunism' is not used, its concept is crucial to our understanding of the major strategic debates which took place in the PCF in preparation for and as a consequence of the Twenty-second Congress which took place early in 1976. The immediate object of controversy was a draft document by the leadership which abandoned the term 'dictatorship of the proletariate', and the (successful) proposal by the leadership for the party statutes to be revised accordingly. The new strategy advocated by the party leadership embodied the Eurocommunist conviction that conditions now existed for a peaceful and democratic transition to socialism. In its French form, this strategy has three main elements. First, a version of the theory of 'state monopoly capitalism', according to which monopoly capitalism has entered a new phase characterised by a 'fusion' of the capitalist state with the monopoly fraction of capital. The problems of over-accumulation of capital relative to opportunities for realisation of surplus value, characteristic of the monopoly phase in the development of Capitalism necessitate massive state intervention to defray the costs of monopoly capital, and so restore its profitability. The capitalist state in the current phase of capitalist development is therefore a single mechanism of economic exploitation and political domination of the rest of the population on behalf of the monopoly fraction of the capitalist class.

The second element in the new strategy follows directly: since even medium and small capital suffers economically from the new form of state power, an immense majority of the population now has an objective interest in social change, and this constitutes the basis for a broad, anti-monopoly alliance, including fractions of the capitalist class, but with the workers as its leading force. The extension of the sphere of intervention of the state, characteristic of this new phase, into every aspect of everyday life simultaneously provides the conditions for widespread popular antagonism to the state.

The third element in the strategy consists in what might best be described as a new 'attitude' to political liberties, representative institutions, and, generally, to the 'ideological' apparatuses. Instead of regarding these as part and parcel of the system of bourgeois class domination, as the 'orthodox' tradition had tended to do, the PCF leadership adopts the somewhat ambiguous perspective of defending and extending 'the liberties' of the French people (something the bourgeoisie has long since abandoned, despite its revolutionary tradition) whilst at the same time struggling for democratisation of the state system. In every stage in the struggle, the multi-party system will persist, and there will be a regular appeal to the French voters. It is here that the significance of the abandonment of the 'dictatorship of the proletariat' is at its most apparent.

Lenin's political theory follows the classics of Marx and Engels in linking the very existence of the state with class domination. As the state is defined in terms of class domination, so the different forms of the state must be related to the different conditions of class rule required by different ruling classes. The capitalist state is the institutional form of the political domination of the capitalist class. The objectives of the class-rule of the working class and its allies – the expropriation of the capitalists, and the establishment of a classless society, which means, in the end, the withering away of the state as such – are quite different from those of the capitalist class. In consequence, a quite new form of state has to be built. In Russia, this meant recognising, as the embryonic organisations of the political power of the working people, the Soviets, and it meant working to consolidate and develop them as an alternative, and opposed centre of sovereignty, administration and direction for social life. The next strategic objective was to resolve this unstable situation of 'dual power' by destroying the Tsarist state apparatus and consolidating the Soviet system.

A fundamental question, then, which is posed by and for Eurocommunism, in the French context as well as elsewhere, is this: how far does a strategy of political struggle within the apparatuses of the capitalist state imply a rejection of the basic theoretical propositions of the Marxist classics linking specific requirements of class rule with specific forms of state apparatus? And the answers given to this question depend, essentially, on how one evaluates the establishment and extension of political liberties (the universal franchise, rights of political and trades union organisation and so on), and the social advances which have been won by working people with these means during the twentieth century in most of the advanced capitalist countries.

The reformist strategies in practice adopted by the largest working-class parties in these countries, the 'social democratic' parties, have been subjected to 'Leninist' criticism on three main grounds. First, they confuse 'democracy' with 'parliamentary' democracy. Parliamentary democracy, even where it is fully developed, though it presents itself as a system of universal political 'representation' is, in its effects, a system of *exclusion* of the dominated classes from power. This itself is a consequence of three main features of parliamentary politics. First, the separation of economics and politics specific to capitalism makes possible the formation of a specialist stratum of political professionals whose presence in the political system as 'representatives' of the mass of workers is simultaneously the exclusion of the latter from direct participation in it: workers themselves are always at 'one remove' from actual political decision-making. A second effect of the separation of economics and politics is a dispersion of the bases of working-class power into more or less independent political and economic organisations. This is, in turn, a condition of possibility of the third feature of parliamentary politics – the mode of individual participation in it. In so far as this is an exercise of the citizenship rights of individuals, defined as such by what Balibar calls 'bourgeois legal ideology',[18] then political participation is experienced not as an aspect of class struggle, but as a contribution made by free and equal citizens to a synthetic 'general will'. The working *class* is excluded from politics as the price paid for participation by workers as individual citizens. This latter mode of participation is one in which individuals figure as 'consumers' of a pre-established range of options, not as *producers* of the political choices on offer.

Parliamentary politics, therefore, as a form of exclusion of workers from political power, needs to be replaced by political forms in which, to use a phrase again borrowed from Balibar, 'the masses intervene in person on the political scene'.[19] Against the representative democracy which characterises bourgeois rule (at its best) is counterposed a 'direct' democracy in which there is active control by the represented over their representatives. Mandating of delegates, right of recall of delegates, definition of units of political participation in terms of interest groups rather than geographical or demographic units, rotation of functions and so on are among the many institutional means for securing such control.

The second element of the Leninist critique of reformism is that, associated with the failure to distinguish parliamentary democracy from direct ('real') democracy is a failure to distinguish governmental power from state power. The relative autonomy of the apparatuses of the state *vis-à-vis* the elected government is such that, should, against all the odds, a socialist government ever be elected, the implementation of its policies may still be frustrated by independent initiatives on the part of the administrative bureaucracy, the judiciary, and, in the last resort, the armed forces. To these resources of bourgeois power can also be added, of course, the various powers of direct coercion available to a class which owns the decisive means of material production. These power resources are sufficient to ensure – and this is the third element in the Leninist critique – that such measures as are implemented by governments susceptible to presssure from the subordinate classes are implemented either in a form which serves the interests of the dominant class, or in such a way as to consolidate the legitimacy of the existing form of class domination, even if at the cost of sacrifices of ruling class short term interests.

Dictatorship and democracy

Among the prominent Althusserian contributions to the French controversy over the abandonment of the 'dictatorship of the proletariat' that of Balibar comes closest to a replication of this Leninist critique of reformism and a re-assertion of the general validity of the concept 'dictatorship of the proletariat' as a basic strategic precept. Althusser himself, cautious about the *phrase*, also defends the scientific validity of the concept. But through a distinction between what is 'essential' to Leninism, and what is merely 'contingent' (that is, specific to the historical circumstances of the Russian Revolution) Althusser is able to develop a line of strategic argument which is distinct both from that of the official party leadership and from the more or less 'conservative' opposition to it offered by Balibar and others. The position adopted by Poulantzas, on the other hand, whilst quite close to Althusser also establishes an *explicit* critical distance from Lenin. In what follows I shall attempt a brief critical evaluation of these different strategic arguments.

Balibar's defence of the 'dictatorship of the proletariat' makes two important contributions, viewed from this perspective. First, it attempts to separate the concept 'dictatorship of the proletariat' from the institutional forms prevailing in the Soviet Union.[20] For Balibar the soviet system was a genuine form of popular power in the revolutionary period. But old ways of working, old habits of mind and divisions of social labour cannot be abolished at a stroke – they re-emerge *within* the organs of popular power themselves. Balibar attempts to show that there is a clear break between Lenin's halting and 'descriptive' recognition of these problems in the consolidation of soviet power, and Stalin's methods of resolving them by a combination of purges, police terror and privileges of office. It is therefore a mistake to identify the system of bureaucratic and authoritarian rule in Russia – a dictatorship *over* the proletariat – with the dictatorship *of* the proletariat from which it degenerated. To oppose the 'model' of socialist construction represented by the USSR, then, is not necessarily to reject the 'dictatorship of the proletariat'. On the contrary, this concept embodies a view of democratic power which is an indispensible critical weapon against both the representative democracies of the West and the authoritarian states of the East.

Secondly, Balibar attempts to reveal the theoretical meaning of the Leninist conception of 'dictatorship.[21] It is not the antithesis of 'democracy', but simply refers to the basis of *all* political systems, democratic or otherwise, in a relation of class power. Individual moral or legal rules may be justified in terms of a moral or legal system, but the system itself, based as it is in a relation of power, is an imposition. In this sense, coercion and violence is at the basis of every system of class rule, that is, every system of state power. This includes hegemonic leadership, and the ideological interpellation which is the effect of the ideological state apparatuses, for, in the end, the repressive and non-repressive forms of domination cannot be separated. This is, in fact, the core of Balibar's argument for the generalisability of Leninism to advanced capitalist democracies: though the *form* of class rule has changed in significant ways, and more or less effectively mobilises the consent of large sections of the dominated classes, the apparatuses of the state are no less the material forms of class domination, and the strategic priority to destroy them and replace them by organs of mass democracy remains central.

Now, amidst the serious, and politically rather dangerous confusions in this argument, there remains a small but important nugget of truth. The confusions first. Balibar speaks of systems of law resting upon relations of power, and therefore being founded upon coercion. There are several confusions compounded here, but the most important one for our purposes is that it relies on a conception of 'power' such that it is constituted somehow prior to and independently of the legal system which ratifies it. Balibar derives this idea from Rousseau. First of all, this rules out *a priori* the possibility that law is itself a power resource for the dominant class: that is, implicitly, Balibar is recognising as 'power' only non-legitimate forms of domination. If that is so, then the essentially coercive nature of class power is reduced to a mere tautology. The 'other side' of this same point is that the basis of the power relation which supports the system of law must be either possession of a monopoly of means of violence or *de facto* possession of the means of production. If the latter position is adopted, then we are back with economic reductionism, whilst the former leads to a serious conflation of hegemonic domination with rule by systematic and unrestrained repression: one legitimates itself, the other does not, but considered as *de facto* systems of power relations they are identical. With proper respect for Balibar's undoubted personal opposition to

Stalinism, it is nevertheless true that this conflation is closer to Stalin's concept of dictatorship than Lenin's. It is the same conflation that we find commonly in conservative thought, and is, for example, at work in Durkheim's concept of 'social facts' as coercive.[22]

The effect of this theoretical confusion is to render insignificant the differences *between* social orders in the *extent* to which they are able to secure the consent of their citizens, or, conversely, have to rely on the use of repressive means. This is a very important difference from the standpoint of the quality of life and subjective experience of those who live their lives within a social order, and it is also a very important difference from the standpoint of the availability of means of organised opposition and the achievement of social change.

Having said all this, the remaining 'nugget' of truth in Balibar's argument is that it doesn't at all follow from the Gramscian analysis of advanced capitalist democracies as characterised by hegemonic domination, that these regimes are any the less systems of class domination: legitimate domination may nevertheless be domination, and the strategic priority for alternative forms of class rule may be no less pressing. This seems to me indeed the most plausible way of reading Gramsci himself. If this is so, then the new strategic perspective of the leadership of the PCF and its abandonment of the 'dictatorship of the proletariat' can still be faulted for failing to recognise this strategic necessity. In particular, its failure to distinguish a *democratic* road to socialism (favoured, incidentally, by Balibar, too), from a *parliamentary* democratic road, and its proposal to preserve and extend existing liberties can easily be seen to rest on an abstraction of these liberties from their character as aspects of a prevailing system of class domination. In this respect, at least, the new strategy is not distinguishable from reformism, and faces the same practical and theoretical problems.

But the new strategy is not unambiguously reformist – the objective is not simply to *use* the existing means of political struggle, but to extend and transform them in the process. In fact, Balibar himself, no less than Poulantzas and Althusser, is also committed to a view of the state apparatuses as both *objectives* of struggle and '*sites*' or '*arenas*' of struggle. This is, indeed, very much in the Leninist tradition. But, if the state apparatuses are an arena for class struggle, then there are but two possibilities. Either the class struggle waged by the dominated classes there is necessarily without effects (in which case the concept of class struggle in the state apparatuses is empty of content, and Althusserianism reduced to functionalism) or these classes do make some advances. The thesis that hegemony is secured through concessions to this struggle recognises just this point. Now, if class struggles in the state apparatuses do enable the dominated classes to make gains, gains that are worth fighting for, any worthwhile strategy must *include* the commitment to at least preserving these gains. Secondly, if such gains can be won through struggles in and upon the existing state apparatuses, what is the *precise theoretical meaning* of continuing to see those apparatuses as unequivocally organs of the power of the dominant class? Connectedly, where is the clear-cut dividing line between a revolutionary strategy which destroys the existing state apparatuses and replaces them by alternatives, and a reformist one which struggles 'on the terrain' of the existing apparatuses and achieves their transformation?

Balibar is very much aided by his failure to say anything concrete about what 'smashing the state apparatuses' would actually be in an advanced capitalist democracy. Althusser on the other hand, is somewhat more specific:

> In fact ... in order to 'smash' the bourgeois State and to replace it with the State of the working class and its allies *it is not enough simply to add the adjective 'democratic' to each State apparatus*, it is something completely different from this formal and potentially reformist operation, it is to revolutionise in their structure, their practice and their ideology the existing State apparatuses, suppressing some of them, creating new ones, thus to produce a *transformation in the forms of the division of labour* between the repressive, political and ideological apparatuses, to *revolutionise their methods of work* and the *bourgeois ideology* which governs their practical activity, and to *construct new relations between these apparatuses and the masses* on the basis of a new, *proletarian* ideology, in order to prepare the 'withering away of the State', i.e., its replacement by organisations of the masses.[23]

Both Althusser and Poulantzas, working with a conception of the state as internally contradictory, and as already 'traversed' by the struggles of the popular masses, are quite explicit that a democratic road to socialism is possible (indeed, as Poulantzas points out, socialism will either be democratic or it will not happen at all) and that this route must involve a combination of struggles *within* the state apparatuses to transform them and their mutual relationships together with struggles 'at a distance' from the state apparatuses, whose effects on the apparatuses will be to change the relationships between them (the apparatuses) and the masses outside.

But Poulantzas[24] is more explicit than Althusser in arguing that this combination of diverse sites and forms of struggle will involve, in particular, a combination of both direct and representative democratic forms, both as means of struggle, and as actually constitutive of socialist democracy. The institutions of representative democracy – universal suffrage, ideological and party pluralism, political freedoms, including those of opposition – are no longer to be seen as definitive of the 'dictatorship of the bourgeoisie' but as themselves popular conquests. Struggles to extend these representative institutions and transform the other state apparatuses are not incompatible with, but are, in fact, a *condition of possibility* of the simultaneous flourishing of forms of direct democracy and self-management. This is the point at which we really can see the seeds of Stalinism in Leninism. Lenin counterposed representative and direct democracy in the strategy of dual power and the 'smashing' of the state, but as Rosa Luxemburg foresaw, this had the effect of killing off the democratic vitality of the country as a whole and so crippled the democratic life of the soviets themselves until all that remained was a bureaucracy. It is important to see, here, that Poulantzas in no way allies himself with opponents of direct democracy, who argue that it is incompatible with the technical requirements of administering a complex division of labour, or that it inevitably degenerates into a dictatorship of the 'active minority'.[25] On the contrary, direct democracy is indispensable to democratic socialism, but direct democracy is itself dependent for its democratic character upon the preservation and extension of the political liberties established in the form of representative democracy.

But if the identification of direct democracy with dictatorship of the proletariat has been challenged by Poulantzas, what of the identification of representative democracy with dictatorship of the bourgeoisie? By these later writings, Poulantzas is clearly committed to a conception of the 'relative autonomy' of the capitalist state, which goes beyond what is necessary to secure cohesion within the power bloc and its hegemonic domination over the dominated classes. It must be recognised, now, that the latter have the possibility to transform the apparatuses of the state to a point where the balance of their interventions tilts in favour of the popular masses. There is no longer an essential connection between representative democracy and capitalist class rule. Poulantzas is not, of course, alone among Marxists in questioning this link. On the basis of comparative historical studies, Goran Therborn[26] has argued that, for that relatively small group of capitalist countries which routinely satisfy his criteria of parliamentary democracy, popular struggles have played a large part in its achievement, and always against the resistance of the dominant classes. On the other hand, if there is no necessary connection between capitalist rule and parliamentary democracy, the connection is not entirely contingent, either. Therborn argues, first, that the establishment of certain basic civil liberties is indispensable for a market economy and that this is also a condition of possibility (free speech and association for example) for the emergence of the very popular movements whose pressure has led to the extension of the franchise and other developments of parliamentary democracy. Secondly, the character of the capitalist class as fractioned and competitive at the economic level requires, at the political level, a means of unifying and legitimating state policy *vis-à-vis* the different capitalist class fractions. Limited forms of parliamentary democracy, 'democracy of the bourgeoisie', are an effective way of satisfying this requirement, but are also open to extension under pressure from the popular classes.

Clearly this view of the relationship between parliamentary democracy and capitalist class rule is incompatible with the unqualified 'machine of class domination' thesis, and so some revision of the Marxist classics would be required by it. On the other hand, Therborn's position does retain a close theoretical link between the parliamentary form of the state and the conditions of capitalist class rule. It is a product of specifically capitalist contradictions and social antagonisms. But the revision of the classical Marxist thesis is significant enough. In Poulantzas' work, it seems that the concessions required of the power bloc in order to sustain hegemony over the dominated classes in the face of their struggles within and upon the state apparatuses may be of such an order as to risk conceding these apparatuses to the enemy.

Here, Poulantzas, unlike many advocates of Eurocommunist

strategy, doesn't dodge the obvious question. Even hegemonic leadership involves a close interconnection of consent and coercion. The power bloc may not rely principally on organised violence in 'normal' times, but it still possesses a monopoly of the legitimate use of force. Is it plausible to suppose that the repressive powers of the capitalist state would be held wholly in reserve, whilst a socialist 'counter-hegemony' was built within and without the state apparatuses? Poulantzas speaks of a 'risk' that a democratic socialist strategy such as he advocates may be recuperated into a social democratic framework. Should this risk be averted, a crisis of the proportions required for a socialist transformation of the state would be likely to provoke a police and military reaction. Poulantzas refers to the Chilean experience in this context.

There are no simple solutions on offer, but two points can be made. One is that despite the immensely greater obstacles to popular struggle presented by the RSAs, it should not be assumed that they are entirely internally homogeneous, or impervious to popular struggle. The role of the armed forces movement in the Portuguese revolution is the obvious recent example here. But implicit in the use of this example is the suggestion that a crisis of the state sufficiently profound to threaten the RSAs themselves with disintegration is a necessary precondition for a democratic socialist transition. Historically, war-time defeat or transitions from 'exceptional' forms of the capitalist state (that is, fascist or military dictatorships), or sometimes, as in the Portuguese example, an 'overdetermined' conjunction of the two, have been necessary for crises of this type. This is a long way from the kind of evolutionary perspective on capitalist development as preparing the conditions for socialist advance that we find in most versions of Eurocommunism. It appears to take us back to Althusser's conception of history as an open and contingent process, and of revolutionary 'ruptures' as the outcomes of wholly exceptional fusions of overdetermined contradictions.

The question of alliances

The second 'pointer' Poulantzas offers in connection with the possibility of a military reaction to democratic socialist advance is that it may be prevented, or at the very least weakened, if the popular movement is sufficiently broad and deep. This brings us to the question of the scope and nature of the 'popular alliance' to which all parties to this strategic debate are committed. Though one of the arguments used by George Marchais and others against the concept of the 'dictatorship of the proletariat' is that socialist strategy requires a far broader popular support than the term 'proletariat' allows, the argument is easily dismissed. The whole Leninist tradition advocated just such a broad alliance, and Lenin's own arguments against 'economism' were directed to just this end. What *is* at issue, though, is the scope of the alliance. Who does it include and exclude? As we saw, the variant of Eurocommunism advocated by the PCF leadership relied on a version of the theory of state monopoly capitalism. It follows from this that the oppositional alliance around the working class potentially includes small and medium capital: an 'anti-monopoly alliance'. Althusser and Poulantzas both oppose the theory of state monopoly capitalism, though, as we have seen, Poulantzas himself came increasingly to recognise the dominance of the monopoly fraction *vis-à-vis* the rest of the power bloc, and also to see in these terms the increasingly interventionist character of the capitalist state. But this still is some way from state monopoly capitalism, in that this thesis reduces politics to economics, confusing the hegemonic domination of the monopoly fraction within the power bloc with its economic domination. The continuing global functions of the state may come into conflict with its economic interventions in favour of monopoly capital, and the contradictions arising out of this are of great strategic importance. They cannot be recognised adequately within the theory of state monopoly capitalism. On the alliance between workers and fractions of capital itself, Althusser notes that it relies on the 'minor theoretical wonder' of the concept of objective interests – as though all that were needed were agitation and propaganda to persuade non-monopoly capitalists to throw in their lot with the workers' revolution.

But perhaps the most important feature of the debate on alliances has to do not with their scope, but with their nature. Althusser, especially, is passionate in his denunciation of the PCF's interpretation of alliance as a mere electoral 'compact' conducted by party leaderships over the heads of their members.[27] A class alliance must be more than this, it must be deeply rooted in the life experiences, traditions of struggle and cultural forms of the mass of the people themselves. Though Althusser himself still appears to think of alliances built, in this way, in the course of mass struggles, as a way of extending the influence of the PCF, there is no mistaking the difference in approach between him and the PCF leadership. And, whilst there is still room in some of Althusser's formulations for a somewhat 'instrumental' view of the popular alliance around the working class, the form of his attacks on the pary leadership suggest that this is not the general *tendency* of Althusser's approach. As we have already seen, Poulantzas' concern for a form of alliance in which real recognition is given to the distinct interests, outlooks and traditions of the alliance partners, leads him to advocate a view of the 'intermediate strata' as a fraction of a quite distinct class.

Both Althusser and Poulantzas, then, are committed to a democratic transition to socialism achieved through the construction of a class alliance deeply rooted in popular life experiences, traditions and cultures. Since the alliance will have to span classes and fractions with different, even contradictory, interests, objectives and outlooks, this will have to be reflected in a common programme which resolves such contradictions non-coercively and in legitimate over-arching institutional forms through which programmes and other forms of common action are decided. This conception of class alliance, together with other features of the new strategic ideas associated with Althusser and Poulantzas, poses fundamental questions, first, for the Marxist theory of ideology, and second, for the Leninist theory of the 'vanguard' party. I'll deal with these problems, very briefly, in turn.

First, the idea of a broad class alliance, rooted in the popular traditions and cultural forms of the allied classes, and with common, legitimate organisational forms of decision-making requires the discovery or formation of symbolic identifications, cultural forms and the establishment of social practices which move within a 'cultural space' wider than that of the class ideologies of the partners to the alliance. Even if Althusserian theory is capable of resolving the problem that its theory of ideology identifies ideology with the ruling ideology (and Althusser sometimes speaks of 'proletarian ideology' as if this theoretical revision were already achieved) then a further break is still required with almost the whole of the Marxist tradition. The theoretical tie between specific ideologies and specific classes has to be broken. In a very interesting criticism and development of Althusser's concept of interpellation, Ernesto Laclau[28] has argued against the notion of a necessary class connotation attaching to the elements of ideological discourse. Instead, the character of a discourse is to be discovered through the nature of the subject it constitutes through its distinctive interpellation. Since, for Laclau, the contradiction between the popular alliance and the power bloc is the location *par excellence* of ideological struggle then we should understand popular democratic discourses as autonomous forms, and not as in some sense artefacts constructed out of elements of the class ideologies of the partners in the popular alliance.

But a still more radical reappraisal of the traditional Marxist model of ideology is required. Althusser himself mentions the important range of new issues which have entered into contemporary politics as marking a decisive shift in the balance of political forces: health-care, transport, the environment, the family and education.[29] We might also add nationality, sexuality, peace, race and others.

Such issues 'mobilise' or recruit individuals to them in various ways. Very broadly, demands for universal state education, for socialised health care, for public transport provision, and so on, often are rooted in the experiences of specifically class forms of social oppression: historically, European social democratic parties have taken up these issues as the political 'other face of the coin' from the economic struggles of workers in their trades unions. For other issues, though, such as nuclear disarmament, environmental questions and others, individuals may be attached to these causes through their relationship to pre-existing ideological–cultural commitments which may not be, in terms of either tradition or content, significantly related to social class membership: pacifism, humanism, various forms of religious commitment, as well as very specific features of personal life history may dispose an individual to link his or her identity with such a cause. Depending on the nature of the movement, and of the individual's attachment to it, such attachment may or may not be the beginning of a 'radicalisation' – the constitution of a more broadly 'oppositional' subjectivity.

Thirdly, though, there are issues such as racial equality, sexuality, and those raised more generally by the women's movement (Althusser mentions 'youth' in this category, too) which *may* recruit individuals on a basis comparable with nuclear disarmament and the like, but which also, and perhaps more centrally, recruit or 'interpellate' individuals on the basis of shared conditions of oppression and/or exploitation in society which are nevertheless not reducible to class. This is of fundamental importance in that the possessors of repressed or stigmatised sexuality, and the victims of racially or gender-based forms of social oppression may come to acquire more or less autonomous (*vis-à-vis* class relations) forms of oppositional consciousness, and means of representation at the political level (either within, or outside the traditional political parties).

Stalinism and the reform of the Party

All of this means that the question of alliances has to be posed, not as a question of *class* alliances only, but as one of alliances between subordinate classes and social categories which cut across class boundaries, together with diverse groupings of individuals bound together, not by any specific shared conditions of social oppression, but by common commitments generated at the political level itself. This immense range of diversity in the social composition of any genuinely popular and democratic oppositional alignment means that the potential for internal strife and contradiction is permanent and pervasive. In such a context, the expectation, implicit in the idea of a 'vanguard' party, and apparently not fully abandoned by Althusser, that a single party can establish itself as the sole, or even predominating, political expression, uniting behind its leadership the whole oppositional popular movement is clearly absurd. Not only is it wildly impractical, it is also highly undesirable, if popular opposition is to retain its full diversity and genuinely democratic nature. The classical Leninist conception of a 'vanguard party' is clearly unsuited to these political conditions, and, in practice, is liable to lead in the direction either of doctrinal purity and consequent political marginalisation, or of an empty, platitudinous electoralism.

This brings us, finally, to some brief comments on Althusser's increasingly bitter denunciations of the PCF leadership in the late 1970s, and his calls for party reform. The task of a vanguard party, to give direction and leadership to the mass struggle, cannot be carried out by a party which has separated itself from the popular initiatives and aspirations of the masses. This is something which lies 'at the heart of the Marxist and Leninist tradition: the practice of letting the masses which make history speak for themselves, of not simply attempting to serve the people but of listening to them, learning from them and understanding their aspirations and their contradictions, and being attentive to the powers of imagination and invention of the masses'.[30] The PCF has become a 'fortress' which defends its position in French politics through an apparatus which enforces 'unity' upon the leadership and obedience on its rank-and-file militants. Such an apparatus for control from above implies suspicion from the leadership of everything which it does not control – from the mass strikes of 1968, to independent theoretical work which challenges the official line of the Party.

Althusser, again, seeks a 'third way' on the question of Party reform: against *both* the 'Stalinist practices' which eliminated the living links between mass spontaneity and the apparatus of the Party, *and* the conversion of the PCF into a reformist, parliamentary party, 'just like the rest'.[31] Both types of party, Althusser argues, reproduce bourgeois politics within the working class movement, in that both ensure the exclusion of the masses, the rank-and-file, from effective participation in politics. Althusser denounces a tradition of secrecy among the leadership: effective party democracy demands access by the membership to information. There must be full and free opportunities for open debate in the Party – this means, among other things, abolishing the vertical separations in the party organisation, especially between workers and intellectuals, it means making possible *horizontal* flows of information and opinion, and it means opening up the Party press to free debate: Althusser himself has to deliver these criticisms in the form of a series of articles in *Le Monde* since the Party press has been closed to him.

But for all the power of Althusser's denunciations, and for all their undoubted libertarian intent, the intervention remains limited and contradictory. What is at stake is a whole form of party organisation – democratic centralism – and its rationale. The reforms demanded by Althusser are *reforms in the practice* of democratic centralism, not its revocation. The purpose of democratic centralism is to create unity of thought and action in the Party. Such unity is vital to the winning of the class struggle against the bourgeoisie. The mechanism through which this objective is to be achieved is free discussion at all levels of the Party, with democratic decisions made at the highest level – the Party Congress – becoming subsequently binding on all militants in their political activity.

But at no stage does Althusser present the case for his supposed necessity of 'unity in action'. A Party-monolith of this sort has no means of opening itself to the mass initiatives and imagination which Althusser elsewhere advocates, and no means of sustaining the democratic internal life of the Party which Althusser avowedly desires. Clearly any Party activity, and, indeed any participation in democratic processes involves forms of discipline on activists: to respect and to abide by the decisions of the majority. This is especially true for the electoral representatives and the leadership. But the continuation of democracy as a living form depends also on the responsibility of minorities to continue to voice their opposition and to fight for change. Unless we suppose this voicing of opposition to be done in secret, behind the backs of the masses (certainly not Althusser's *practice* by 1978, whatever happened before that), then it must to a degree disrupt the 'unity of thought and action' of the Party. A telling instance of Althusser's failure to fully carry through his critique of the Party apparatus is his unequivocal opposition to the formation of stable and recognised 'tendencies' within the PCF.[32] If oppositional groupings and minorities of various kinds are not entitled to *organise* their opposition in the formation of tendencies, then the liberty of expression and debate to which Althusser is committed must reduce to a matter of *individual* liberty: that is to say, in effect, the liberty of a famous Marxist intellectual, such as Althusser himself is, to be heard in the Party press. In the absence of organised tendencies, the buzz of the freely expressed individual opinions of the thousands of rank-and-file members can cancel itself out and need hardly be heard by the party leadership.

Part III
Critics and Crusaders

Part III

Cities and Crusaders

8

The Rebellion of Subjectivity

Vincent Descombes, seeing in Althusser's later philosophical position an abandonment of the attempt to give Marxism an epistemological foundation, argues that with this the Althusserian undertaking is brought to 'an official close'.[1] I do not think the position is so simple as this, but there is no doubt that others, several of whom had shared the project of Althusser's earlier work, took the self-critical path much further than did Althusser himself. In some ways, the very audacity of that original project, and the scope of its implications (some of which I have briefly sketched in Chapters 6 and 7) provoked a critical rejection which could be no less all encompassing. Out of what may be seen as the internal decomposition of structural Marxism as a more or less unified programme of philosophical and social scientific research was to emerge a revolt on behalf of the subject and subjectivity, and an irrationalism, both no less global in their implications than had been the Althusserian commitment to the exclusion of the demands of the subject in the name of scientific reason. I shall, in this chapter, be concerned with some of these developments on the French intellectual scene, and with their echoes in the English-speaking world. In Chapter 9 I shall be considering some critical responses to Althusserianism form historians and sociologists which are more limited in scope, if often not less passionate and intemperate in their denunciations.

The 'new philosophers' and their ancestry

In 1977, the centre of the French intellectual scene was suddenly occupied by a group of writers hailed by adulatory media attention as *Les Nouveaux Philosophes*. Though not a wholly unified philosophical movement, the New Philosophers (B. H. Levy, G. Lardreau, C. Jambet, A. Glucksmann, J.-M. Benoist, J.-P. Dolle and others) shared common assumptions, themes and attitudes, not unconnected with a shared background of leftist political activity and militancy from the 'events' of May 1968. One persuasive interpretation[2] of the militantly anti-Marxist celebration of individual rebellion and dissidence which is a common theme of their writings is that it was an attempt to preserve something of the values and experiences of 1968 in the face of the disillusionment and failure of the leftist opposition to the orthodox organisations of the Left (most especially, of course, the PCF). For these writers, the imminent prospect of electoral success for the Eurocommunist strategy (which did not, after all, materialise) seemed to set the seal on the recuperation of the implications of the spontaneous cultural revolt of 1968, and to promise the final re-imposition of oppressive, ordered existence.

The late 1960s and early 1970s had seen a fusion of the 'spontaneist' student movement with the Maoist current of Althusserianism in avowedly 'Maoist' organisations to the left of the CP. These groupings, though they retained something of a Marxist theoretical rhetoric, and what Peter Dews has called a 'guiding political fantasy',[3] had really abandoned most of the main principles and doctrines of orthodox Marxism and Leninism. This experience, and its failure was a shared feature of the political biographies of several of the 'New Philosophers', and their retrospective interpretation of it, and the 'policing', recuperative role of the PCF in those years, is to see in Marxism and its institutional expression nothing but the most developed form of what the revolt of 1968 was a revolt against. From this standpoint, the project of a Marxist opposition to totalitarianism and oppression was a contradiction in terms. The cultural revolution espoused by the 'gauchiste' militants of that time could never have been advanced, but only recuperated by the Marxist idea of an ideological transformation which would usher in a new mode of production. Indeed, as the examples of Eastern Europe show (so the 'New Philosophers' claim) this new mode of production can do no more than to consolidate and rationalise the centralisation of state power and the systematic totalitarian control over personal life already initiated by the bourgeoisie.

The *New Philosophy* was initially presented, partly because of the political biographies of its leading exponents, as a critical response to Marxism from the Left, though the 'movement' was diverse in its political and ethical commitments, taking leftist, liberal, libertarian and Christian forms. Its characteristic themes were, first, through an abstract and metaphysical use of such concepts as power and order, to effect a generalised and pessimistic rendering of all forms of institutional ordering of life as oppressive and totalitarian. Since the state is for the 'New Philosophy' the ultimate organiser and central-iser of systematic social power, then it is but a short step to the perception of the Marxist movement in both its 'orthodox' East European and its Eurocommunist forms as the main enemy of the moral values of individuality and liberty. An almost exclusive focus on the human-rights violations of the regimes of Eastern Europe, and a championing of their victims and dissidents (most especially Solzhenitzin) readily opened up the often genuinely leftist intent of the 'New Philosophy' for the purposes of the right.

A second, related, theme of the new movement was its identifica-tion of forms of thought, even of rationality itself with the institu-tional powers they serve. Western philosophical and scientific rationality is a totalising and oppressive 'doctrine of order' which renders nature and human relations alike calculable, predictable, and controllable. Marxism, especially in its most rigorous, totalising and 'scientific' Althusserian form, is the completion of this intellectual–political trajectory. The subversive pretentions of Marxism fit it all the better to recuperate rebellion and disruption and to facilitate the imposition of ever more totalitarian forms of order. What else could be expected of a doctrine which poses the question of human liberation in the form of a seizure and exercise of state power? The critique of structural Marxism, then, turns out to be a critique of all Marxism, and, eventually, of systematic, totalis-ing rationality, of theory itself, as all unified by an inner commit-ment to systematic social órder, to the concentration camp and the Gulag.

Set against this unity of institutional and intellectual totalitarian-ism exists only the individual right and responsibility of spontane-ous, intuitive rebellion and resistance, without the expectation that our individual rebellions will coalesce, or will be capable of effect. Evaluation of such action can have nothing to do with strategic calculation, but solely with its ethical or aesthetic quality. Just as there is a parallel here with Romantic assertions of the 'truth' of sentiment and feeling as against the cold, calculating reason of the

Enlightenment, so there is a parallel in the New Philosophers' choice of its heroes and heroines: the poets and vagabonds, peasants and shopkeepers, the individual dissidents and dreamers, the excluded, outcast and suppressed. With this goes a celebration of the simple, unsystematic and intuitive wisdom born of experience, as against the formal, academic and intrinsically oppressive rationality of the 'Masters' of Western philosophy and science.

But just as the contemporary opponents of the Enlightenment had to face the problem of a critique of reason which did not beg the question by using the methods of reason, the New Philosophers themselves make cognitive claims (about the inevitability of the recuperation of revolutions, for example) whilst renouncing epistemology, and seem to fail to recognise the origins of the very individualism and conception of human rights to which they appeal in the self-same Enlightenment project which they reject. In some respects, the New Philosophers' attack on 'Western rationality' was anticipated in Jacques Derrida's project of 'deconstruction', which was also turned against 'structuralism' as its most formidable target, but Derrida's work was always distinguished by a sophisticated methodological consciousness of the paradoxical character of so fundamental an attack upon everything which falls within the horizon of our contemporary thought and culture.[4]

But there are other, closer, antecedents, in the previous generation of French intellectuals, some of them, most notably Lacan and Foucault explicitly recognised by the New Philosophers themselves. Notwithstanding the borrowings made from Lacan by the arch-rationalist Althusser, there remains space in the former's work for quite contrary readings. The parallel exclusion of the 'subject' from scientific discourse and the alienation of the unity of the subject with its entry into the symbolic order allows for the possibility of a 'revenge' on the part of the subject in the form of an irrationalist opposition to scientific discourse, and a wilful destabilisation of the order of language. Gilles Deleuze and Felix Guattari (despite the later mutual hostility between the former and the New Philosophy) also significantly anticipated themes of the New Philosophy in their *Anti-Oedipus*,[5] representing all forms of order, including systematic theory as indifferently oppressive, and interpreting the events of May 1968 as a rebellion of 'desire' against power and order, including the power and order of the supposedly revolutionary party.

Power and knowledge

The work of Michel Foucault is, perhaps, the most important of these anticipations, and certainly more important than the work of the New Philosophers themselves. Despite obvious differences, expecially in the richness and complexity of Foucault's work, and his ambiguous attitude to Marxism, there are nevertheless important points of contact between his work and elements in the New Philosophers' critique of Marxism. Despite a sharing by both Althusser and Foucault of borrowings from structuralism and historical epistemology, there was, even in the earliest period of their works, a sharp division between Althusser's requirement for a clear science/ideology distinction and Foucault's methodological insistence on a suspension of questions of truth and falsity. Whereas the Marxist could follow historical epistemology in its relativising of ideological phenomena to their social and political conditions of possibility, and sympathise with Foucault's search for constituting rules for the formation of discourses, there could be no suspension of questions of truth or falsity. For Althusser the epistemological division of science from ideology, as we have seen, corresponded to a difference, also, of socio-historical location and dynamic. In Foucault's later work, this refusal of an epistemological science/ideology distinction eventuates in a displacement of questions of truth and falsity in favour of questions as to the institutional field over which a given discursive apparatus assigns power and control. There is no longer 'truth', but rather 'regimes of truth' which are at the same time apparatuses of power, so close is the relation between power and knowledge as Foucault now sees them.[6]

Foucault works to uncover 'genealogies' of the specific disciplines of the human sciences, locating them in the emergence of institutional practices such as incarceration, imprisonment and confinement, and representing them as inseparable aspects of strategies of surveillance and control. The tendency of scientific knowledge is oppressive in its exclusion and suppression of the plurality of alternative discourses – those of the insane, the imprisoned, the dreamer or the poet.

It is easy to see how these aspects of Foucault's work are complementary to the aims of the New Philosophers. Marxism, expecially in its Althusserian form, is not hard to represent as the Master science, with its field of institutional operation the Party apparatuses and the bureaucratic states of Eastern Europe: a nightmare fulfillment of the Enlightenment project of a predictive and explanatory science of 'Man', leading with implacable logic to the Gulag, the concentration camp society. But, as Peter Dews has shown,[7] there are major obstacles to this easy assimilation of Foucault's work. The teleology of the inference from the Marxist theoretical project as such to its realisation in 'the Gulag' is quite out of keeping with the particularity and contingency implicit in Foucault's approach to his genealogies. In their focus on the state as the site *par excellence* of concentrated power, the New Philosophers seem again at variance with Foucault, who disperses power to the micro-structure of individual bodies and personal interactions. Here, however, there is a certain complicity, in that both conceptions of power are incompatible with any overarching political project of liberation through political transformation. Either this is wholly impracticable, because of the irreducible particularity and diversity of centres of resistance to a correspondingly diverse and localised dispersion of power, or it must lead to a new and indifferently oppressive consolidation of the institutional ordering of power.

In their use of the supposed relationship of power and knowledge as a weapon against Marxism, the New Philosophers concede both too much and not enough to their adversary. They concede too much by implicitly recognising Marxism's achievement of the Enlightenment project of a 'science of Man', which renders human relations predictable and controllable: for it to function as an intellectual technology of power as their moral critique supposes, then Marxism must have already redeemed its cognitive promises. In the West, at least, few contemporary Marxists would share this confidence. But the New Philosophy also concedes too little to Marxism, in that its extrapolation and generalisation of an oppressive and totalitarian side of Marxist theory and practice overlooks another side of its historical 'balance-sheet'. It fails to recognise the diversity of ways in which Asian peasants, Western industrial workers, oppressed racial minorities in all parts of the world, liberation movements against imperialism and others have been able to make use of the ideas of the Marxist tradition as a call to resistance against oppression, and as a source of strategic and tactical guidance. Set against this, it is true, is what now appears to be a systematic inability on the part of Marxism either to establish and sustain genuinely libertarian and democratic post-revolutionary societies, or to adequately come to terms intellectually with this reality.

That this failure is not a historical contingency, that it is a failure in a tradition which the tradition has no resources to correct, that it is, in short, inscribed in the very project of Marxism, and even in the whole intellectual culture of the West seems to be a conclusion with some current fashionability. It is even, I think, an understandable response to the grotesque ideological and political paradoxes of our time. It is, however, a conclusion which, I hope to show, is both unwarranted, and far more problematic than the problems it affects to solve. For myself, the arguments of the New Philosophers are too slipshod, too contradictory, too lacking in a sense of historical and intellectual specificity to carry rational conviction against the rationality they reject, and the irrationalist moral grounds upon which they stand have a historical balance-sheet which is certainly no less bloody and oppressive than the one they attribute to 'Western Rationality' and its Marxist culmination.

Epistemology and relativism

None of this is to deny that the New Philosophers and their allies have identified fundamental moral and political problems which must be confronted by the Marxist tradition. Nor is it to deny that they have, so to speak, given a name to real intellectual weaknesses in Marxist, and especially structural Marxist theory. I shall later return to a more general consideration of some of these problems, but for the moment I want to focus on one argumentative theme which is quite decisive in generating the radical philosophical scepticisms of the New Philosophers and some other 'post-structuralist' writers (such as Derrida and Foucault, especially). This argumentative theme is the marginalisation or 'displacement' of questions of truth and falsity, of cognitive evaluation, in the consideration of theoretical discourses and statements. This displacement is itself a step which facilitates a further move to the rejection or abandonment of objective knowledge as a legitimate intellectual pursuit, to the much proclaimed 'abandonment of epistemological discourse'. In place of cognitive evaluation, the appropriate questions to pose of any discourse are the questions of the social or historical conditions of its emergence, the institutional power it serves, and the exclusions of the 'right to speak' which it effects. This decisive shift, then, is a movement away from interpretation and evaluation of discourses in terms of the relationship between their concepts and the objects to which they refer, in the direction of the relationship between discourses and their constituting values and interests, and the moral evaluation of their institutional–political effects. The end point of this shift in prescribed modes of evaluation and criticism is often a thoroughgoing cognitive relativism or agnosticism. This *need* not be the end-point, of course. It is a quite defensible tactic to assert the logical independence of moral or political evaluations from cognitive, or epistemological ones, but for reasons which should become clearer, many post-structuralist and post- Althusserian writers have been unwilling or unable to avoid the pressure towards conventionalism and relativism.

Any Marxism which claims to be an objective science (and this, of course, includes Althusser's Marxism) has to confront the arguments which sustain this drift to relativism. As we have seen, the problem is an especially acute one for Althusser in that both structuralism and historical epistemology, when they are rendered self-consistent, generate pressure towards relativism. In Chapter 1, I tried to show why this is so in the case of Bachelard's historical epistemology. In the case of structuralism, the decentring of the subject as bestower of meaning, as well as the exclusion of the function of reference from the theory of linguistic meaning cut off the two most obvious ways of 'fixing' meaning or validating knowledge. Meaning and knowledge can no longer be 'anchored' either in the indubitable 'presence to itself' of the human subject, or in the extra-discursive referents of linguistic signs. All that is left is a radical interiority of language as a system of mutually defining differences. Knowledge as a relation between a 'knowing subject' and its external reality becomes simple unthinkable.

This pressure towards epistemological relativism or agnosticism is present in Althusser's work itself, and it issues from his structuralist and conventionalist borrowings. As we saw in Chapter 2, when these borrowings are combined with the requirement to defend a version of historical materialism as objective knowledge, tensions are set up which are not ultimately resolved, despite the systematic later self-criticism. As I suggested in Chapter 2,[8] the key site at which this central tension emerges is in Althusser's distinction and opposition between a 'real object' external to and independent of thought, and an internal, conceptually constituted 'object of knowledge'. The requirement, for the possibility of objective knowledge, of a determinable correspondence of these irreducibly separate and incommensurable 'objects' is at the root of all of Althusser's uncomfortable shifts of position on the question of the distinction between science and ideology. I also suggested in Chapter 2 that this tension in Althusser's position could be resolved only by an abandonment of the real object/object of knowledge distinction, but that this abandonment could take one or other of two opposed forms. Either it could take a realist, or materialist direction, upholding the idea of theory as potentially a source of knowledge about a reality independent of the mind, or it could take a conventionalist and relativist direction which could sustain the idea of the constitution and historical transformation of thought-objects, but not their capacity to refer to a world independent of thought. Almost universally, Althusser's one-time followers have taken this relativist and conventionalist route out of Althusser's epistemological dilemma. This is probably because they have supposed, wrongly, I think, that to take the realist route would be to return to the 'terrain' of already abandoned empiricist and humanist conceptions of knowledge.

In the apparent paradox, then, that structural Marxism attempts perhaps the most uncompromising defence of Marxism as an objective science yet attempted, and yet does so in terms of theoretical traditions radically inimical to the idea of an objective knowledge, is to be found the explanation of the fact that Althusser's most radically relativist and irrationalist opponents were to be found amongst the number of his former followers. To set out in more detail why this should be so, and what is at stake in this argument, I shall turn again to an examination of the more recent work of Althusser's former leading followers in Britain, the work of Barry Hindess, Paul Hirst and their associates. Unlike many of their French colleagues, these writers have tended to remain committed to some form or other of socialist politics, to which they now see orthodox Marxist theory as an obstacle (perhaps the long-lamented absence of an authentic British Marxism has been a blessing in disguise?). Nevertheless, in their opposition to 'epistemological discourse', and to the idea of 'knowledge in politics' and in their commitment to political values as determinants of theoretical perspectives they generally replicate much of the work of their French counterparts.

We have seen how,[9] in their *Pre-Capitalist Modes of Production*, Hindess and Hirst embarked on an intellectual project already specified in Balibar's essay, only to produce in their final chapters the critical refutation of their starting-point. The initial focus of this critique was the problem of theorising historical transition. But this problem, it soon emerged, was premised on the defective concepts of mode of production and structural causality which had been right at the centre of their own, and Balibar's theoretical project. These developments were the starting point of a trajectory which led through critiques of the concepts of ideology, of political class struggle, of 'relative autonomy', of reproduction, of mode of production and others, into a critique of the rationalist epistemology which supposedly underlies them. This critique of rationalist epistemology was integrated into a critique of epistemology as such and in general. As we shall see, this critique is so radical in its implications that it swallows up the specificity of the critiques of the other concepts and arguments of Althusserian Marxism, and issues in a wholesale abandonment of the view of theoretical work, whether in history or in any other field, as providing knowledge of a reality beyond itself. Hindess and Hirst do, of course, attempt to provide an alternative account of theoretical work and its relation to politics which purports to do without this cognitive dimension but I shall argue that this conception is fundamentally flawed.

The critique of epistemology and its implications[10]

Since the central argumentative strategy in all this is the critique of epistemology, I shall begin with an exposition and some criticism of it. The critique of epistemology is presented differently in different texts, and often formulated in an extremely sloppy way. The following is my attempt to present the argument in its most defensible form. First, the Althusserian critique of empiricism is generalised to cover all forms of epistemological discourse. This latter is characterised as governed by the problematic of a subject – object structure. A distinction is made, in epistemological discourse, between a knowing subject and the object of its knowledge. But, for the subject to possess knowledge, the distinction must be complemented by a correlation: the knowledge 'reflects' or 'expresses' its external object. How is this correlation effected? Epistemological discourse leaves open two possibilities here. In the first, there is some form of direct or privileged access to the real which is somehow accorded to the knowing subject (the model for this form of knowledge would be self-knowledge, as in Descartes' '*cogito*', or, where the subject is a collective one, in Lukács' identical subject/object of history). This option can easily be demolished, it seems: it supposes a miraculous 'pre-established harmony' between the object of knowledge and the knowing subject, such that the latter has essential cognitive capacities (recognition, experience, and so on) and the former exists in a form such that it is available to these cognitive capacities of the subject.

Alternatively, epistemological discourse may accept that the representation of the external object cannot be achieved without *means* of representation. But in this case, how do we establish that what is represented by these discursive means really is the external object? How, in other words, is the existence of a correlation between subject and object to be established? Allowing the impossibility of a direct access to the real, this variant of epistemological discourse has to concede that the establishment of a correlation between discourse and reality has to be effected through the intervention of some other discourse or level of discourse: one discourse has to serve as the 'standard' or 'measure' of the correspondence to reality achieved by other discourses. For empiricism the level of discourse which is privileged in this way is that of the 'observation' or 'sense-datum' statements that are the supposed evidential basis of theories. For rationalism, a set of abstract concepts (the categories and forms of intuition in Kant, for example) or forms of argument (Descartes' 'four rules') guarantee the correspondence to reality of discourse generated according to it.

For Hindess and Hirst it is this privileging of one form or level of discourse which constitutes the central objection to epistemology, since it next has to be asked, what is the rational justification for assigning privilege? Epistemologies, it seems, have three possible responses: resort back to some form of 'pre-established harmony' or 'direct access' theory at least for the privileged levels of discourse; simply effect a dogmatic closure of debate, treating the privileged level as an unquestionable bedrock; or, thirdly, attempt a scientific theory of the knowledge relation. The first two responses are objectionable on the grounds of their dogmatism, and the way they 'close' discourse within fixed boundaries, whilst the third epistemological strategy (some approaches to a cognitive psychology, the sociology of knowledge, and Althusser's own 'theory of theoretical practice' would be examples) fails on account of its circularity: the correspondence of scientific discourse to its object is what has to be proved, whilst the method of proof presupposes this, at least in its own case.

The critique of rationalism, as a specific form of epistemological discourse, is pursued more vigorously in these texts than is the critique of empiricism. This is partly because the critique of empiricism is already taken as established within Althusserianism, and partly because the object of the argument is to include structural Marxism itself within the terms of the critique of epistemology by representing it as an example of rationalism. The basis for this case can already be found in the discussion of Balibar, and in the method of concept construction and validation adopted at the beginning of *Pre-Capitalist Modes of Production*.[11] Here, the basic concepts and propositions of historical materialism are treated as 'privileged' both in the sense that they are the source of the conceptual problems and means of their solution within historical materialism, and in the sense that particular concepts in this discourse may be validated or otherwise only by reference to these basic concepts. This clearly is an instance of a 'dogmatic closure' of discourse.

But this rationalism has other serious ill-effects. Since it is dogmatically supposed that the 'basic concepts' are linked to their external objects through some unexplained pre-established harmony which guarantees that discourse generated according to their protocols *really is* an 'appropriation of the real in thought', it follows, Hindess and Hirst argue, that the forms of thought must determine the order of connections in the real: the logical relations of inclusion and exclusion between concepts determine what is and is not possible in reality. Although this form of presentation of the argument is typical, it seems that what is being objected to is not so much the 'rationalist' assumption of a 'determining' role of thought in relation to reality (in another part of their argument Hindess and Hirst present it as a *strength* of Althusser's theory of ideology that it allows for this), but rather that it leads to an effective collapse of the order of the real into the order of theoretical discourse. Rationalist epistemology cannot, in the end, *sustain* the recognition of reality as independent and autonomous, though it necessarily *presupposes* it.

Several elements of the Althusserian project of a science of history appear susceptible to this argument. Hindess and Hirst endorse the argument advanced by Badiou and others that, disclaimers notwithstanding, the theory of modes of production projected in Balibar's essay is in effect a structuralist philosophy of history in that the concepts of the particular modes of production are already 'given' in the general concept of mode of production, as the possible forms of combination of its invariant elements.[12] This is indeed a fair criticism of the intellectual project with which Hindess and Hirst begin *Pre-Capitalist Modes*, but, as we have seen, the essays of Althusser and Balibar themselves are much more ambiguous and contradictory. At a lower level of generality, the concept of a mode of production as a unity of levels governed by structural causality is also held to be rationalist in its epistemological assumptions, since the necessity and form of the reproduction of the relations of production is supposedly derivable from their concept. The unthinkability of transition and the commitment to modes of production as 'Spinozistic eternities', is, as we have seen, a supposed consequence of this rationalism.[13]

The critique of epistemology as such, as distinct from its specifically rationalist forms, has a further bearing on several of the other key concepts of Althusserian Marxism. Hirst's critique of Althusser's concept of ideology,[14] for example, makes decisive use of it. Althusser's concept of ideology as representation of the lived relations between a subject and its conditions of existence avoids the dichotomy between true and false consciousness typical of pre-Althusserian Marxist theories of ideology. But Althusser's functionalist theory of ideology requires its re-introduction at one remove in the form of the necessarily *imaginary* relation of subjects to their conditions of existence: the ideological interpellation of subjects serves the reproductive requirements of the system only if subjects live their subjection *as if it were* freedom and self-determination. And again, in the theory of the ISAs, the unity of these is a functional unity given by the ideology of the ruling class. The only foundation for this unity, Hirst argues, is in supposed class interests which can be 'read off' from the relations of production.

In both areas of the theory of ideology, Althusser requires a conception of ideology such that what is represented in it exists independently of its representation in ideology, and a way of demonstrating that this representation is a *mis*representation. The subject – object structure of epistemological discourse is clearly still present even in Althusser's later work on ideology, and may be subjected to essentially the same form of critique. Either the *means of representation* are given some determining role in relation to what is represented, or they are not. If they are not (as in the case of 'class interests' given in advance by the economy) then the position reduces immediately to a form of simple economic determinism. If, on the other hand (and this is clearly Althusser's *objective*) 'means of representation' are to be given some determining role, so that the notion of ideology as a *relatively autonomous practice* can be sustained, then the insoluble question of the correspondence or non-correspondence of the represented to the means of representation is posed once again. In Althusser's case this problem is resolved dogmatically by the rationalist imposition of functional necessities onto the mechanism of interpellation. For Hirst, the only route out of this theoretical impasse is the abandonment, in the theory of ideology as in epistemology, of the very conception of discursive forms as 'representing'/'misrepresenting' independently existing realities.

But in the case of the concept of ideology this epistemological argument is supplemented with an ontological one:

> Ideology is not illusory for the reason we've given before; it's not illusion, it's not falsity, because how can something which has effects be false? It may derive from forms of the imaginary but it is not false. It would be like saying a black pudding is false, or a steam roller is false.[15]

Althusser is here commended for establishing, through the idea of ideology as a practice located in the relations and rituals of the ISAs, the social *reality* of ideology: it is not 'mere' mystification and illusion in the minds of agents. Another way of making the same point is to say that ideology has effects: anything which has effects must be real. We then have an ontological claim about the possible predicates of candidates for the title 'real'. The paradigms here (steam rollers and black puddings) are undoubtedly real and un-questionably have effects, characteristics they share with ideology. Of course, being real, and having effects, black puddings and steam rollers cannot be either true or false. Likewise, ideology being real and having effects, may not be true or false. I have done my best to make this argument seem plausible – I fear I may have failed. One

might usefully reflect that ideologies, though real and having effects, cannot be eaten nor driven.

Structural Marxist political theory is a further field of application
of the critique of epistemology. Again, parties, and other organisations are held to 'represent' classes, class fractions and so on. Either
the means of political representation affect what is represented or
they do not. If they do not, then the position is that of simple
economism: politics 'reflects' or 'expresses' without modification
interests which are constituted at the economic level. To sustain the
Althusserian thesis of the relative autonomy of the political, it is
necessary to concede that what is represented (that is, class interests) are actually constituted in and through the means of representation. It follows that the relationship between classes as categories
of economic agents and the various organisations which are present
on the political stage cannot be one of representation by the latter of
'interests' already constituted by the former. The relation between
them is, rather, one of 'necessary non-correspondence'.[16] This
leaves the political analyst free to identify political forces at work in
a conjuncture without the requirement to 'sociologistically' or
'economistically' reduce their specificity to social or economic
classes.

Finally, a variant form of the critique of epistemology is used to
demolish the whole enterprise of a scientific study of history.[17]
History, it is argued, must always take its object, 'the past', as given,
whereas the past, by definition, no longer exists. All that exists are
'preserved records and documents'. Historical practice treats these
'representations' as its means of access to the concrete reality of the
historical past, but this past is by its nature inaccessible. All that is
possible is the interpretation of preserved records. It is these which
constitute the object of history, the particular modes of writing
history providing so many ways of constituting and reading these
records as 'texts'. Marxist history could hope to be no more than one
such reading among the rest. Since Marxist history would then share
with other ways of writing history their central misconception that
they have a 'given' object ('real history', 'the past') it would, like
them, be susceptible to the established Althusserian critique of all
philosophies of history: 'Marxism, as a theoretical and a political
practice, gains nothing from its association with historical writing
and historical research. The study of history is not only scientifically
but also politically valueless.'[18]

The main purpose of this extended exposition of what has now become a widely accepted 'post-Althusserian' critique of epistemology is to show just how corrosive it is, not just of the Althusserian project, but of an immense range of intellectual activity, including the other traditions of Marxist work and the disciplines to which they relate. It is hardly an exaggeration to say that Althusserian Marxism includes an implicit or explicit critique of every other form of intellectual work. The epistemological critique of Althusserianism, far from *restoring* the status of those other forms of intellectual work, simply extends the critique to include Althusserian Marxism itself. It remains seriously problematic whether any form of intellectual work (not excluding the subsequent work of Hindess and Hirst) whatsoever could escape the strictures entailed in this critique.

A defence of epistemology[19]

My response to this critique of epistemological discourse and its associated alternative conception of the relation between theory and politics will have five main elements. These are:

1. Although it is true that sustaining the idea of discourse as referring to or 'representing' some reality independent of discourse does involve various forms of 'privileging' of specific discursive items, levels or forms, these forms of privileging characteristically do not operate in the way Hindess and Hirst suggest. Moreover, they do not operate in the way Hindess and Hirst require if they are to sustain their claim that such 'privileging' is necessarily dogmatic and/or circular.
2. I shall argue that the idea of discourse as referring to realities outside itself, as 'representational', can also be advocated consistently with *both* the main elements of Althusser's critique of empiricism *and* the idea of the 'constitutive' role of means of representation.
3. I shall argue that social practices in general, and discursive practices in particular, presuppose the achievement of reference to more or less enduring extra-discursive realities. Since Hindess and Hirst are at least committed to the existence of discursive practices, then they are also committed, whether they recognise

it or not, to the existence of reference to extra-discursive realities.

4. I shall argue that the arguments used at various points in the Hindess and Hirst critique of epistemology commit them to both rationalism and cognitive agnosticism. Not only are these positions mutually inconsistent, but both are also dogmatic on their own conception of dogmatism.

5. Their moral and/or political relativisation of forms of discourse not only deprives moral or political practice of the possibility of being genuinely informed by intellectual work, but also relativises moral and political outlooks themselves in a way that is dogmatic in a rather different sense.

In this set of arguments, those included under sub-headings 1. and 2. are mainly deployed to show that Hindess and Hirst's arguments are not sufficient to secure their conclusions. In my view, my expository outline of the costs for intellectual work of the success of their arguments amounts in itself as a *prima facie* case for the rejection of their conclusions, in the absence of quite decisive arguments in their favour. Nevertheless the main burden of elements 3. to 5. is to show that the alternative position adopted by Hindess and Hirst is entirely untenable in its own terms.

Discourse, privilege and dogmatism

I accept as decisive the Hindess and Hirst case against both 'direct access' (usually empiricist) and 'necessary correspondence' (usually rationalist) ways of attempting to secure thought to its extra-discursive referants. I recognise, in other words, that any attempt to defend the idea of the 'representative' or externally-referring character of discourse must assign some constituting role in the process of representation to the means of representation themselves. This is, indeed, a thesis common not only to French conventionalist and historical epistemology, but is now widely accepted in most contemporary philosophies of science. In some places,[20] Hindess and Hirst seem to think this is enough of itself to erode the idea of discourse as representational. For the idea of discourse as representational to be applicable, there would have to be a clear distinction between what is represented and what does the representing, but since it is admitted that the objects of discourse are (at least partially) constituted by discourse, the relation between them cannot be one of representation. But this argument is quite spurious since it confuses the role of 'discursive means' in constituting the *process* of representation with that of constituting its *object*, and so begs the question. For example, the linguistic and conceptual practices ('discursive means') of seventeenth century mechanics may be said to have played a constituting role in the formation of the *concept* of inertia, but it doesn't at all follow from this that they constituted inertia itself. This could only be made to follow if there were further, supplementary arguments to show that the reality of inertia were somehow dependent on our having a physical science sufficiently advanced to conceptualise it.

But are Hindess and Hirst right, at least, in their claim that maintaining the referential, representational character of discourse necessarily involves some form of privileging of at least some forms or levels of discourse in a dogmatic way? Let us suppose that any cognitive claim must take a discursive form, say, be expressed in a statement. Any challenge to, or attempt to criticise that cognitive claim must also take a discursive or statement form. Now, the maker of the cognitive claim may either adopt an agnostic stance in relation to such statements, or accept them as tending to confirm or disconfirm the original claim. In this very limited sense, then, it is true that avoidance of pervasive cognitive agnosticism necessarily involves making decisions to accept or reject rival propositions – that is, 'privileging' some against others. But for their argument to be effective, Hindess and Hirst need more than this. They need to be able to show that such privileging is always implicitly based on some ultimate court of appeal in a single form or 'level' of discourse, and is 'ultimately immune from further evaluation'.[21] But the cognitive claims and counter-claims which we make in everyday life involve appeals to evidence, considerations, arguments and so on which need not be and usually aren't systematised beyond the conceptually and chronologically localised practical contexts in which they are made. 'I know its there because I saw it yesterday' is a cognitive claim which 'privileges' a certain evidential basis, but there is no necessary implicit commitment here to an ultimate court of appeal in visual sense-datum language. 'It', here, might be a jar of apricot jam which I'd mistaken for a jar of marmalade – I might be persuaded (tomorrow) to revise today's judgement that 'I'd seen the marmalade.' Nothing about this simple domestic scene makes me the least bit uncertain about the capacity of language to enable extra-discursive reference. After all, I did see *something*, and I now know what it was (I could be wrong again, of course).

But the main target of the critique of epistemological discourse is not everyday contexts, but scientific knowledge claims, and in scientific contexts there is, indeed, an attempt to systematise, codify, and even measure types and degrees of evidential support for porpositions. In some respects the classical epistemologies of rationalism and empiricism can be understood as attempts to generalise different aspects of these scientific systematisations into universal and ultimate foundations for all knowledge-claims. If it could be shown that the argumentative and critical procedures employed in scientific contexts could be effective only on condition that some such philosophical generalisation could be sustained, then, again, Hindess and Hirst's critique would be effective. There would, of course, be a certain air of paradox in having to regard those discursive practices which are usually distinguished from others in their systematically critical attention to, and regular revision of, their own knowledge-claims as also the most dogmatic. Fortunately, however, we don't have to embrace the paradox: the critical procedures of scientific work, though usually more systematic than those of everyday life, remain relatively localised both chronologically and in their disciplinary scope, and there is no requirement in scientific work for any judgment to be regarded as 'ultimately immune from further evaluation'.

Not only is the Hindess and Hirst lumping together of all types of application of critical standards under the single category 'privileging', very misleading, it also cuts off any worthwhile investigation of the implications of recognising the force of these different types of critical standards. There are, for example, amongst the critical standards used in everyday and scientific contexts, purely formal ones such as consistency. Such standards as these do not presuppose, dogmatically or otherwise, any privileged relation to 'the real', but are essential conditions for intelligible discourse. There is, too, an obvious difference between, as empiricism does, 'privileging' observation statements, and, as Althusser and Balibar are held to do (I've already tried to show that this criticism applies more readily to Hindess and Hirst's earlier work than it does to Althusser) 'privileging' the basic concepts of a particular scientific theory. The latter would, indeed, be a dogmatism, but the former would allow for a critical revision of all claims that were not identical with or reducible to observation statements. Sciences dominated by empiricist canons of enquiry do, after all, still manage to have conceptual revolutions!

Reference and description

As we have seen, the central difficulty in Althusser's theory of knowledge derives from his particular way of attempting to reconcile the 'conventionalist' commitment to the socially constructed or constituted character of knowledge, with the requirement that at least some knowledge-claims make an objective reference to a reality independent of mind. Now there is really nothing at all problematic in admitting that all theories have social and political conditions of possibility, whilst at the same time claiming that the questions of their truth or falsity and referential capacity can be settled independently of questions of their social conditions of origin. Althusser himself at some times appears to recognise this clearly enough.[22] But what makes it *difficult* for Althusser to consistently reconcile the possible objectivity and the necessarily socially-constituted character of knowledge is the *particular* philosophical heritage in terms of which he tries to pose the question, and most especially his distinction between internal and external objects of knowledge. Hindess and Hirst recognise this and, in effect, abandon the distinction in favour of exclusive reliance on internal objects.[23] A realist strategy is, however, both possible and defensible, so long as it is recognised that one and the same object may be known and/or referred to under many different, and sometimes incompatible descriptions. On this strategy at least some of the terms of our everyday and scientific discourses may be held to make reference to discourse-independent realities, and propositions constructed with those terms may be held to embody revisable knowledge-claims about them. No dogmatic or ultimate linkage of any discursive items with their external referents need be presupposed. My coming to realise that what I had previously referred to under the definite description 'the jar of marmalade' is better described as 'the jar of apricot jam', and the descriptive, argumentative and ostensive (showing, pointing, and so on) procedures that might be employed to persuade me, may be treated, for our purposes, as a model also for the grander processes of conceptual change and paradigm-shift[24] in science. Of course, the extra-discursive realities will not be everyday material objects like jars of jam (the example of 'inertia', which I used above illustrates this, too) and across scientific paradigm-shifts the difficulties of securing identity of reference through a radically changed conceptual scheme and set of explanatory procedures are much greater. There will, for example, be partial and overlapping continuities and discontinuities in the external referents of the terms of pre- and post-revolutionary theories. (Newtonian 'mass' has a different but *overlapping* extension from that of the new physics, Darwinian and pre-Darwinian concepts of species require different classifications of some organisms to be made, but also taxonomic groupings remain unchanged for a great many more), but from the standpoint of either, the rationale for the other can made out in terms of the prior and independent existence of a single world, of which the two theoretical systems provide competing descriptions.

Social practice, discursive practice and reference

But the argument for a realist strategy for understanding discursive practices can be made stronger than this. I think it can be plausibly argued that it is not only defensible, but indispensable. Such everyday practices as discovering one made a mistake about the marmalade, learning how to read or to listen to music, changing one's mind, persuading or being persuaded, all rely on the possibility of learning to apply new descriptions to things and processes previously described in different ways. Learning to recognise 'that noise' as 'a quartet by Bartok' or a 'tenor solo by John Coltrane' doesn't count as 'learning' at all unless the relevant indentities of external reference are presupposed. As Roy Bhaskar[25] has shown, comparable arguments can be made in relation to such scientific practices as scientific education, the application of scientific knowledge, scientific experiment, and scientific revolutions. This is an important further step in the argument: it suggests that not only is the realist philosophical assumption which Althusser inherits from the materialist philosophical tradition of Marxism compatible with recognising the social constitution of scientific knowledge, but the very intelligibility of scientific social practices depends on this realist assumption.

But since persuading, learning, changing one's mind, applying assumptions from one context to another, and so on, are embedded in such an immense diversity of social practices, it begins to look as though the realist perspective on cognitive discourse can be stated in a more general form. Quite generally, human social practices involve actors in performing calculations, acting on expectations, predicting and interpreting outcomes and other broadly cognitive performances. These practices of prediction, calculation and interpretation presuppose the existence of a broadly recognisable, re-identifiable, predictable and calculable natural and social context of action. It is not necessary that these practices 'work' all the time, but that they work most of the time is a necessary condition of social life, and, indeed, of biological life for human beings.

Now, if this is true quite generally of social practices, it is also true of specifically discursive practices (if, indeed, any case could be made out for regarding discursive practices as a delimitable sub-set of social practices in general). Since Hindess and Hirst are committed to the existence of discursive practices, if of nothing else, then they are also committed to their condition of possibility: successful reference to extra-discursive realities on the part of at least some discursive terms. There is even a partial recognition of this at one stage[26] in their argument, when they object that rationalist epistemology, in effect, cannot sustain a distinction between the order of discourse and the order of its objects. This, as we saw, was the basis of their argument against ideas such as structural causality and mode of production: a 'reality' is deduced from a concept. But, of course, if the Hindess and Hirst critique of epistemology is effective, then this counts for rather than against rationalism.

At this point, however, it might be argued against the realist strategy, as I have represented it, that it is itself susceptible to the Hindess and Hirst critique of rationalism (Hindess and Hirst themselves tend to treat realism as a form of empiricism)[27]: I may appear to be arguing deductively to the necessary existence of certain mind-indepedent features of the world. In fact, the strategy is rather different. It takes as its main premise the claim that social practices exist, and under descriptions which are intended to be uncontroversial. It then moves to conclusions about what the world *must* be like *if* it is to contain social practices. The main premise is contingent and so is the conclusion, *the relation between them* being a necessary one. The world *might* have been different, and so *might* not have been capable of social practices and human cognition.

Ontology and the abandonment of epistemology

If, as Hindess and Hirst propose, discourse is not to be rationally evaluated in terms of its adequacy or inadequacy to any extra-discursive referent, then either it must be rationally evaluated only by criteria of a purely formal kind, or rational evaluation must be wholly replaced by other modes of evaluation: aesthetic, moral or political standards, for example. On the first possibility, the Hindess and Hirst position turns out to be a form of rationalism. This is borne out by a good deal of their own critical activity which, while itself not generally logically consistent or conforming to particularly rigorous standards of proof, certainly faces other discourses with that requirement (see, for example, their critique of Marx's theory of value in *Marx's Capital and Capitalism Today*).[28] But this rationalism is inconsistent both with the rejection of epistemology as such, and also with the rationale for displacing questions of truth and falsity in the direction of moral or political evaluation of discourse. This rationale is a philosophical agnosticism, which is consistent with the rejection of epistemology, but gives rise to special problems in its own right!

The denial of epistemology, Hindess and Hirst argue, causes them 'no intellectual discomfort when we refrain from walking out of the top windows of high buildings'.[29] But should it? They are committed, they say, not to the *denial* of an extra-discursive reality, but to a denial 'that existence takes the form of objects representable in discourse'.[30] They are committed, in short, to a dualist ontology: on the one side, discourse, on the other, an external reality to which discourse has no access. It is this ontology which is the source of the principal arguments against Althusser, Marxism, and History which we have so far discussed: they are all premised on the knowability of the real by discursive means, whereas the real is unknowable. In what sense can this form of argument be less dogmatic than what it opposes? Why is the epistemological denial of the knowability of reality any less dogmatic than its epistemological affirmation?

Can there be knowledge in politics?

Central to Marxism has always been the question of the relationship of theory to transformative and emancipatory political practice. There have been many ways of posing and solving this problem. It is a crucial site of theoretical difficulties for Althusser himself. Hindess and Hirst, despite their abandonment of 'epistemological discourse', nevertheless continue to insist on the centrality of the link between theoretical discourse and politics. But the idea that political practice is guided by theoretically derived knowledge of its conditions and possible effects is dismissed: 'There can be no "knowledge" in political practice'.[31] Instead: 'Politics and political calculation generate problems for theory, and theoretical forms provide means, whose value is variable, for calculation.'[32] Apparently theory is now to be understood as the discursive elaboration of problems recognised initially in the course of political practice. This is the beginning of an answer to the problem of how criticism and debate is to occur in theoretical discourse if the cognitive dimension is abandoned: theoretical and cognitive standards of criticism are to be replaced by political ones. This is precisely what happens in *Marx's Capital and Capitalism Today*: 'Many of the central concepts and problems of *Capital*, far from constituting a point of departure, are actually *obstacles* to the new kinds of theoretical work socialists need to undertake if they are to come to terms with modern capitalism.'[33] There are two ways of reading this: either the concepts and problems of *Capital* are to be rejected because they misrepresent the character of modern Capitalism, and so obstruct socialist politics, or they are to be rejected simply because they do not conform to the requirements of an independently established practice of socialist politics. The former reading is ruled out for Hindess and Hirst if they are to remain consistent, so only the latter remains: first, engage in socialist politics, then use as a criterion of adequacy in theoretical discourse its pertinence to that practice. In short, the abandonment of epistemology leads from a supposedly dogmatic privileging of levels of discourse to the genuinely dogmatic privileging of a 'given' political practice.[34] As the *source* of theoretical problematisation, political positions and values cannot be the *object* of theoretical evaluation and consequent rational debate and persuasion. Ideological and political struggle can have no cognitive content. The theoretical discourse of the various political tendencies must be incommensurable and so talk at cross-purposes. Moral and political perspectives can never be educated or informed, but simply confront each other. This is the underlying dogmatism of all relativisms: rational debate between value-determined perspectives is impossible.[35] The alternatives? Abandon the struggle, or resort to coercion. For this, if for no other reason, autonomy of theory from the requirements of immediate political practice is of the first importance not just intellectually, but also politically.

'Representation' and relative autonomy

P. Q. Hirst's critiques of Althusserian theories of ideology and politics,[36] and especially of the notion of 'relative autonomy', as we have seen, raise serious and important problems for existing theoretical positions but, I shall argue, they dogmatically shut off the possibility of further theoretical work by imposing the terms of their agnostic epistemology. For example, Hirst's critique of Althusser's use of the concept of interpellation is extremely effective. He is able to show that the mechanism of interpellation has to pre-suppose what it is supposed to explain: the constitution of concrete individuals as subjects. The recognition of 'self' and 'others' in the dual mirror relationship *pre-supposes* a subject *capable* of this recognition. As we have already seen, the idea of interpellation faces other, connected difficulties: how and why is interpellation simultaneously the constitution of a subject *and* its subjection. What, exactly is the ontological status of the domain of the 'imaginary' within which the constitution of subjects occurs? How is the constitution of subjects also the constitution of *gendered* subjects? Hirst poses some, though not all, of these problems in an effective and provocative way, only to dissolve their specificity away in an epistemological critique of the whole conception of ideology as involving (mis)recognition and (mis)representation.

In Hirst's critiques of Althusser's theories both of ideology and politics, the argument takes the form of a claim that Marxism posits a relation, 'representation', holding between, on the one hand, social classes (or their 'interests') and, on the other, their representations in politics or in ideology. On this basis, the terms of the critique of epistemology (the denial that discourse can 'represent' the real) can be directly applied. Economic (or class) reductionist versions of Marxism in which politics or ideology appear as mere insubstantial epiphenomena, or 'surfaces' of the realities they represent, share the fate of 'direct access' forms of epistemology. More sophisticated Marxisms, however, like Althusser's, assert the specific reality, or 'relative autonomy' of politics and ideology *vis-à-vis* what they represent; they assign a positive, constituting role to the 'means of representation'. Again, what 'represents' cannot play a part in constituting the thing it represents, and so the attempt to 'save' historical materialism from its apparent exceptions by means of the idea of 'relative autonomy' must fail.

Obviously, this argument is dependent upon the validity of the analogy between the discourse–object relation and the politics (ideology)–class relation. This can be challenged in at least two ways. First, the 'relative autonomy' thesis does not necessarily reduce to a matter of assigning a 'constituting' role to political organisations. Poulantzas, for example, gives it a rather different meaning in terms of a disparity between the economic–corporate interests of a class and the requirements of its hegemonic dominance in the context of complex patterns of political alliance.[37] Secondly, the argument rests on a concealed ambiguity in the term 'representation'. Its use in the argument against epistemology (already metaphorical) gives it a sense close to 'depict' or 'refer', whereas political parties, for example, are not held by Marxist theory to represent in this sense, but in the sense of 'acting for' or 'on behalf of'. Ideologies may be said to 'represent' in either of these or still other senses. But since, in any case, the argument against epistemology has been shown to be ineffective, perhaps we need not pursue these dis-analogies? Unfortunately, the argument cannot be concluded so quickly, since in at least one respect, the dis-analogies are actually helpful to Hirst. The 'representative' character of political organisations is problematic in a way that the 'representational' character of cognitive discourse is not. To say that a political organisation is representative (or not representative) of a particular class assumes that the class may be identified independently of the organisation which represents it. Now, the 'constituting' role of the 'means of representation' (political discourse, political institutions, electoral procedures, and the like) is not, here, as it is in the epistemological argument, confined to constituting the form of representation (for example, a specific type of Party, or political programme). If it were, this, too, would be unproblematic. But the more sophisticated contemporary Marxisms, including Althusserian Marxism, also assign to political organisations and types of political intervention a constituting role *vis-à-vis* the *class they are held to represent.* This really does seem to undermine the basis for thinking of this relationship as one of any kind of representation at all.

But is this conclusion inescapable? Hirst himself argues that claims on behalf of parties that they represent classes can be interpreted in any of three ways. Either they are dogmatic derivations from theory, or they rest upon illicit definitions of 'class interests' as constituted at the economic level, in which case the position reduces to a simple economic determinism. The third possibility, adopted by Hirst himself, is that the claim is a very misleading political value-judgment.[38] But Hirst overlooks what is perhaps the most obvious interpretation. If 'representation' in this context has to do with acting for or on behalf of the represented, then theoretical content can be given to it in terms of the existence and type of democratic procedures linking categories of socio–economic agents with specific forms of political organisation. Categories of socio–economic agents can be specified independently of their forms of political representation in ways which are not at all inconsistent with the recognition that different systems and forms of political representation (for example, parliamentary democracy versus council democracy) play an effective role in constituting these agents as political agents, and also have effects in modifying and re-structuring the socio–economic categories.

In attempting, here, to preserve a broad strategy of Marxist interpretation of relationships between classes and political organisations against Hirst's variant of the critique of epistemology, I do not want to be taken as suggesting that this strategy is unproblematic. In this field, as in the theory of ideology, Hirst and other writers have identified major theoretical difficulties in Althusserian Marxism. My claim is, rather, that the dogmatism of the political relativisation of theory which is common to Hirst and his associates here, and many of the French 'post-structuralist' writers, shows itself in the way that their critical strategies effectively shut off attempts to solve theoretical difficulties *at the level of generality at which they arise.* Instead, each local difficulty becomes a symptom of a general crisis of theoretical 'Reason' itself.

9
Crusaders and Sociologists

The subjects of my last chapter were those critical rejections of Althusserian Marxism, and sometimes of Marxism itself, which had as their starting-point positions internal to Althusserianism or, at least, in other tendencies of thought which shared with it important common sources and assumptions. My concern in this chapter will be with a series of critical encounters which have come from other directions – intellectually and politically. Leszek Kolakowski was the author of a mainly philosophical critique of Althusser which appeared in the *Socialist Register* for 1971.[1] *New Left Review*, as well as publishing translations of Althusser's work from the later 1960s onwards, also published several important critical assessments, most notably those by Norman Geras, André Glucksmann, and Pierre Vilar.[2] These, together with Alex Callinicos' excellently clear and well-balanced study *Althusser's Marxism*[3] served to ensure that the reception of Althusser's work in Britain was not a matter of 'lying prostrate before the theorist(s) of our choice'.[4]

In the wake, however, of the internal 'decomposition' of Althusserian Marxism, the broad outlines of which I attempted to trace in my last chapter, there has emerged a more aggressive and self-confident, even, sometimes, spiteful and abusive spate of critical activity. Perhaps the most polemical of these recent attacks was an extended essay by one of Britain's most distinguished Marxist historians, E. P. Thompson. Thompson, himself a former member of the British Communist Party, is a veteran of successive attempts to conduct effective intellectual and political activity on the Left independent of both the CP and the British Labour Party. Thompson's departure from the Communist Party in the wake of the Soviet repression in Hungary in 1956, and the suppression of his own critical intellectual work by the British CP led to the formation of a left-wing periodical the *New Reasoner*, the forerunner of the *New Left Review*. Divisions over editorial policy here were the occasion for Thompson's departure in 1963, also the year in which his major historical work, *The Making of the English Working Class*,[5] appeared. He is at present perhaps best known as a powerful voice in favour of unilateral nuclear disarmament. An outstandingly gifted historian and an effective political polemicist, Thompson has rarely committed himself to work of sustained theoretical reflection. It was, indeed, rather late in the day (1978) when his onslaught on Althusser was finally delivered.[6] Perhaps, as he says, it was his final recognition that this 'weird apparition', this 'freak of intellectual fashion' would 'not for that reason go away'.[7] Perhaps, also, it was the ultimate absurdity of the Hindess and Hirst renunciation of the study of history as 'not only scientifically but also politically valueless'[8] that finally stung Thompson into action. But whatever it was that occasioned the timing of Thompson's assault, there is no mistaking its motivation: Althusser is the theoretical systematisation which Stalin lacked in his lifetime: 'It is only in our own time that Stalinism has been given its true rigorous and totally coherent theoretical expression. This is the Althusserian orrery ... So far from being a "post-Stalinist generation", the Althusserians ... are working hard, every day, on the theoretical production-line of Stalinist ideology.'[9] It is appropriate that Perry Anderson, editor of *New Left Review* since just before Thompson's departure and the object of an earlier critical piece by Thompson, should have taken on the task of replying to this outrageous and unhistorical abuse. I have already commented briefly on this question in my introductory chapter, and refer the interested reader to Anderson's work.[10]

As Thompson himself says, his essay 'is a polemical political intervention and not an academic exercise'.[11] The objective is not a critical encounter with the ideas of another intellectual, but a kind of warfare, an attempt to extirpate the enemy. It is a crusade to oust the infidel from the temples of Marxism:

> Althusser and his acolytes challenge, centrally, historical materialism itself. They do not offer to modify it but to displace it ... And if (as I suppose) Althusserian Marxism is not only an idealism, but has many of the attributes of a *theology*, then what is at issue, within the Marxist tradition, is the defence of reason itself.[12]

Perry Anderson's reply to Thompson is a measured, and often critical assessment of Althusser, as well as an extended commentary on E. P. Thompson's position in the light of his main historical writings.

Other, more welcome additions to the ever-growing bandwagon of critical work on Althusser and structural Marxism come from a quite different source. Sociology, and European sociology especially, is a discipline which has always taken Marx and Marxism seriously. Though its encounters have often been polemical and its image of Marx a caricature, there have also been scholars who, while standing outside the Marxist tradition, have nevertheless respected it enough to give it the sustained critical attention it deserved. In some ways, despite its weaknesses, structural Marxism has a sophistication which demands of the present generation of non-Marxist sociologists a renewal of their critical effort. In what follows I shall offer all too brief and schematic responses to the work of just two who have met this challenge, David Lockwood and Anthony Giddens.[13] In discussing their work, and that of Thompson, I shall consider arguments of a broadly theoretical kind only. In Chapter 1, I have attempted to show why I think attempts to discuss Althusser's work by reducing it to an ideological legitimation either of Stalinist politics, or the professional privilege of an academic élite, or both, are inadequate. The theoretical questions around which controversy has centred can be ordered as follows: 1. problems in Althusser's theory of theoretical practice, and his associated 'anti-empiricism'; 2. the concepts of structure and of agency and the associated problems of conceiving deliberate social change; and 3. the frequently alleged 'functionalism' of Althusser's theoretical position.

Experience, empiricism and historical methodology

In E. P. Thompson's critique, the first and second theoretical problems are linked through his re-assertion of the centrality of the concept of 'experience' both to historiography and to the constitution of the historical process itself. Althusser's 'structuralist' demotion of human agents to the status of mere bearers or supports of social structures amounts to a denial of the possibility that human actors may play a part in the making of history, but it also denies them a role in the making of the *understanding* of history. Actors become conscious of their conditions of social life through 'experience', so that Althusser's denial of the pertinence of experience in his theory of theoretical practice is a devaluation of the contribution to the theoretical understanding of history made by working people themselves. Althusser's critique of empiricism is therefore a covert consolidation of the division between mental and manual work, and of the privileges of an intellectual élite. In a complementary argumentative procedure, Thompson attempts to demonstrate that the abandonment of empirical means of validation in the writing of history itself leads to a rationalism in which theoretical concepts are self-validating and become a means of imposing a pre-conceived pattern on the flow of real events. Thompson follows Sartre in opposing this as a form of idealism, and goes on to link this aspect of Althusser's epistemology also to intellectual élitism and Stalinism.

I have tried to deal with what I consider to be the error of conducting critiques of intellectual positions on the basis of the supposed politics of their authors. In so far as there is any substance in Thompson's argument it has to be spelled out in theoretical terms. First, the use of the term 'experience'. As Perry Anderson points out in his critical discussion of Thompson's work, the term is used in several quite different ways by Thompson, and the distinctions make a significant difference for his argument. For our purposes it is necessary to distinguish three uses of the term. First, a philosophical use in which the 'experience' of the knowing subject is taken to be a theory-neutral arbiter in cases of competition between theories. I shall call this the 'raw intuition' concept of experience. Second, a concept of experience such as is at work in everyday practices of description of events witnessed. I shall call this the 'descriptive' concept of experience. Finally, there is a concept of 'experience' according to which someone with long-established participation in an activity requiring skill and learning may be said to be 'experienced', and so to have a certain basis for spkeaking with authority. I will call this the 'practical wisdom' concept of experience.

Now, Althusser's critique of empiricism, taken strictly, rejects 'experience' in the 'raw intuition' sense only. In this, as Kolakowski and other critics have pointed out, Althusser is doing no more than reiterate one element in a long-established conventionalist critique of empiricism. It is important to recognise that the implication of this critique is to refute *empiricist accounts* of the pertinence of experiential evidence to scientific work; it is *not* to deny that experiential evidence has any pertinence at all. The basis for the refutation of empiricism is the denial that 'raw intuition' can figure as evidence. For any item to figure as 'evidence' at all, its experiential content must be presentable in *propositional form*. Theories may confront evidence, but first the evidence must be stated. A 'raw intuition' can neither confirm nor refute a theory. Now E. P. Thompson, John Scott, Chris Pickvance, Leszek Kolakowski[14] and many other critics of Althusser concur on this point. Empiricism in *this* sense is rejected by all of them, yet each wants to maintain that some room remains for history and the other social sciences to be practised as *empirical* disciplines. Althusser's alleged rationalism appears to leave no such room, and to conflate the 'empirical' with the 'empiricist'.

Is there a basis for this criticism in Althusser's work? First, it needs to be said that Althusser has too frequently been read through the grids of his more rationalist followers. Thompson, for example, compliments Hindess and Hirst for having carried 'Althusserian logic to its own *reductio ad absurdam*, "History is condemned by the nature of its object to empiricism." '[15] *Reductio ad absurdam* it certainly is, but the absurdity results from the logic of Hindess and Hirst. That the passage he quotes comes from a *critique* of Althusser seems to have escaped Thompson's attention, so suitable is it to his intellectual purposes to believe otherwise. Notwithstanding the frequency of Althusser's castigation for 'rationalism', there is nothing in his texts which is incompatible with his granting a pertinence to experience, both in the shape of 'practical wisdom' and as 'descriptive experience', in the formation of scientific knowledge. For Althusser, theoretical practice is a work of transformation of raw materials by means of theoretical categories. These raw materials will include the theoretical categories which were the product of previous phases of theoretical work, but they also include 'practical' concepts and notions provided by other practices – such as political and ideological struggles. Althusser's anti-empiricist stipulation here is that these raw materials are themselves *already* 'generalities': that is to say, they already exist in conceptual or propositional form. Both 'descriptive experience' and 'practical wisdom' satisfy this requirement.

But this will not satisfy Althusser's critic. The point E. P. Thompson makes has to do with the nature of the operation described as 'transformation' in the account of theoretical practice. If the raw materials are transformed by the conceptual means of production, then this seems to imply an absolute cognitive authority of the theoretical problematic over the descriptive material and practical reflections which enter into the knowledge process as raw materials. If this really is an implication of Althusser, then the charges of idealism and intellectual élitism are well-founded. Here, it seems to me, we are returned to the unresolved tensions of Althusser's texts. On the one hand, it is quite true that Althusser more than once acknowledges a debt to the rationalist philosopher Spinoza, and that he never actually provides us with *either* an illustration *or* a general discussion of how empirical evidences may be pertinent to a revision of basic theoretical concepts. It is also true that Althusser's difficulty in reconciling realism and conventionalism is such that the notion of the independent existence of the object of knowledge has little more than gestural status.

On the other side of the balance, Althusser's account of theoretical practice does require that the theoretical problematic which operates as means of production in one phase of theoretical production is open to revision on the basis of that practice itself. This is present in the inclusion of 'Generalities III' (products) of previous theoretical work in the category 'Generalities II' (means of production) in future phases. Now, if the basic categories of a science are held to be subject to continuing revision at all, this is some distance from the philosophical rationalism sometimes attributed to Althusser. More significantly, what is entailed here is a concept of a transformative practice in which the means of transformation are also transformed. If we take the metaphor of 'production' seriously then it implies two things: first, that the form taken by the means of production has to embody a recognition of the character of the raw materials, and second, the form taken by the product will embody only such transformations as are allowed by the character of the raw materials, given existing means and conditions of production. In woodwork, for example, the design of tools has to take into account both the material character (the hardness, the porosity, the direction of the grain and so on) of the wood and the physical powers of the human agents who are to use the tools. Similarly, the range of products which can be made of wood will be conditioned by these same qualities of the material, the character of the tools, and the skills and know-how of the carpenter. If taken seriously, then, the metaphor of theory as 'production' involves *precisely* recognising the independent reality, and 'transformability only within limits', of the raw materials upon which it works.

To say, moving back to the analysis of theoretical practice, that experiential evidence and theoretical problematic are related as raw materials and means of production, is to concede that certain items of experiential evidence may turn out to be resistant to transformation in the directions required by the available theoretical problematic. Is this possibility compatible with Althusser's anti-empiricism? In my view it is. To deny that 'raw intuition' can figure in the validation or falsification of scientific theories is *not* to be committed to the thesis that there is complete elasticity in the propositional presentation of experience, or that different ways of describing the same event cannot be evaluated against one another. The famous experiments of the gestalt psychologists, which have been adduced by conventionalist philosophers of science such as Thomas Kuhn, are very effective in demonstrating the involvement of conceptually-derived expectations in perception. The diagram of a duck that may be seen as a rabbit, or the sets of playing cards in which 'spades' are coloured red, show this conceptual ordering of experience. They do not, however, show that a playing card may be indifferently described as a light bulb or even a black pudding. In fact, E. P. Thompson's very interesting and valuable description and classification of the ways in which 'discrete facts' are critically interrogated in historical research could well be integrated into an account of history as a 'theoretical practice' if Althusser is read in this realist way.

There are, however, several specific points in Thompson's alternative conception of the relationship between historical method and its object which are neither consistent with Althusser, nor defensible in themselves. The philosophical imperialism supposedly exercised over historical research by Althusser takes the form of demanding a rigour in the definition of concepts and a fixity in their meaning, which, Thompson argues, is quite out of keeping with the nature of the object of historical enquiry. First, the processes to which historical concepts are applied are in constant flux, and it follows that historical concepts must themselves change to keep pace with their referents. Second, historical concepts are derived by generalisations from many examples, and are brought to bear on evidence as 'expectations'. 'They do not impose a rule, but they hasten and facilitate the interrogation of the evidence, even though it is often found that each case departs, in this or that particular, from the rule.'[16] This necessary flexibility, or elasticity of historical concepts, Thompson claims, irritates philosophers for whom 'a rule is not a rule unless the evidence conforms to it'.[16]

To take the first objection first, both Simon Clarke[17] and E. P. Thompson concur in their condemnation of Althusser's use of trans-historical theoretical categories, and there are other arguments deployed by both of them which lead in the same direction: Althusser is incapable of explaining social change. Now, whether or not the *conclusion* of these arguments is true, the main premise is quite specious. Presumably no-one would wish to claim that *all* social change required conceptual change for its interpretation: a growth in the birth rate, a decline in the standard of living, a change of government, and so on, can all be registered in propositions without a change in the analytical categories employed in the propositions. What, however, is to be said of qualitatively new phenomena on the historical stage: the emergence of a new form of property ownership, of industrial production, of social, as distinct from political, revolution, and so on? Here, it seems that for the actors involved, and for the historians of the period, new categories have to be invented to capture a changing reality. This much is true, but it does not in any way affect the crucial point that to register such changes, certain concepts must remain unchanged: recognising a new form of property ownership requires the general concept of property of which it can be recognised as a new instance. Similarly with the other examples. Of course, the new instance may indicate an imprecision or suggest a correction in the established general concept. In this respect, though, there is no difference in principle between this situation and that in any other science where a phenomenon is newly discovered (it may have *been* there all along, waiting to be found) which renders problematic existing classifications.

On E. P. Thompson's second point, the supposedly necessary elasticity of historical concepts, founders his whole case against Althusser's 'rationalism'. It is essential to that aspect of Thompson's critique that historical concepts should be susceptible to revision or rejection in the face of empirical evidence. But it is only if such concepts are clearly and rigorously defined that conformity or otherwise to them on the part of evidence can be even detected, let alone ignored. The requirement of clarity and rigour in theoretical concept construction is not a foible peculiar to Stalinist philosophers and sociologists, but is an essential condition of serious, substantive intellectual work. Theoretico–political polemics aside, of course, Thompson is as aware as anyone else of this. There is, however, another, independent reason why Thompson thinks there must necessarily be an 'openness' in the expectations derived from historical concepts, and I shall return to this in a moment.

In general, my argument has been that Althusser's critics have been right to argue against rationalist or wholly conventionalist conceptions of theoretical practice, and right, too, in seeking to make room for a conception of the social sciences as *empirical* disciplines, which is, at the same time, not an *empiricist* conception. Where they have, in my view, been mistaken is in supposing that Althusser's work is unequivocally rationalist, and that there is no basis for a development of the idea of theoretical practice in a realist direction. In the work of Thompson, especially, the overriding intention to theoretically and politically devastate Althusserianism obstructs any fruitful intellectual encounter of this kind.

Structure, process and agency

Turning now to E. P. Thompson's criticism of Althusser's devaluation of the role of 'experience' in the historical process itself, this is clearly linked to a range of overlapping problems concerned with conscious agency and the structural conditions of action. For Thompson, despite Althusser's denials, his position is a structuralist one, and, as such, incapable of grasping history as 'process'. This latter concept is a central one for E. P. Thompson. Althusser's structuralism is incompatible with it:

History as process, as open-ended and indeterminate eventuation – but not for that reason devoid of rational *logic* or of determining *pressures* – in which categories are defined in particular contexts but are continuously undergoing historical redefinition, and whose structure is not pre-given but protean, continually changing in form and in articulation – all this (which may be said to constitute far more truly 'the most profound characteristic of the Marxist dialectic') must be denied.[18]

History as 'process' has to give a central place to human agency, and as such must have an element of indeterminacy about it. There is a 'logic' of process, and the actions of historical actors are subject to 'shaping and directing pressures': human agents are both the makers of history and are made by it: they are 'the ever-baffled and ever-resurgent agents of an un-mastered history'.[19]

In excluding human agents from the process of history, and representing them as mere 'bearers' of complex 'structures in dominance' Althusser renders himself incapable of conceptualising historical process at all. This is so for two reasons. First, however complex their combination, the variables of Althusserian theory 'maintain their original fixity as categories'.[20] They are categories of 'stasis' even when set in motion as moving parts. Second, what motion is conceivable is motion within the limits of a pre-given structure. In short, Althusserian structuralism, however complex, is capable of thinking of historical change only in the form of a metaphor with *mechanical* motion, within set boundary conditions. This is a conception into which Marx himself retreated, and is to be found in the *Grundrisse*, a text in which Marx works out the dynamics of capitalism in the form of an auto-development of its basic structures. The contemporary retreat of Marxists such as Althusser into a static structuralism is rooted in the immobilism of cold-war confrontation. Thompson's version of historical materialism, however, struggles to overcome this stasis, and its conceptual source is in texts such as the *Communist Manifesto* and the *German Ideology* which articulate the required conception of history as process, and give a central place to human agency in the making of history.

In his commentary, Perry Anderson attempts both a conceptual clarification and an historical relativisation of the issues at stake between Thompson and Althusser.[21] Both, he says, operate with universal philosophical concepts of agency, each of which articulates opposed meanings of the term in everyday speech. Sometimes we speak of 'free agents' as the spontaneous source of their own actions and initiatives, but also we may speak of 'agents' as the instruments of an external force (as in 'foreign agent'). What Althusser's philosophical and structuralist adoption of the latter conception achieves is an inability to conceive historical change as the consciously willed outcome of a social movement: if Socialism is to be possible at all it must be brought about 'behind the backs' of those whose struggle brings it about, and they must continue to live their history as 'subjects' in the element of imaginary misrecognition. But, by contrast, what Thompson's obverse philosophical schema commits him to is a reading back into history of the specificity of modern social movements. For Anderson, the Marxist conception of human agents as entering into relations 'independently of their will' is generally true of historical periods prior to the emergence of the modern proletariat, when individuals were usually the victims of circumstance, and classes were not self-conscious and active forces in history. It is to this historical past that Althusser's structural determinism is more appropriate.

But it seems to me that, clarificatory though it is, Anderson's commentary does not take us far enough. It is not simply a matter of adjusting the proportions of agency and structure to account adequately for the conditions of different historical periods, but, as Anderson partly recognises, the duality of 'agency' and 'structure' itself has to be questioned.[22] To begin with the concept of agency, two questionable assumptions are made by Thompson and other critics of Althusser. First, that historical change, if it is to be explained at all, has to be explained in terms of voluntary agency, and connectedly, that all agency is, or is reducible to individual human agency. The first assumption is, of course, challenged by Althusser himself, in the notion of history as a 'process without a subject'. Overdetermined structural contradictions may 'fuse' to bring about revolutionary change, according to Althusser's earlier work, whilst in the later work the 'motor of history' is class struggle. In both cases the analogy is with mechanical motion and therefore unacceptable to Thompson. The key *explicit* objection here is that mechanical action can only be conceived as occurring within fixed boundary conditions. But Thompson mentions in passing, only to off-handedly reject, the impact of evolutionary biology on the Marxism of the Second International. There are indeed several historical sciences such as evolutionary biology and geology, as well as developmental sciences such as embryology, in which the methodological problems of structural transformations and the emergence of qualitatively new forms have had to be posed *without benefit of voluntary agency or any analogue of it*. I am not, of course, arguing that these sciences contain ready-made solutions to comparable problems in the human sciences, but the mere existence of such explanatory strategies in other sciences is enough to show that qualitative change, change which transforms its 'boundary conditions', is thinkable in other historical sciences which have no place for teleology or voluntary human agency. It was indeed this methodological implication of Darwinist biology which attracted both Marx and Engels to it.

On the second assumption, that all agency is, or is reducible to individual human agency, Thompson's discussion contains a critical commentary on Engels' famous treatment of the problem of the relationship between individual motivation and historical outcomes.[23] Historical outcomes need not, Thompson argues, be seen as the unintended consequence of the clash of individual wills. If, instead, we suppose that individuals share common conditions of existence, then we may expect their experience of these conditions to issue in a *collective* response to them, and historical outcomes will be the outcomes of the clash of collective wills – of *class* conflicts. But if classes can be collective agents, in this sense, then how are we to understand the relationships between individual agency and class action? And if classes can, under certain circumstances, be active in history, why not other forms of association – political parties, pressure groups, voluntary associations of various kinds, unions, firms, state apparatuses, armies and so on? Of course, Thompson would not deny the pertinence of these questions, but they take us a long way from the centrality of conscious human agency in history. Unions, parties, firms, and so on, certainly operate as historical forces – they may be said to make decisions, act or not act on them, form alliances and so on. But the decisions and actions of these bodies are not the actions or decisions of their individual members, and are not generally reducible to such decisions. The eventual course of action may be one neither willed nor foreseen by any individual member. In many cases, actions and decisions of collective agents are ones which *could* not even be made by individuals (a decision by the Bank of England to devalue the pound, of a firm to go into liquidation, or of a party to field candidates in an election, are 'decisions' which could be made by no person, but only by a collective actor, politically or legally constituted). Again, Thompson is far too good an historian to be unaware of the importance of unintended consequences. His notion of 'ever-baffled and ever-resurgent agents of an unmastered history' captures this beautifully, but it does not avoid the problem that much of the work of history is done 'behind the backs' of human agents.

Now to the concept of 'agency' itself. Thompson's opposition to fixity and precision of historical concepts, and his insistence on the character of historical process as indeterminate, though 'shaped' by determinate 'pressures', is rooted in a notion of human agency as a source of indeterminate initiatives: external structures exert determinate 'pressures', but the interpretation of these pressures and the action which results occurs in a realm of free play allowed by external conditions. These conditions thus 'shape' and 'exert pressure', whilst not wholly determining action. But, since human agency is, for Thompson, the immediate source of all historical change, it follows that he, no less than Althusser, is incapable of explaining historical change. An indeterminate event is one whose explanation is beyond the reach of causal explanation.

It is precisely the unsatisfactory character of this philosophical conception of human subjectivity and agency that motivates structuralist approaches to explanation in the human sciences, but in general, where structuralism leaves intact this philosophical conception of subjectivity and intentional action, simply 'decentring' it, theoretical difficulties re-emerge. In Althusser's case, these difficulties take the form of a retention of subjectivity as an 'imaginary' relation which nevertheless has effects, and of agency as mere fulfilment of functional requirements of the social system. So long as the opposition between structure and agency governs theorising about historical causality, the extremes of structural fatalism and vacuous voluntarism can be avoided only by arbitrary combinations of the two.

The beginnings of a way out of this impasse can, I think, be established through a recognition of three methodological principles in the use of structural explanation. First, the widely held assumption that structural determinants of action are external to the actor has to be questioned. Psychoanalysis is one intellectual tradition in which psychic life is itself understood to be structured in such a way that the conscious life associated with intentional action and subjectivity is subject to unconscious determinations which are nevertheless internal to the individual psyche. The notion of unconscious determination of conscious life provides theoretical space for a conception of human actors as more than mere 'bearers' of external structures, without resort to the essentially theological notion of action as an 'uncaused cause'. Second, the widespread assumption that structural conditions of action are *constraints* on action should be questioned. Rules of grammar and semantical rules, for example, certainly impose a discipline on the speaker, as structuralists have shown. But to speak of such structures as constraints is highly misleading, since, beyond a certain limit, to assert one's will against constraints like these is not to gain freedom of speech, but to lose the power to speak intelligibly at all. Certain structural features of social and psychic life, then, should be seen not as 'constraints', but as facilitating conditions, or conditions of possibility of action. When this is recognised, the identification of structural explanation with fatalism is hard to sustain. Thirdly, explanation in terms of structures is not the same thing as explanations in terms of *immutable* structures. Any more or less enduring pattern of relationships between agents (which may be individual persons, parties, associations, and so on) or between agents and objects may be thought of as constituting a 'structure'. Relationships may confer causal powers on the agents which they relate and they may effect constraints on their behaviour in various ways. The susceptibility of relationships to deliberate dissolution or transformation by agents is similarly immensely variable – from the delicacy of the bonds constituting a friendship to the immense resilience of the relations constituting a mode of economic production.

Marxism and the utilitarian concept of action

I have so far suggested that a broadly 'structuralist' strategy for explaining both social action and historical change, which makes no use of any indeterminist philosophical category of human agency, is defensible from the kind of attack mounted by E. P. Thompson. But even if this is granted, it is still a long way from a Marxism in which revolutionary class action could be conceived as a deliberate and fully conscious act of self-emancipation. Disputes over the role of intellectuals and vanguard parties aside, it has been a characteristic feature of all traditional Marxisms to represent this as, at least, a historical possibility. More than this, Marxists have usually recognised a requirement to explain, in terms of the dynamics and historical tendencies of capitalist societies, the mechanisms which generate revolutionary class action. Within Althusser's own work, and in the work of structural Marxism, more generally, there is a clearly detectable shift away from the initial postulation of mechanisms of historical change (the 'fusion' of overdetermined contradictions) which give no essential place to the mediation of impersonal social forces through the consciousness of historical actors. In Althusser's own later emphasis on class struggle as the 'motor of history' as well as in Poulantzas' later attempt to distinguish the structural determination of social classes from the political positions adopted by them in conjunctural class struggles, we can detect attempts to come to terms with the problems posed by such a view of history for any emancipatory political strategy which purports to be genuinely democratic.

Unfortunately, however, the opening up of a 'space' between structural determination and conjunctural action introduces an untheorisable indeterminacy into the explanatory framework, which is precisely analogous in its effects to Thompson's retention of an indeterminist philosophical conception of agency. In an important and challenging critical discussion of Marxist attempts to theorise the possibility of revolutionary class action (and its failure so far to materialise) in terms of systemic properties of capitalist societies, David Lockwood[24] focusses on this alternation between 'positivist' determinism and 'idealist' voluntarism. This instability of explanatory strategies is argued to be a general characteristic of Marxism, and it, together with other more specific failings in the class theories of Poulantzas, Erik O. Wright and others, is taken to be symptomatic of a fundamental flaw in the Marxist conception of action. Lockwood's view is that this conception, despite some limited modifications, remains essentially utalitarian. This residual utilitarianism is a fundamental obstacle in the way of the integration into Marxism of a recognition of normative and value-related constraints upon action. Though Marxists have often recognised at an empirical level the significance of the phenomena of status, citizenship, and incorporation, their insights have remained vague, *ad hoc* and often contradictory. This is not just a contingent feature of Marxist work, but inseparable from the fundamental features of the Marxist conception of action.

The utilitarian conception of rational action consists in the application to actions of a means–ends schema of interpretation, in which 'ends' are taken to be randomly distributed and 'given'. Action is interpreted as the outcome of a choice in which the agent selects the most efficient and, in this sense, 'rational', means of achieving his or her 'given' ends. Lockwood recognises that this conception of action had already been modified in one respect in the tradition of classical political economy upon which Marx draws: the ends of action are now treated not as ultimate variables, but as themselves the result of social determinants. Marx adds two more modifications. First, there is an asymmetry between the rationality displayed by capitalists and workers, in that the means–ends egoism of the utilitarian concept of action is retained for the former,[25] but significantly qualified in the case of the latter. The ends ('immediate interests') imposed on workers by their location in the economic system are subject to what Lockwood calls an 'end-shift' towards the adoption of objectives which presuppose the abolition of the very system which produces the ends (higher wages, shorter working week) characterised as 'immediate interests'. Workers, then, must be supposed to be able to move from forms of action which adopt efficient means for securing immediate interests towards forms of action which adopt efficient means for securing their fundamental interest in socialism. This, in turn, presupposes that they are capable of a second-order exercise of 'reason', on the basis of which utilitarian 'rational' action in pursuit of immediate ends can be seen as self-defeating. This is the second departure from the original utilitarian scheme.

Now, despite these departures, Lockwood argues that Marx's conception of action still shares with utilitarian action theory one important feature: neither can give due weight to the possibility that actors' choice of actions may be normatively constrained by ultimate values, and that the ends of action might be integrated through a common value system. This has serious consequences for Marxist attempts to explain the failure, in the advanced capitalist societies, of the predicted 'end-shift' to occur. The characteristic Marxist explanations here conform to the utilitarian model in that they represent departures from 'rational' action as essentially cognitively induced 'irrationalities'. Departures from rational action have to be explained as a result of misapprehension of pertinent facts of the situation of the action, or as a failure to appreciate which of the available means is really the most efficient. Typically, Marxist theories of ideology attempt to identify systematic sources of limitation, distortion and falsity of working-class consciousness as the basis of the supposedly 'irrational' action of the working class. Only in the face of the increasingly obvious weaknesses of these accounts have Marxists started to appeal to wider, and not specifically cognitive, cultural forms to explain working-class incorporation. Gramsci's work is mentioned favourably in this context. But such appeals are not susceptible to stable or systematic integration into Marxist theory because they rely on a conception of action as normatively governed by ultimate values, in a way incompatible with the residual utilitarianism of the Marxist theory of action. Here, Lockwood draws upon the Parsonian distinction between 'irrational' and 'non-rational' action, arguing that the latter can, whereas the former cannot, sustain explanations of working-class incorporation in terms of a status order through which actions are normatively integrated.

As I shall be arguing in my concluding chapter, I agree that it is a fundamental error in the principal traditions of Marxist work that they represent the main sources of both attachment and opposition to the prevailing social order as cognitive. David Lockwood's argument goes a long way to displaying the source of this error in the Marxist theory of action. But to be effective against the whole Marxist explanatory strategy, as distinct from the work of many of its principal exponents to date (a large enough claim, indeed!), Lockwood has to be able to show that there is a radical incompatibility, or, at the very least, no prospect of a theoretical linkage, between the means–ends schema of action which is certainly an essential feature of Marx's treatment of the action of individual capitalists, and the rather different kinds of action-explanation required in accounting for both working-class incorporation and its potential for revolutionary action. It is this further step which, I think, is not licensed by Lockwood's argument. For him, the Marxist explanatory strategies are vitiated by their failure to distinguish 'irrational' from 'non-rational' action. But to insist on this distinction is, in my view, still to concede too much to the utilitarian position. In particular, it doesn't put into question the appropriation by that tradition and its descendants (including, in this respect, Max Weber) of the concept of 'rationality' to designate and 'privilege' one normative constraint (cost/benefit 'efficiency') against all others. From this standpoint, the broad category of 'non-rational' action, as defined by Lockwood can be seen to *include*, as a special case, both 'rational' and 'irrational' action in the utilitarian sense (i.e. both types of action are normatively governed).

Not only does this show that both types of action-explanation *can* be linked within a single theoretical system, but, more importantly, it shows a way of avoiding a serious weakness in Lockwood's commitment to the irrational–non-rational typology of action. This weakness is that cognitive and normative conditions of and constraints on action are, for him, not simply analytically distinct, but are further separated out as the basis of a typology of action. Such a typology is obstructive of any theoretical recognition of the means–ends rationality of capitalists as anything more than an instrumental adaptation to system-produced ends (profit-taking). That 'efficiency' as a standard governing action may be more than a cognitive recognition of external constraints on action, but might itself come to be felt as an 'ultimate' value, may have few, if any, implications for Marx's theory of the system-effects of capitalists' action, but it certainly is pertinent to explanation at the level of social integration and what Lockwood calls the status order. Conversely, the sentimental and moral attachments of workers to non-revolutionary trades union practices, traditions and goals are interwoven with a conceptual ordering of social reality and a commitment to specific beliefs about its nature and prospects which are indisputably cognitive in character.

If this is right, then attempts, such as Gramsci's, to develop a theory of ideology which recognises the inseparable interweaving of cognitive, sentimental and moral aspects of social action are not incompatible with the conception of action required for theorising the system-consequences of the rationality of capitalist class-actors. It is true that, as Lockwood points out, this has the effect of making the concept of ideology a heterogeneous 'rag-bag' category, but it is hard to see how Lockwood can avoid the counter-charge in relation to his own favoured term, 'status'. Moreover, the capacity of this theoretical strategy to retain an important place in the explanation of class action for the cognitive capacities and achievements of actors, does at least suggest a possible way of making intelligible links between system properties, on the one hand, and social action on the other. This, after all, is an objective which Lockwood shares with the Marxist tradition: 'the problem is rather to understand how action is jointly determined by both realistic and normative elements, and particularly by the way in which changes in these elements are mutually interdependent'.[26]

But, it should be noted, what I have so far offered is a very minimal defence of the possibility of the Marxist explanatory strategy. What further can be done in support of the more substan-

tive claims by Marxists to be able to detect in the historical tendencies of the capitalist system a mechanism which generates, mediate-
ly or immediately, the 'end-shift' of the working class towards
revolutionary objectives? Lockwood's argument here seems to be
that, although Marxism's recognition of the possibility of an 'end-
shift' of any sort is a departure from the utilitarian conception of
action, which takes ends as 'given', the currently dominant traditions in Marxism remain committed to viewing the proletarian
'end-shift' in ways which are still residually utilitarian. Erik
Wright's way of defining class interests as 'hypotheses about the
objectives of struggles which would occur if the actors in the
struggle had a scientifically correct understanding of their
situations'[27] is a particularly transparent example of this. Features
of especially the early work of Poulantzas commit him to a comparable notion of an 'objective' or 'fundamental' interest in Socialism
on the part of the working class. I have argued elsewhere[28] that it is a
mistake to suppose that interests can be assigned in this way
independently of any consideration of the actual normative – and
value – commitments of actors, but this is not the only difficulty for
Wright and others who share his theoretical device. The further
difficulty is that the 'gap' between the commitment of workers to
their 'immediate interests' and any future commitment to revolutionary objectives has to be seen as spanned by (a) a cognitive
rectification which is (b) in some sense already inscribed as an
objective tendency of the capitalist system. The foregoing discussion shows the first assumption to be defective, but note, in a way
that *Marx's* conception of the proletarian 'end-shift' is not. There is
nothing in the Marxist conception of action which precludes thinking about this 'end-shift' as the outcome of ideological and political
struggles in which workers and their organisations may (or may not)
succumb to prevailing forms of normative integration. The second
assumption, it seems to me, is not logically absurd, but empirically
highly unlikely to turn out to be true. In so far as Wright and
Poulantzas (in some of his work) do theorise the relationship
between the objective position and class action of the working class
in ways which render this assumption unproblematic, Lockwood
provides an effective argument against them.

The outcome of this argument, it seems to me, is that Marxism
may well be able to identify ways in which system-properties of
capitalist societies present inbuilt obstacles to stable normative

integration, or 'incorporation', of their subordinate classes. What it cannot do, however, is show that these system-properties generate universal tendencies towards the adoption of revolutionary consciousness on the part of the working class, less still that revolutionary class action will generally, or ever, be effective in bringing about socialist transition. The adoption by the whole, or a large part, of the working class of the advanced capitalist societies of socialist objectives must be seen as a problematic and contingent possible outcome of ideological and political struggles. Whether this more modest revision of the explanatory and predictive claims sometimes made on behalf of classical Marxism does or does not constitute a tacit abandonment of Marxism is a question I leave to others of a more taxonomic cast of mind.

Functionalism, historical change and class struggle

Finally, I shall turn to what has become the most widespread of all the critical weapons used against Althusser – the charge of 'functionalism'.[29] This term, like the term 'positivism' has been so commonly used as a term of abuse that it has ceased to convey a precise theoretical meaning so a brief definition is in order. A functionalist social theory, I shall assume, is one which specifies a number of general prerequisites for the existence of any form of society whatsoever (there must, for example, be means of ensuring that the subsistence needs of the population are in general met, that sexual and procreative activity is regulated, that means exist for integrating subjective motivation with the requirements of the division of labour, and so on). The approach to the typology of social forms or the analysis of the institutional framework of particular societies then takes the form of a specification of the various ways in which these general prerequisites are met in particular cases. Functionalism is susceptible of a good deal of flexibility beyond this minimum stipulation, moreover, and is capable of recognising institutions without functions, institutions with multiple functions, and institutions which obstruct the fulfilment of functional requirements ('dysfunction'). Crucially important for the whole approach is the (broadly structuralist) thesis that the forms of understanding under which actors participate in institutional activity may rationalise it in ways which have nothing to do with its 'latent function'.

There is a great deal in Althusser which conforms to this characterisation of functionalism. First, the thesis of the omni-historical
necessity of ideology is only intelligible as the consequence of an
assumed universal functional requirement that human individuals
be constituted as 'subjects' who are 'subjected' to the requirements
of the social division of labour. The Althusserian conception of the
state, to, can be seen as functionalist in this sense. The state
apparatuses are assigned the function of reproducing the relations
of production: that is to say, they operate to fulfil functional
requirements established at the economic level. Poulantzas' earlier
conception of the state as operating to secure the cohesion of the
social formation is similarly functionalist. Finally, Althusser's conception of the role of the ideological state apparatuses in the
reproduction of the relations of production shares with Parsons'
functionalism a failure to distinguish 'system' and 'social'
integration.[30] Althusser's theory of interpellation of subjects
through participation in the functions of the ISAs is a theory of the
constitution and distribution of subjects who will be the *bearers* of
relations. It is not a theory of the reproduction of the relations
themselves. Indeed, convincing arguments[31] have been presented to
the effect that Marxists have tended to greatly overestimate the
extent to which social reproduction under capitalism relies on the
consent of compliant 'subjects'. Economic constraints are themselves generally effective in securing compliance, irrespective of
ideological dispositions. But even if this were not true, Althusser's
conception of the determining character of the structures *vis-à-vis*
their 'supports' is such that a theory of the reproduction and
distribution of 'supports' is a long way from a theory of the
reproduction of what it is they support.

I shall briefly mention four significant objections to these areas of
correspondence between Althusserian Marxism and the functionalist paradigms of sociology and anthropology. Whilst broadly en-
dorsing these objections, I shall try to show that important aspects
of the relevant explanatory strategies remain defensible. First, the
required relationship between the properties of social systems and
actors' conscious apprehension of those systems sets up serious
problems not just from a moral or political point of view, but also
from the standpoint of theorising the connections between action
and system. As Anthony Giddens argues, the parallel here with
Parsons's sociological functionalism is very close: 'each reaches a

position in which subject is controlled by object. Parsons's actors are cultural dopes, but Althusser's agents are structural dopes of an even more stunning mediocrity.'[32]

Secondly, functionalist explanations are objectionable in that they embody what might be called a 'systems teleology: a supposed functional requirement is held to call into existence the institutional complex (a state, ideological apparatus, or whatever) which satisfies the requirement. In the case of Althusser, the decentring of the individual subject is achieved at the apparent cost of a re-emergence of conscious agency, or its analogue, at the level of the social system itself. I have argued elsewhere that there is, indeed, a tendency towards a functionalism of this sort in Althusser. However, a good deal in the 'reproduction' approach to the state and ideology can, in my view, be sustained without it. It seems to me to be perfectly legitimate to ask, either at the level of society as such, or at the level of specific sets of social or economic relations, 'what are their conditions of possibility?' As Hindess and Hirst correctly argue, the specification of, say, capitalist production relations, necessarily involves specification also of those conditions which have to be satisfied if capitalist relations are to persist.

In a parallel argument against functionalist explanations in Marxism, Anthony Giddens seems prepared to accept the legitimacy of such questions, so long as they are presented as counterfactuals ('What would have to be the case for social system x to come about, persist or be transformed?').[33] But if we can genuinely establish answers to such conditional statements, there is no logical reason why we should confine inferences from them to purely counterfactual situations. To use Giddens' own example, 'in order to exist in a relatively stable form, the capitalist economy has to maintain a certain overall level of profit':[34] if this proposition does genuinely state a necessary condition of stability in the capitalist economy, then it is perfectly legitimate to infer the existence of the required level of profit, on the basis of a confirmed empirical instance of a stable capitalist economy. More generally, given that in a particular society capitalist relations do exist and do so relatively stably over a long period of historical time, it follows that their conditions of existence must be more or less stably satisfied by *some* social mechanism or other. Now, the attempt to identify and classify the institutions and practices (for example, the state apparatuses) in terms of the *effects* they happen to have on the reproduction of the conditions of existence of economic practices is, again, quite legitimate given these assumptions. Whether or not this is still a type of functionalist explanation is a debatable matter, but it is not functionalist in the sense defined above, and, in particular, it could not be argued against this type of analysis that it explains the existence (either the coming into being or the maintenance in being) of institutions in terms of their effects in satisfying the conditions of existence of other social institutions or relations: that is, no appeal to a systems-teleology is involved. There is, in other words, a legitimate place for analysis of the systemic interconnections between institutions and institutional complexes, so long as this analysis is not confused with the quite separate task of analysing the specific historical processes through which such institutional complexes and systemic interconnections are formed and transformed.

The third argument against the 'functionalism' of structural Marxism is closely related. Even if one could accept the functionalist assumption that the existence of a functional requirement calls into existence its satisfaction, this still falls short of an explanation of how it is that 'answers' to functional needs are distributed among institutional complexes in the way that in fact are. Even granted a 'need' for a 'factor of cohesion' in the social formation, for example, why should the satisfaction of this need fall to the state, in particular? Here again a separation of questions about the systemic effects of institutional complexes and questions about the conditions of their emergence is sufficient to offset this objection, though it does pose other problems for Marxist theory. In particular, if these questions are separated for analytical purposes they must at some stage be connected up again. The cost of not doing so would be to make the existence of societies as more or less enduring systemic unities a product of untheorisable fortuitous circumstances. The functionalist conflation of questions of genesis with questions of system integration, as we have seen, leads to the opposite problem that societies are interpreted as eternally self-reproducing. This, indeed, is the fourth major criticism of functionalism, that it renders social change untheorisable.

Althusser's own attempt at avoiding both these two extreme positions is the introduction, rather late in the day, of the idea of class struggle as the 'motor' of history. Quite apart from any intrinsic difficulties with this idea, how is it to be integrated into the rest of the theoretical framework? One difficulty, already noticed, is that the concept of ideological interpellation leaves no room for oppositional forms of subjectivity, and conflates ideology with ruling ideology. A second area of difficulty concerns the conceptualisation of relationships between the structural determination and the effectivity of class struggles. If, for example, the functional account of the role of state apparatuses in the reproduction of the relations of production is to be reconciled with the classical Marxist conception of the state as a machine of class domination, even in its qualified Althusserian form, then we must suppose a necessary correlation between the formation and implementation of political strategy on the part of the ruling class, and the fulfilment of the functional requirements of the relations of production which sustain its dominance.

There are two very important and highly questionable assumptions here. One is that the ruling class is possessed of adequate knowledge of its interests and of how to secure them. The second is that, short of social revolution, the oppositional struggles of the working class (and other subordinate classes) are *wholly* ineffective in obstructing the realisation of ruling-class objectives in the state. The second assumption, at least, has to be rejected if a conception of class struggle as an *effective* practice is to be sustained at all. And if this assumption is rejected, then the classical Marxist conception of the state as a machine of class domination has to be modified, and with it the necessary correspondence between ruling-class interests and the system-effects of the state. The conception advanced by Poulantzas in a later text, of state institutions as a 'condensate'[35] of the given balance of power between social classes captures this well. But then, the function of the state in securing the 'cohesion' of the social formation can only be performed at a price to the class interests of the ruling class. Non-Marxists as widely separated as T. H. Marshall[36] and Margaret Thatcher have recognised that state recognition of union rights, welfare provision and like measures to secure the incorporation of working-class opposition, may at the same time impede capital accumulation.

It seems, then, that Althusser's attempt to avoid the functionalist conception of societies as necessarily self-reproducing unities, through the introduction of the idea of class struggle, implies a more radical revision of the original theoretical schema than Althusser envisaged. Nevertheless, if carried far enough, the revision is a promising one. It does not conflate questions about the systemic *effects* of institutions with questions about their genesis, but it allows for theoretical and empirical investigation of their connections. The achievement of political and social institutional forms through which the reproductive requirements of capitalist relations can be met, is not a magical result of the teleology of the system, nor is it a purely contingent and fortuitous happening. It is, instead, the uncertain, uneven, qualified and contradictory outcome of struggles between opposed social and political forces. In these struggles, neither side is *guaranteed* success, and neither side has a God-given perception of its interests and how to secure them. That, however, either side even partially achieves its objectives is a testimony to the real cognitive content of the ideologies through which these social conflicts are fought. However partial and distorting these ideologies are, they must necessarily have a degree of correspondence to the practical requirements of struggle. In this, E. P. Thompson is certainly vindicated against both Althusser and Hindess and Hirst.

10

Instead of a Conclusion

Like many other socialists of my generation, my own ideas and political activities have been influenced over the last decade and a half by the ideas and arguments presented in this book, sometimes beneficially, sometimes in ways that I now regret. So much a part of everyday life have they become that, when I was approached with the idea of writing this book it seemed that it would be an easy thing to do. In fact, it has been one of the most difficult things I've ever attempted, and has turned into a kind of settling of accounts with my own intellectual and political biography. I have, in the course of the book, argued for views I never knew I held, seen problems in ways that had never occurred to me before (realising, at the same time, that others had *always* seen them this way!) and engaged in arguments whose implications are still beyond my grasp. This chapter, then, is a kind of provisional staging-post, not a conclusion. I want to indicate in a brief, and not especially rigorous way, how I now see some of the themes and debates I've described and engaged with in my earlier chapters.

As to the question of Marxism, considered as a vehicle for intellectual work in the human sciences, I am aware of a range of serious intellectual challenges to each of its major contemporary versions. These challenges, as well as difficulties generated by Marxists themselves as they have tried to develop their paradigm, have made me more circumspect than I used to be in my use of the word 'science', and I now think that the prospects for intellectual work within the space defined by Marxism have to be viewed far more modestly than in the heady days of the early 1970s. Nonetheless, I see no *other* intellectual tradition with a comparable scope in the human sciences or with a comparable richness of resources, and none of the challenges so far offered to Marxism seem to me to be fatal.

Whilst there are, it is true, immense difficulties to face in the form of precise theoretical specification and detailed historical research, the broad outlines of the Marxist perspective seem to me to be indispensable: the fundamental importance of economic relations and practices for the form taken by other social processes, the insistence on the specificity of each historical form of social existence, the understanding of political processes in terms of patterns of socio–economic antagonism, the analysis of the state as a relation of political domination also to be understood in these broad socio–economic terms, and, above all, a tendency to seek generalising and fundamental explanations of particular fields of empirical phenomena. On the other hand, these programmatic features are all consistent with theoretical weaknesses which have been both cognitively and politically disastrous. The fundamental importance of class relations to our understanding of political struggle can, and has, led to a refusal of the specificity and irreducibility of other forms of emancipatory struggle: the struggles for the emancipation of women, and against the oppression of ethnic and national minorities and of homosexuals, for example. Other issues, such as disarmament and the ecological crisis cannot be simple reduced to questions of class. They affect the whole of human kind. But the economic and class 'reductionisms' which have sustained these failures of theory and practice are not 'written into' the Marxist intellectual programme. On the contrary, a critical and creative use of the resources of the Marxist tradition seems to me to offer the best prospect for positive advances in these fields.

To turn, now, to the case of Althusser and his followers, the position is still more complex and ambiguous. I don't propose to repeat the specific arguments of the book, but instead to look at the implications of Althusser's answers to one specific question: 'What is Marxist philosophy?' Althusser's answers were all governed by a single central assumption: that Marxism had to be defended as a science. This meant that a whole historical tradition of speculative philosophy of history, and its associated developments in political and moral philosophy that had considered itself to be Marxist, had to be rejected. The consequence was a drastic narrowing of philosophical work to a concern with epistemological 'servicing' of Marxist historical 'science'.

As is well known, the problematic character of Althusser's attempts to advance this epistemological requirement, by combining 'conventionalist' borrowings from structuralism and historical epistemology with elements drawn from Marxism's legacy of materialist philosophical foundation, made his work vulnerable to objections to it at the epistemological level (such as, for example, the critical work of E. P. Thompson and Barry Hindess and Paul Hirst). But perhaps more serious are the effects of this epistemological failure at the level of substantive theoretical work. As I have suggested already, one of the great strengths of the Marxist tradition is its commitment to generalising and deepening its explanatory power. The source of this is in the materialist heritage in Marxist philosophy, which involves commitment to a conception of the ultimate, if not immediate unity of the sciences both of nature and of human history. This philosophical commitment persistently calls into question the fixity and pertinence of disciplinary boundaries. It seeks more fundamental and inclusive explanations of the relatively discrete and homogeneous fields dealt with by the particular social science disciplines. None of these disciplines – political science, sociology, economics, history, psychology, archaeology, anthropology, linguistics and so on – can, for a materialist Marxism, be seen as having more than a provisional autonomy and self-sufficiency.

The materialist tradition is also committed to seeing in the human species *both* a distinctive capacity for culture and a distinctive form of historicity *and* a kinship with other living organisms. The human species, though a special case, is nevertheless part of the order of nature. This perspective is absolutely essential if integral, interdisciplinary work is to be developed in such fields as human ecology and the constitution of gender relations. Other theoretical problems to which I have alluded in the course of earlier chapters also require, I think, a comparably interdisciplinary approach. The conceptualising of social reproduction which gives structural Marxism so much difficulty is a case in point. It is quite right, of course, to point out that social reproduction cannot be reduced to biological reproduction, but, equally, social reproduction cannot adequately be conceptualised in abstraction from biological reproduction. The reproduction of social relations also has its conditions of possibility in the external organic and inorganic environment of the species: a central theme of Marx's early work which is marginal to the point of exclusion in structural Marxism. In the attempt to theorise the social constitution of subjectivity, too, it seems to me that the objections to which Althusser's theory of ideology are open (especially the concept of interpellation) are irresolvable without a grounding of the theory in a broadly biological conception of the human individual and its basic tendencies, capacities and developmental processes.

The work of Althusser is not only no help in dealing with these questions, but it is actually obstructive even to their being posed. To a considerable extent, I think this is a result of the operation of conventionalist protocols for theory building and criticism. In their most extreme form in Althusser, these protocols assert the 'spontaneous' capacity of each field of discourse to generate its own, autonomous forms of proof and criteria of validity: maths, for example, doesn't have to wait for physics to prove its theorems. Taken seriously, this entails a commitment to the absolute conceptual autonomy and mutual incommensurability of theoretical disciplines, which is radically incompatible with the kind of interdisciplinary programmes I've just sketched.

But the materialist philosophical tradition carries its own inherent dangers – the danger of a banal and often reactionary reduction of the specificity of human social and historical life to the biological. The predecessors of today's sociobiologists were diverse currents of social Darwinism in the later decades of the nineteenth century, and the outlines of a non-reductionist, but still materialist, critique of them can be excavated from the works written by Marx, Engels and Bebel at the time. I have attempted some of this work of excavation and continuation as have others, such as Hilary and Steven Rose, in this country, and such writers as Timpanaro and Gerratana in Italy.

If we cannot agree with Althusser, then, in his narrowing of the field of philosophy to epistemology, or in his specific epistemological theories, it does at least seem that work in the philosophy of science, defending the materialist project of a non-reductionist unity of the sciences, is both viable and important. Whether, in the end, Marxism can be defended as a science is a question that no longer seems to me to be resolvable one way or the other. I certainly think it is appropriate for workers in the human sciences to work with a model of their enterprise which commits them to the highest standards of rigour that are obtainable, that commits them to specifically cognitive objectives, and which allows for the development of conceptual and methodological links with other sciences, especially the life-sciences. On the other hand, if the model of 'science' to which the appeal is made includes commitment to the levels of quantification, precision of theoretical language, predictive adequacy and standards of verification which have been achieved in the contemporary physical sciences, then the exercise can only be stultifying, empty and scholastic.

But still, this partial and qualified defence of the cognitive claims of classical Marxism will ring alarm-bells in some quarters. What does it imply for the classic questions of the relation of theory to practice, and of intellectuals to party and class? The writings of classical Marxism have given rise to two broad traditions for thinking about these questions. On the one hand, there is a view of intellectual activity on the Left which organically links it to 'spontaneous' popular cultural forms of resistance. Theory may elaborate, render consistent, and deepen the available cultural means of resistance and opposition, but always from a position *within* the cultural space already occupied by popular oppositional movements. We may refer, loosely, to this tradition as having a view of theory as 'critique'. The main alternative to this has been to take seriously, as both Althusser and the 'orthodox' Leninist tradition of Marxism have done, the cognitive claims of Marxism. If Marxist intellectual work is to be conducted as a specific cognitive, even 'scientific' discipline, then it is to be expected that it will develop its own technical concepts and language, and maintain, at the level of its most fundamental propositions, a growing distance from the thought and language of everyday life and 'common sense'.

The objections to the 'orthodox' tradition are well rehearsed: the theory which is supposed to carry the emancipatory potential of the popular movement has to be provided from outside. The institutional vehicle of this 'introduction' of theory to the masses, the 'vanguard' party has proved to be unable to sustain either the independent development of intellectual work, or the pursuit of its political objectives in an effective or democratic way. This provides at least the experiential basis of the militant renunciation of Marxism by the 'New Philosophers' and others. But the tradition of 'critique' is also radically flawed. Its rationale depends on a positive valuation of at least the general tendencies and outlooks of the forms of popular resistance in which it locates itself. Where appropriate forms do not, in fact, exist, the tradition of critique easily degenerates into an uncritical 'populism' or 'workerism', or, alternatively, a self-deluding historical romanticism. But the 'orthodox' tradition, too, is at its most dangerous in such times, and is tempted to launch 'coercive' or 'adventurist' political initiatives, out of step with popular consciousness, under the legitimation of the 'correctness' of its theory.

This, it seems to me, suggests that there is no general philosophi-

cal or theoretical solution to the classic questions of Marxism about
the relation of theory to practice. The conditions under which either
'orthodox' Marxism or the tradition of critique can make a genuine
and 'living' contact with an emancipatory popular movement are
historically contingent, and not producable at will. However, even
where a culturally rich, vital and combative popular movement does
exist, the relationship of Marxist intellectual work to it is highly
problematic. In such contexts, there remains a need for systematic,
objective work of analysis of the conditions, tendencies and possibilities which define the situation. Such analyses are indispensable, if coherent and realistic political strategies are to be worked out
and put into effect. This could only be denied on the basis of a
thoroughgoing political voluntarism which I regard as untenable.
The tradition of 'critique', not specifically or centrally cognitive in
its concerns, is unlikely, it seems to me, to be able to supply the basis
for such exacting strategic calculation. There is a political, as well as
an intellectual case, then, for the continuation of Marxist intellectual work which is broadly analytical, cognitive, and empirical and for
philosophical work which sustains this activity.

But how can the results of this work find their place in popular
struggles without the mediation of a 'vanguard' party or some other
politically or morally unacceptable vehicle? It seems to me that
there are three important considerations to be taken into account in
trying to solve this question. First, important problems associated
with the absence of internal democracy in vanguard parties also
constrain and subordinate intellectual work to the requirements of
political strategies decided in advance. Serious and genuinely informative intellectual work cannot be done in such circumstances but
only under conditions of political independence. Historically, the
'academic freedom' offered by the universities and other institutions of higher education has provided conditions of possibility for
such intellectual work on the Left, for the tiny minority of
academics who have been disposed to carry it out. Even these
minimal conditions are now, of course, under intense political
pressure in several European countries, and there is an enormous
political responsibility to defend them, at the same time as working
to develop conditions for free and effective intellectual work outside the specifically educational institutions. Fortunately, the conditions which might sustain such intellectual work are already present
in the form of the growth in most Western countries of diverse

oppositional and emancipatory movements (around such issues as ecology, peace and women's rights) both within, and cutting across, the established parties.

The second consideration is that the dogmatism which has so often characterised the 'orthodox' tradition when it has turned to politics has rested intellectually on a conception of 'science' which is philosophically indefensible. Even Althusser, despite his familiarity with modern non-Marxist work in the philosophy of science, seems finally unable to break from the idea that scientific work is incompatible with the co-existence of diverse theoretical perspectives and the openness to revision of established theories. One of the main arguments of this book has been to show that far from being incompatible, these features are *inseparable* from genuine scientific work.

The third consideration has to do with the conjunction of knowledge and power which many of the most bitter critics of contemporary Marxism see as intrinsic to it. As I have suggested elsewhere, the 'élitist' implications of the undoubted tendency of 'orthodox' Marxism to embue its intellectuals with political authority flow, not from the idea of Marxism as a science, but from a technocratic degeneration of this idea. But there is another source, rooted not in Marxism's claim to the status of science, but, on the contrary, in a quite specific theoretical error. This error is quite characteristic of the 'orthodox' tradition, and has its roots in the conception of ideology advanced by Marx in *Capital*, but is really far more widespread than this might suggest. The error is to suppose that the attachment of individuals to their subordinate position in the social order, the 'subjection of social subjects', is secured exclusively or even primarily by cognitive means. The elaboration of illusions by the ideologists of the ruling class, and the systematically misleading appearances taken on by capitalist social relations may well both have a part to play in the attachment of individuals to their place in society. To the extent that they do, the correction of ideological illusions, too, has a part to play in the formation of an oppositional consciousness. But in reality, the cognitive distortions imposed by capitalist forms of domination are interwoven with a capacity to organise and direct desires, and to mould moral sentiments. Some thinkers and traditions with their roots in classical Marxism have recognised this – Wilhelm Reich, and writers in the tradition of the 'Frankfurt School', such as Herbert Marcuse, for example – but they have been untypical. An adequate theory of what one might call the moral and motivational dynamics of subordination and emancipation is lacking in 'orthodox' Marxism, and this is a weakness which has serious politcal effects.

The 'orthodox' conception of the relationship between intellectuals and popular movements, as defined exclusively or principally in cognitive terms, cannot be sustained in the face of such a projected correction of the traditional Marxist conception of ideology. The political pertinence of other kinds of intellectual engagement – in literature, theatre, photography and other creative arts, in speculative political philosophy and moral theory, and so on – must be given a theoretical recognition, not as an alternative to, but as complementary with, the more 'conventional' kinds of theoretical work.

And this brings me, finally, to a few brief words about the 'epistemological break'. Returning, in the last couple of years to a serious rereading of some early works of Marx – especially the *1844 Manuscripts* – for teaching purposes I was immediately captivated as I had been many years before by the scope and attractive power of their vision of a possible future for humankind, as well as by the depth and continuing pertinence of their moral critique of capitalist social relations. At the same time, none of this could persuade me to abandon the Althusserian criticisms of philosophical humanism and speculative philosophy of history. As a means of sustaining historical enquiry and socio–political analysis and explanation, the categories of the early Marx are, in my view, hopelessly flawed. I think it can be shown that Marx came to this view, too. But, as I have argued above, intellectual work on the Left cannot be, and should not be, confined to what goes under the name 'scientific' analysis, necessary though that work is. There is also a fundamentally important place for avowedly committed speculative and creative philosophical work, which engages directly with the popular culture and oppositional 'discourses' of its time and place. The mistake has been to suppose that these quite different parts could be played by a single, self-consistent theoretical discourse.

Notes and References

Preface

1. Douglas Johnson, in an excellent and very informative review article in the *London Review of Books*, 16 Apr–6 May 1981, pp.13ff.
2. 'To My English Readers', in *For Marx* (London, 1969).
3. See Stuart Hall's appreciation in *New Left Review*, no.119, Jan/Feb 1980, pp.60ff.
4. I have in mind, for example, Simon Clarke's essay in S. Clarke *et al.*, *One-Dimensional Marxism* (London and New York, 1980), and E. P. Thompson's 'The Poverty of Theory' in *The Poverty of Theory and Other Essays* (London, 1978).
5. In defence of his doctoral 'thesis'. See *Radical Philosophy*, no.12, Winter 1975, p.44.
6. In a review of V. Descombes, *Modern French Philosophy*, published in *London Review of Books*, 16 Apr–6 May 1981, p.16.

Chapter 1: Introduction

1. Louis Althusser, *For Marx*, trans. B. R. Brewster (London, 1969); Louis Althusser and Etienne Balibar, *Reading Capital*, trans. Ben Brewster (London, 1970); Louis Althusser, *Lenin and Philosophy and Other Essays* (London, 1971).
2. Published in English translation as ch.3 of *For Marx*, the essay originally appeared in *La Pensée*, Feb 1963.
3. Louis Althusser, 'What Must Change in the Party', *New Left Review*, no.109, May/June 1978, see especially p.36. The pieces translated under this title first appeared in *Le Monde*, during Apr 1978.
4. Louis Althusser, *For Marx*, pp.27ff.
5. See K. Marx and F. Engels, *The German Ideology*, pt1, ed. Chris Arthur (London, 1970) p.48.
6. For an interesting analysis of this episode written by a scholar greatly influenced by Althusser, see D. Lecourt, *Proletarian Science? The Case of Lysenko*, trans. B. R. Brewster (London, 1977).
7. E. Bernstein, *Evolutionary Socialism*, trans. E. C. Harvey (New York, 1978).
8. G. Lukács, *History and Class Consciousness*, trans. R. Livingstone (London, 1973). See also P. Anderson, *Considerations on Western Marxism* (London, 1976), and the useful collection of articles published as *Western Marxism: A Critical Reader* (London, 1977). Specifically on Lukács, see G. Lichtheim, *Lukács* (London, 1970).
9. Mark Poster, *Sartre's Marxism* (London, 1979), and Ian Craib, *Existentialism and Sociology* (New York, 1976) are both excellent

introductions to Sartre's work. For commentaries which set his work in a wider context see G. Lichtheim, *Marxism in Modern France* (New York and London, 1968), and V. Descombes, *Modern French Philosophy* (Cambridge, 1980). See also F. Jameson, *Marxism and Form* (Princeton, 1971).

10. René Descartes, *Discourse on Method*, trans. and ed. F. E. Sutcliffe (Harmondsworth, 1968). See especially pp.53ff.

11. In this book I shall use the word 'epistemological' to mean 'pertaining to the philosophical theory of knowledge'.

12. J. P. Sartre, *Critique de la Raison Dialectique* (Paris, 1960), translated by A. Sheridan-Smith as *Critique of Dialectical Reason* (London, 1976).

13. F. de Saussure, *Course in General Linguistics* (New York, 1966). Helpful accounts of French structuralism are to be found, for example, in A. Giddens, *Central Problems in Social Theory* (London and Basingstoke, 1979), ch.1; V. Descombes, *Modern French Philosophy*, ch.3, and F. Jameson, *The Prison-House of Language* (Princeton, 1974).

14. C. Levi-Strauss, *The Savage Mind* (London, 1966), ch.9.

15. 'Cartesianism': the philosophical legacy of Descartes.

16. 'Solipsism': the doctrine that only one's own existence is demonstrable.

17. For example, see Levi-Strauss, *The Savage Mind*, pp.249ff.

18. See 'To My English Readers', in L. Althusser, *For Marx*, p.9.

19. This is the view of, for example, E. P. Thompson. See his *The Poverty of Theory* (London, 1978), p.333.

20. J. Rancière's criticisms are a good example of this. See, for example, his 'On the Theory of Ideology (the Politics of Althusser)', in *Radical Philosophy*, no.7, Spring 1974. See also commentary by myself (*Radical Philosophy*, no.9) and Ian Craib (*Radical Philosophy*, no.10).

21. A sophisticated and interesting example is Paddy O'Donnell's 'Lucien Sève, Althusser and the Contradictions of the PCF', *Critique*, no.15, 1981, pp.7–29.

22. Alasdair MacIntyre writes: 'So far as French philosophy was concerned, he de-Stalinised Marxism more thoroughly than any other Marxist did.' (*London Review of Books*, 16 Apr–6 May, 1981, p.16.)

23. See, for example, Althusser's introduction, 'Unfinished History', to D. Lecourt's *Proletarian Science? The Case of Lysenko*, and also 'What Must Change in the Party'.

24. See V. Gerratana, 'Althusser and Stalinism', *New Left Review*, no.101–2, Feb/Apr 1977, pp.110–21.

25. The secondary literature on Gramsci is now enormous. Two useful introductions are C. Boggs, *Gramsci's Marxism* (London, 1976), and P. Anderson, 'Antinomies of Antonio Gramsci', in *New Left Review*, no.100.

26. 'Philosophical Ontology': a general philosophical (as distinct from, for example, scientific) theory of the nature and basic kinds of existence.

27. Useful introductory accounts of conventionalism in the philosophy of science are to be found in R. Harré, *The Philosophies of Science* (London, 1972), and R. Keat and J. Urry, *Social Theory as Science* (London, 1975). A more historically oriented discussion is J. Losee, *A Historical Introduction to the Philosophy of Science* (London, Oxford and New York, 1972), ch.11. On the French tradition of 'historical epistemology', see D. Lecourt, *Marxism and Epistemology: Bachelard, Canguilhem, Foucault*, trans. B. R. Brewster (London, 1975).
28. This aspect of scientific advance is well exemplified in one of the few works by Bachelard to have been so far translated into English: *The Psychoanalysis of Fire*, trans. A. C. M. Ross (Boston, 1964).
29. L. Althusser, *For Marx*, pp.12–13.

Chapter 2: Althusser and Marxist Philosophy: Science and Ideology

1. In the essay 'On the Materialist Dialectic' in *For Marx* (London, 1969), pp.184ff.
2. Marx's 'General Introduction' to the *Grundrisse*, trans. M. Nicolaus (Harmondsworth, 1973), pp.83–111. Also included as a supplementary text in K. Marx and F. Engels, *The German Ideology*, pt1, trans. Chris Arthur (London, 1970).
3. Louis Althusser, *Reading Capital* (London, 1970), p.38.
4. Thomas Kuhn, *The Structure of Scientific Revolutions* (Chicago and London, 1962), especially ch.10.
5. See, for example, *Reading Capital*, p.59.
6. Ibid, p.62.
7. T. Benton, *Philosophical Foundations of the Three Sociologies* (London, 1977), pp.185ff.
8. Louis Althusser, *Reading Capital*, p.41.
9. See, for example, Marx's famous preface to *A Contribution to the Critique of Political Economy* (London, 1971), p.20.
10. Louis Althusser, *For Marx*, p.166.
11. Louis Althusser, *Reading Capital*, p.27, second emphasis added.
12. This book, ch.1, pp.28–30.
13. Louis Althusser, *For Marx*, pp.219–42.
14. Ibid, p.231.
15. Ibid, p.235.
16. Louis Althusser, *Reading Capital*, p.52.
17. Ibid, p.53.
18. Louis Althusser, *For Marx*, p.169.
19. For a more extended discussion of this 'scientific metaphysics', and what can be salvaged from it, see my contribution, 'Natural Science and Cultural Struggle', to J. Mepham and D. H. Ruben, eds, *Issues in Marxist Philosophy*, vol.II (Brighton, 1979).

Chapter 3: Marx's 'Epistemological Break'

1. Louis Althusser, *For Marx* (London, 1969), pp.34ff.
2. K. Marx, afterword to 2nd German edition of *Capital*, vol.I (New York, 1967), p.20. Similar statements by Engels can be found in *Anti-Dühring* (Moscow, 1969), the essay 'Ludwig Feuerbach ...' (*Selected Works*, vol.II, London, 1953), and elsewhere.
3. K. Marx, *A Contribution to the Critique of Political Economy* (London, 1971), p.22 (from the preface).
4. K. Marx and F. Engels, *Collected Works*, vol.3 (London, 1975), pp.229–346.
5. K. Marx and F. Engels, *Collected Works*, vol.5, p.4. Also in Marx and Engels, *The German Ideology*, pt1, ed. Chris Arthur (London, 1970), p.122.
6. Ibid, p.94.
7. Marx and Engels, *Selected Correspondence* (Moscow, 1955), pp.311ff.
8. Ibid, p.313.
9. Both essays are included in *For Marx*.
10. Louis Althusser and Etienne Balibar, eds, *Reading Capital* (London, 1970), ptII, ch.9.
11. Ibid, p.186.

Chapter 4: The Basic Concepts of Historical Materialism

1. 'The Basic Concepts of Historical Materialism', in Louis Althusser and Etienne Balibar, eds, *Reading Capital*, (London, 1970), pt III, pp.199–308.
2. Marx, *Capital*, vol.III (Moscow, 1971), p.791.
3. Marx, preface to *A Contribution to the Critique of Political Economy* (London, 1971), p.21.
4. Balibar, *Reading Capital*, p.214.
5. Marx, *Capital*, vol.III, ch.52, pp.885–6.
6. *Reading Capital*, p.233.
7. Ibid, p.223.
8. Louis Althusser, *For Marx* (London, 1969), pp.113–4.
9. See Marx's preface to the first edition of *Capital*, vol.I (Harmondsworth, 1976), pp.90–1.
10. *Reading Capital*, pp.207, footnote.
11. Ibid, p.273–308.
12. Ibid, p.302.
13. See ch.7 of this book.

Chapter 5: Self-criticism and Revision

1. See, for an example of this, V. Descombes, *Modern French Philosophy*, trans. L. Scott-Fox and J. M. Harding (Cambridge, 1980), p.135.
2. See, for example, Rancière's essay 'On the Theory of Ideology (the Politics of Althusser)', in *Radical Philosophy*, no.7, Spring 1974, pp.2–15. See also comments by myself and Ian Craib in *Radical Philosophy*, nos.9 and 10, respectively.
3. 'Ideology and Ideological State Apparatuses' in *Lenin and Philosophy and Other Essays* (London, 1971), pp.121–73.
4. Althusser and Balibar, *Reading Capital* (London, 1970), p.8.
5. Althusser, *For Marx* (London, 1969), p.15.
6. Louis Althusser, *Essays in Self-Criticism*, trans. G. Lock (London, 1976).
7. Mao Tse-Tung, *Selected Readings from the Works of* (Peking, 1976), pp.70–108.
8. *Essays in Self-Criticism*, p.121.
9. See, on this, the very interesting essay by Balibar, 'From Bachelard to Althusser: the Concept of "epistemological break"', *Economy and Society*, vol.7, no.3, Aug 1978, pp.207–37.
10. *Essays in Self-Criticism*, p.110.
11. V. I. Lenin, *Materialism and Empirio-Criticism* (Moscow, 1970). The principal source for Althusser's new conception of philosophy is the essay 'Lenin and Philosophy', but see also the interview, 'Philosophy as a Revolutionary Weapon', and 'Lenin before Hegel' collected together in the same volume, *Lenin and Philosophy and Other Essays*.
12. See also Louis Althusser, *Philosophie et Philosophie Spontanée des Savants* (Paris, 1974). An important commentary on this text, and the implications of Althusser's 'new' conception of philosophy is T. O'Hagan, 'Althusser: How to be a Marxist in Philosophy', in G. H. R. Parkinson, ed., *Marx and Marxisms* (Cambridge, 1982).
13. See, for example, the foreward to *Lenin and Philosophy and Other Essays* of June 1970.
14. See ch.7 of this book.
15. E. P. Thompson, for example. See ch.8 of this book.
16. *Essays in Self-Criticism*, p.121.
17. Ted Benton, 'Natural Science and Cultural Struggle', in J. Mepham and D. H. Ruben, eds, *Issues in Marxist Philosophy*, vol.II (Brighton, 1979), pp.101–142.
18. See Douglas Johnson, 'Althusser's Fate', *London Review of Books*, 16 Apr–6 May 1981, pp.13–15.
19. Pamphlet issued by the Foreign Language Press (Peking, 1966), p.1.
20. *Lenin and Philosophy and Other Essays*, p.128.
21. Ibid, p.132.
22. Ibid, p.140.
23. See ch.6 of this book.

24.   *Lenin and Philosophy and Other Essays*, p.141, footnote 12.
25.   See E. Balibar, 'Self Criticism – an Answer to Questions from "Theoretical Practice"', in *Theoretical Practice*, no.7/8 Jan 1973, pp.56–72.
26.   *Lenin and Philosophy and Other Essays*, p.160.
27.   P. Q. Hirst, 'Althusser's Theory of Ideology', in *Economy and Society*, vol. 5, no.4, Nov 1976, esp. pp.404ff.
28.   This book, chs8 and 9.

Chapter 6: Mode of Production, Articulation and Social Formation

1.   Louis Althusser and Etienne Balibar, eds, *Reading Capital* (London, 1970), p.21.
2.   The distinction I make here closely parallels in its intent the points made by Richard Johnson with his concept of 'absolutism': 'The absolutist excess comes in when this partial description of how an account is organised warrants a wholesale dismissal... The whole work is consigned to the scrapheap of ideologies or of superseded problematics.' 'Against Absolutism', in R. Samuel, ed., *People's History and Socialist Theory* (London, Boston and Henley), 1981.
3.   Althusser and Balibar, *Reading Capital*, p.201.
4.   I would like to acknowledge the help of Maxine Molyneux and Alison Scott, especially with bibliographic references, for this section of the book. A very useful recent attempt to evaluate the modern French Marxist work in the field of anthropology is J. S. Kahn and J. R. Llobera, eds, *The Anthropology of Pre-Capitalist Societies* (London and Basingstoke, 1981). See especially ptIII. The journal *Critique of Anthropology* is also an important English-language source for much of the debate covered in this section.
5.   C. Meillasoux, *L'Anthropologie Economique des Gouro d'Côte d'Ivoire* (Paris, 1964).
6.   In Terray's 'Le Marxism devant les sociétés primitives', which was subsequently criticised by P. P. Rey in a paper translated in *Critique of Anthropology*, no.3, Spring 1975, pp.27–79, under the title, 'The Lineage Mode of Production'. A later version of Terray's original paper appeared in English translation as the second part of his book *Marxism and 'Primitive' Societies* (New York, 1972), and incorporates responses to Rey's criticisms.
7.   There were also anthropologists working within the structuralist tradition itself who attempted to reinterpret and use Marxist categories. M. Godelier is one of the best known of these. See especially, M. Godelier, *Perspectives in Marxist Anthropology*, trans. R. Brain (Cambridge, 1977), and 'Modes of Production, Kinship and Demographic Structures', pp.3–27 in M. Bloch, ed., *Marxist Analyses and Social Anthropology* (London, 1975).

8. Terray, *Marxism and 'Primitive' Societies*, p.141.
9. Meillasoux, *L'Anthropologie Economique des Gouro d'Côte d'Ivoire*, pp.168–9, quoted in Terray, p.142.
10. B. Hindess and P. Q. Hirst, *Pre-Capitalist Modes of Production* (London and Boston, 1975), ch.1.
11. Ibid, pp.1–2.
12. G. Dupré and P. P. Rey, 'Reflections on the Pertinence of a Theory of the History of Exchange', in *Economy and Society*, vol. 2, no.2, May 1973, pp.131–63.
13. Hindess and Hirst, *Pre-Capitalist Modes of Production*, p.22.
14. Ibid, p.67.
15. Ibid, p.65.
16. Ibid, p.67.
17. Ibid, p.2.
18. T. Asad and H. Wolpe, 'Concepts of Modes of Production', in *Economy and Society*, vol. 5, no.4, Nov 1976, pp.470–506, see p.474.
19. Hindess and Hirst, *Pre-Capitalist Modes*, p.44.
20. E. Laclau, 'The Specificity of the Political', in *Economy and Society*, vol. 4, no.1, Feb 1975, pp.87–110, see especially pp.103–9.
21. M. Molyneux, 'Androcentrism in Marxist Anthropology', *Critique of Anthropology*, vol. 3, nos9–10, 1977, pp.55–81. Molyneux also includes within the scope of her critique the later and significantly revised position presented in Terray's 'Classes and Class Consciousness in the Abron Kingdom of Gyaman', in M. Bloch, ed., *Marxist Analyses and Social Anthropology*; see also Meillasoux's later work, *Maidens, Meal and Money* (Cambridge, 1981).
22. See John Taylor's review article, '*Pre-Capitalist Modes of Production*', part 1, *Critique of Anthropology*, nos.4–5, Autumn 1975, p.130, and part 2, *Critique of Anthropology*, no.6, Spring 1976, pp.56ff. See also the reply by Hindess and Hirst, *Critique of Anthropology*, no.8, Spring 1977, pp.49–58.
23. Louis Althusser, 'Contradiction and Overdetermination', in *For Marx* (London, 1969), see esp. pp.99ff.
24. See also E. Balibar's, 'Self-Criticism: An Answer to Questions from *Theoretical Practice*', in *Theoretical Practice*, nos.7–8, Jan 1973, esp. p.57.
25. See ch.4 of this book, pp.77–8.
26. Hindess and Hirst, *Pre-Capitalist Modes*, p.1.
27. See for example, Charles Bettelheim, *Economic Calculation and Forms of Property*, trans. J. Taylor (London, 1976).
28. See especially the work of John Taylor. His important book, *From Modernisation to Modes of Production* (London and Basingstoke, 1979), was of great help to me in the preparation of this section of the present work. Other writers, such as Barbara Bradby, Harold Wolpe and Claude Meillasoux have used this approach, and a useful collection of their work is H. Wolpe, ed., *The Articulation of Modes of Production* (London, Boston and Henley), 1980.
29. This work, ch.7.

30. For example, Christine Delphy, *The Main Enemy*, pamphlet (London, 1977).
31. See Wally Seccombe, 'The Housewife and her Labour under Capitalism', in *New Left Review*, no.83, Jan–Feb 1973, pp.3–24, see esp. pp.7–10.
32. See the critique of Seccombe by Jean Gardiner, 'Women's Domestic Labour', and by Coulson, Magas and Wainwright, '"The Housewife and her Labour under Capitalism" – a critique', in *New Left Review*, no.89, Jan–Feb, 1975.
33. For example, John Harrison, 'The Political Economy of Housework', in *Bulletin of the Conference of Socialist Economists*, Winter 1973.
34. See, for example, C. Meillasoux, *Maidens, Meal and Money* and H. Wolpe, 'Capitalism and Cheap Labour-power in South Africa: from Segregation to Apartheid', in H. Wolpe, ed., *The Articulation of Modes of Production*, note 27.
35. See especially Maxine Molyneux, 'Beyond the Domestic Labour Debate', in *New Left Review*, no.116, July–August 1979, pp.3–27, which also contains useful reviews and assessment of the literature of the debate.
36. See, for examples of work within, or influenced by this perspective, the papers by Mary McIntosh and Ann-Marie Wolpe in *Feminism and Materialism* (London, Boston and Henley, 1978), and R. Dean, *Women and Schooling* (London, 1978).
37. See Juliet Mitchell, *Psychoanalysis and Feminism* (Harmondsworth, 1975).
38. See Michèle Barratt, *Women's Oppression Today* (London, 1980), ch.2, for an excellent discussion of these and related problems in feminist theory. Veronica Beechey's 'On Patriarchy', *Feminist Review*, no.3, 1979, pp.66–82 includes a very helpful critical commentary on Juliet Mitchell's work, along with other feminist uses of the term 'patriarchy'.

Chapter 7: Class, State and Politics

1. See K. Marx 'The Eighteenth Brumaire of Louis Bonaparte', in K. Marx and F. Engels, *Collected Works*, vol.II (London, 1979), pp. 99–197.
2. L. Althusser, *For Marx* (London, 1969), pp.87–128.
3. See, especially N. Poulantzas, 'On Social Classes', in *New Left Review*, no.78, March–April, 1973, pp.27–54, and *Classes in Contemporary Capitalism*, trans. D. Fernbach (London, 1975).
4. Poulantzas defends this view in 'The New Petty Bourgeoisie' in A. Hunt, ed., *Class and Class Structure* (London, 1977). This collection contains a number of other useful contributions on this and related themes. See also A. Giddens, *The Class Structure of the Advanced Societies* (London, 1973), esp. ch.10.

5. See S. Mallet, *La Nouvelle Classe Ouvrière* (Paris, 1963 and 1969), and also Duncan Gallie's critical study, *In Search of the New Working Class* (Cambridge, 1978).
6. Poulantzas, 'On Social Classes', p.34.
7. See especially E. O. Wright, 'Class Boundaries in Advanced Capitalist Societies', in *New Left Review*, no.98, July–Aug 1976, pp.3–41.
8. Ted Benton, '"Objective Interest" and the Sociology of Power', in *Sociology*, no.15, May 1981. See also Barry Hindess, 'Power, Interests and the Outcomes of Struggles', in *Sociology*, no.16, Nov 1982.
9. See especially N. Poulantzas, *Political Power and Social Classes* (London, 1973), and the exchange between Poulantzas and Miliband published as 'The Problem of the Capitalist State' in Robin Blackburn, ed., *Ideology in Social Science* (London, 1972).
10. N. Poulantzas, *Fascism and Dictatorship*, trans. J. White (London, 1974), and *Crisis of the Dictatorships* (London 1976).
11. See, for example, Miliband, in Blackburn, ed. *Ideology in Social Science*, p. 259.
12. See, especially, N. Poulantzas, *State, Power, Socialism*, trans. P. Camiller (London, 1978). See, also, the useful commentary on this text by Stuart Hall in *New Left Review*, no.119, Jan–Feb 1980, pp. 60–9.
13. Poulantzas, ibid, pt3.
14. Ibid, p.203.
15. See, especially, M. Castells, *The Urban Question*, trans. A. Sheridan (London, 1977).
16. See, for example, M. Harloe, 'Marxism, the State and the Urban Question: Critical notes on two recent French theories', in C. Crouch, ed., *State and Economy in Contemporary Capitalism* (London, 1979), and C. G. Pickvance, 'Historical Materialist Approaches to Urban Sociology' in C. G. Pickvance, ed., *Urban Sociology: Critical Essays* (London, 1976).
17. Evidence of this, with a suitably modest disclaimer is given by Castells in the afterword to his *The Urban Question*, p.465ff.
18. E. Balibar, *On the Dictatorship of the Proletariat*, trans. G. Lock (London, 1977), pp.66ff.
19. Ibid, p.111.
20. Ibid, pp.43ff.
21. Ibid, pp.66ff.
22. See E. Durkheim, *The Rules of Sociological Method* (New York and London, 1964), ch.1.
23. Louis Althusser, 'The Historic Significance of the Twenty-second Congress', in Balibar, *On the Dictatorship of the Proletariat*, pp.206–7. A revised version of this text is published in *New Left Review*, no.104, July–Aug 1977, pp.3–22.
24. See especially part 5, 'Towards a Democratic Socialism', in N. Poulantzas, *State, Power, Socialism*. This text is also published separately in *New Left Review*, no.109, May–June 1978, pp.75–95.
25. See P. Q. Hirst's defence of the idea of popular democracy from

Weber's critique, in P. Q. Hirst, *Social Evolution and Sociological Categories* (London, 1976), ch.7.

26. See, for example, G. Therborn, 'The Role of Capital and the Rise of Democracy', in *New Left Review*, no.103, May–June 1977, pp.3–41.

27. See, in particular, Althusser's critique of the Party leadership which appeared in four parts (on 24–27 Apr 1978) in *Le Monde*. The most easily available version of this is in a translation by P. Camiller under the title 'What must change in the Party?', in *New Left Review*, no.109, May–June 1978, pp.19–45.

28. E. Laclau, *Politics and Ideology in Marxist Theory,* (London, 1977), especially ch.3, 'Fascism and Ideology', pp.92ff.

29. Louis Althusser, 'On the Twenty-second Congress of the French Communist Party', in *New Left Review*, no.104, p.5

30. Louis Althusser, 'The Historic Significance of the 22nd Congress', in E. Balibar, p.200.

31. Louis Althusser, 'What must change in the Party', in *New Left Review*, no.109, p.44.

32. See Louis Althusser, 'On the Twenty-second Congress of the French Communist Party', in *New Left Review*, no.104, pp.20ff.

Chapter 8: The Rebellion of Subjectivity

1. V. Descombes, *Modern French Philosophy*, trans. L. Scott-Fox and J. M. Harding (Cambridge, 1980), p.135.

2. For a fuller version of this interpretation, and for an account of *Les Nouveaux Philosophes* which does more justice to their individual particularities than I am able to do, see Peter Dews, 'The "New Philosophers" and the End of Leftism', in *Radical Philosophy*, no.24, Spring 1980, pp.2–11, and 'The "Nouvelle Philosophie" and Foucault', in *Economy and Society*, vol.8, no.2, May 1979, pp.127–71. My own account is greatly indebted to Dews, and also to as yet unpublished work by Couze Venn. The American journal, *Telos*, no.32, 1977, contains a collection of short articles by some of the New Philosophers and their opponents, whilst further useful background is given in Descombes, *Modern French Philosophy*, and in a recent collection of papers edited by A. Montefiore, *Philosophy in France Today*, (Cambridge, 1983). Alex Callinicos' excellent book, *Is there a Future for Marxism?* (London and Basingstoke, 1982), contains useful expositions and critical responses to many of the French writers mentioned here from a Marxist standpoint. Poulantzas, too, in his last work, *State, Power, Socialism* (London, 1980), responds critically to some of their positions.

3. Dews, 'The "New Philosophers" and the End of Leftism', p.131.

4. Any attempt at an introduction to Derrida's complex and difficult work is well beyond the scope of this chapter, but I refer the reader to Derrida's contribution to the Montefiore collection mentioned above, for confirmation of the specific point made here.

5. G. Deleuze and F. Guattari, *Anti-Oedipus* (New York, 1977).
6. See, for example, M. Foucault, *Discipline and Punish: the Birth of the Prison*, trans. A. Sheridan (Harmondsworth, 1977).
7. P. Dews, 'The "New Philosophers" and the End of Leftism'.
8. This book, ch.2
9. See this book, ch.6.
10. The main sources for this critique are B. Hindess and P. Q. Hirst, *Pre-Capitalist Modes of Production* (London and Boston, 1975), the concluding chapter, and, by the same authors, *Mode of Production and Social Formation* (London and Basingstoke, 1977).
11. *Pre-Capitalist Modes of Production*, p.2.
12. *Mode of Production and Social Formation*, p.36.
13. This book, ch.6.
14. P. Q. Hirst, 'Althusser and the Theory of Ideology', in *Economy and Society*, vol. 5, no.4, Nov 1976, pp.385–412.
15. P. Q. Hirst, *Problems and Advances in the Theory of Ideology*, pamphlet published by Cambridge University Communist Party, 1976, p.16.
16. P. Q. Hirst, 'Economic Classes and Politics', in A. Hunt, ed., *Class and Class Structure* (London, 1977), p.130.
17. Hindess and Hirst, *Pre-Capitalist Modes of Production*, pp.308ff.
18. Ibid, p.312.
19. The arguments presented here repeat and develop the themes of correspondence between P. Q. Hirst and myself which was published in *Economy and Society*, vol.3, no.2 and vol.4, no.1. They also draw upon criticisms of Hindess and Hirst from broadly similar perspectives by Tony Skillen, 'Post-Marxist Modes of Production', and by Andrew Collier, 'In Defence of Epistemology' both in *Radical Philosophy*, no.20, Summer 1978.
20. For example, pp.19–20 of *Mode of Production and Social Formation*: 'the entities specified in discourse must be referred to solely in and through the forms of discourse, theoretical, political, etc. in which they are constituted. What is specified in theoretical discourse can only be conceived through that form of discourse ...; it cannot be specified extra-discursively ... *Objects* of discourse do not exist. The entities discourse refers to are constituted in it and by it.'
21. *Mode of Production and Social Formation*, p.21.
22. See this book, ch.5, pp.87–8.
23. See, for example, the quotation given in note 20, above.
24. See T. S. Kuhn, *The Structure of Scientific Revolutions*, 2nd edn (Chicago, 1970), ch.2.
25. Here, as elsewhere, I am greatly indebted to the work of Roy Bhaskar in the philosophy of science. See especially R. Bhaskar, *A Realist Theory of Science*, 2nd edn (Hassocks, 1978), and *The Possibility of Naturalism* (Brighton, 1979). For a detailed critical response to the latter work, see my 'Realism and Social Science', in *Radical Philosophy*, no.27, Spring 1981.
26. *Mode of Production and Social Formation*, p.24.

27. For example, in Cutler *et al.*, 'An Imaginary Orthodoxy – a Reply to Laurence Harris', in *Economy and Society*, vol.8, no.3, Aug. 1979, p.310. This text contains a brief response to the articles by Collier and Skillen (see note 19). The latter are accused of 'translating our arguments against epistemology into absurd positions in epistemological discourse' (*Economy and Society*, vol.8, no.3, p.310), but nowhere do Cutler *et al.* show how or why this 'translation' is inappropriate or mistaken. Perhaps, for them, the distinction between *thinking* one has abandoned epistemological discourse and *really* abandoning it is one that can have no place? But there is an implicit retreat in the face of the realist argument: 'This is not to say that we should not be concerned with relations between discourses and their objects but rather that there are no grounds for positing a universal mode of relationship (called 'knowledge') between a realm of discourse on the one hand and a unitary realm of objects (called 'reality') on the other' (p.313). It appears, then, that despite the appearance of a vigorous defence of their position against Collier and Skillen, Cutler *et al.* have, without acknowledging it, abandoned the main point at issue (the possibility of reference to extra-discursive objects) in favour of a position not, in fact, contested by either Collier or Skillen (whether 'reality' should be considered as a 'unitary realm of objects', or 'knowledge' a 'universal relation' to it are questions which Bhaskar's transcendental realism, for example, answers decidedly in the negative).

28. Cutler *et al.*, *Marx's Capital and Capitalism Today* (London and Boston, 1977), vol.1, pt1. A critical discussion of this test is Laurence Harris, 'The Science of the Economy', in *Economy and Society*, vol.7, no.3, Aug. 1978, and there is further debate between Cutler *et al.*, and Harris in *Economy and Society*, vol.8, no.3.

29. *Mode of Production and Social Formation*, p.8.

30. Ibid, p.21.

31. Ibid, p.59.

32. Ibid, p.61.

33. Cutler *et al.*, *Marx's Capital and Capitalism Today*, p.3.

34. 'Even in Marxist politics there can be no one form of political calculation for the simple reason that there is no one form of the political conditions of that calculation. For example, calculation for parties committed to parliamentary and legal struggles has quite different conditions from those of parties engaged in directing people's wars' (*Pre-capitalist Modes of Production*, p.59). The political dogmatism implied by this relativism is clear. Theoretical reflection and analysis can never inform debate and decisions as to which of these strategic perspectives is appropriate. At this level, theory can be no more than an elaboration and confirmation of its political premises.

35. This direction of thought is contained in a recent work by Paul Hirst and Penny Woolley, *Social Relations and Human Attributes* (London and New York, 1982), in which they endorse the cultural relativism of

Peter Winch's 'Understanding a Primitive Society', in B. Wilson, ed., *Rationality* (Oxford, 1970).

36. In P. Q. Hirst 'Althusser and the Theory of Ideology', and 'Economic Classes and Politics', respectively.
37. See this book, ch.7, p.148.
38. Hirst, 'Economic Classes and Politics', in Hunt, p.131.

Chapter 9: Crusaders and Sociologists

1. Leszek Kolakowski, 'Althusser's Marx', in *Socialist Register*, 1971, pp.111–128.
2. Norman Geras, 'Althusser's Marxism: An Account and Assessment', in *New Left Review*, no.71, Jan–Feb, 1972, pp.57–86. André Glucksmann, 'A Ventriloquist Structuralism', in *New Left Review*, no.72, Mar–Apr 1972, pp.68–92, Pierre Vilar, 'Marxist History, a History in the Making: Towards a Dialogue with Althusser', in *New Left Review*, no.80, July–Aug 1973, pp.64–106.
3. Alex Callinicos, *Althusser's Marxism* (London, 1976).
4. E. P. Thompson, *The Poverty of Theory and Other Essays* (London, 1978), p.iv.
5. E. P. Thompson, *The Making of the English Working Class* (London, 1963).
6. E. P. Thompson, 'The Poverty of Theory', in *The Poverty of Theory and Other Essays*. This point is also made by Richard Johnson in his contribution to the debate on Thompson's attack on Althusserianism which took place during the 1979 History Workshop at Ruskin College, Oxford. Johnson's work is especially helpful in its attempt to situate Thompson's work within the history of the British post-war left, and in its call for 'careful and respectful', 'brotherly and sisterly' modes of debate on the Left. Unfortunately, Thompson's contribution to the debate is deaf to this call, turning Johnson's phrases back against him as an ironic, taunting refrain. Stuart Hall's contribution to the debate is, like Johnson's, clarificatory and helpful, as is Hall's commentary, published elsewhere, on Poulantzas' later work. (See contributions by Stuart Hall, Richard Johnson and E. P. Thompson, in R. Samuel, ed., *People's History and Socialist Theory* (London, Boston and Henley, 1981), and Stuart Hall's review of Poulantzas' *State, Power, Socialism* in *New Left Review*, no.119, Jan–Feb 1980.)
7. Thompson, 'The Poverty of Theory', p.195.
8. Quoted in Thompson, ibid, p.194.
9. Ibid, p.333.
10. Perry Anderson, *Arguments Within English Marxism* (London, 1980), see especially ch.4. *Economy and Society*, vol.8, no.4, Nov. 1979 also contains critical responses to Thompson from P. Q. Hirst and from K. Nield and J. Seed.
11. E. P. Thompson, *The Poverty of Theory* p.385.

12. Ibid, p.196.
13. I shall refer mainly to D. Lockwood, 'The Weakest Link in the Chain? Some comments on the Marxist theory of action', in R. L. Simpson and I. H. Simpson, *Research in the Sociology of Work*, vol.1, pp.435–81, and A. Giddens, *A Contemporary Critique of Historical Materialism,* vol. 1 (London and Basingstoke, 1981).
14. See L. Kolakowski, 'Althusser's Marx', John Scott, 'Sociological Theorising and the Althusserian Ideal', in *Sociological Analysis and Theory*, vol.4, no.2, June 1974, pp.89–113, and C. G. Pickvance, 'Althusser's "Empiricist" Conception of Knowledge', in *Economy and Society*, vol.2, no.4.
15. Thompson, *The Poverty of Theory*, p.194.
16. Ibid, pp.137–8.
17. See Simon Clarke 'Althusserian Marxism', in S. Clarke, V. J. Seidler, K. McDonnell, K. Robins, and T. Lovell, *One-Dimensional Marxism: Althusser and the Politics of Culture* (London and New York, 1980). In many respects Simon Clarke's piece is disappointing. It reproduces the political stances of Thompson's critique, denouncing Althusser's 'Stalinism' in the name of an alternative and largely unargued Marxist orthodoxy. This is not true of some of the other texts in the same volume.
18. Thompson, *The Poverty of Theory*, pp.275–6.
19. Ibid, p.280.
20. Ibid, p.275.
21. Anderson, *Arguments within English Marxism*, pp.18ff.
22. I have previously criticised this theoretical 'couple' as it appears in sociological theory, in T. Benton, 'How Many Sociologies?', in *Sociological Review*, vol.26, no.2, May 1978, pp.217–36.
23. Thompson, *The Poverty of Theory*, pp.278ff.
24. D. Lockwood, 'The Weakest Link in the Chain?'.
25. Soon after writing these lines I came across a quotation from Marx which, it seems to me, refutes Lockwood's basic thesis (as to the closeness of the conceptions of action of Marx and the utilitarians) much more decisively than I have been able to do. Marx not only criticises the utilitarian conception for 'the apparent stupidity of merging all the manifold relationships of people in the *one* relation of usefulness' but relates this to 'the fact that in modern bourgeois society, all relations are subordinated in practice to the one abstract monetary–commercial relation'. The correspondence of the utilitarian conception of action to reality, its analytical appropriateness for the analysis of capitalists' action ('All this is actually the case with the bourgeois. For him only one relation is valid on its own account – the relation of exploitation') *is* asserted by Marx. In this Lockwood is right. But this assertion by Marx is not evidence of a failure on his part to break sufficiently from the utilitarian philosophical conception of action. It is, on the contrary, the outcome of a simultaneous theoretical critique and historical and sociological localisation of the source and pertinence of the concept. (My quota-

tions from Marx are drawn from a much longer quotation used for other purposes by M. Sahlins in his *The Use and Abuse of Biology* (London, 1977), pp.55–6. The original source is K. Marx, *The German Ideology* (London, 1965), pp.460–1.)

26. Lockwood, 'The Weakest Link in the Chain?', p.466.
27. E. O. Wright, *Class, Crisis and the State* (London, 1978), p.89, quoted in Lockwood, 'The Weakest Link', in Simpson and Simpson, p.440.
28. T. Benton, '"Objective Interests" and the Sociology of Power', in *Sociology*, no.15, 1981.
29. An ambitious attempt to extend this criticism to the work of Poulantzas as well as each of the other main contemporary Marxist approaches to state-theory is K. Koch, 'The New Marxist Theory of the State or the Rediscovery of the Limitations of the Structural–Functionalist Paradigm', *Netherlands Journal of Sociology*, n.16, 1980, pp.1–19.
30. D. Lockwood, 'Social Integration and System Integration', in G. K. Zollschan and W. Hirsh, eds, *Explorations in Social Change* (Boston, 1964), pp.244–57.
31. N. Abercrombie, S. Hill and B. S. Turner, *The Dominant Ideology Thesis* (London, 1980).
32. A. Giddens, *Central Problems in Social Theory*, London, 1979, p.52.
33. A. Giddens, *A Contemporary Critique of Historical Materialism* (London and Basingstoke, 1981), pp.19–20.
34. Ibid.
35. N. Poulantzas, *State, Power, Socialism* (London, 1978), pt2.
36. See T. H. Marshall, *Citizenship and Social Class and Other Essays* (Cambridge, 1950).

Index of Names

Index of Subjects and Texts

Index of Structural Marxist Terms